Diane Wilkes

TAROT OF
JANE AUSTEN

Artwork by Lola Airaghi

LO SCARABEO

GW00691974

Tarot of Jane Austen

First printing, 2006

By Diane Wilkes
Illustrations by Lola Airaghi

Editing and book design:
Pietro Alligo, Valentina Bolatto, Riccardo Minetti, Margaret Sullivan

Printed in the EU

Lo Scarabeo S.r.l. Via Cigna 110 - 10155 - Torino - Italy
info@loscarabeo.com - www.loscarabeo.com

ISBN 13: 978-888395607-2

Acknowledgments

Despite the fact that I am bound to forget someone, I can't not acknowledge the people who provided
assistance and/or friendship during the lengthy process involved in completing this book.
My husband, Jeffrey Gemmill, provided editing and support beyond the call of duty.
Lee Bursten helped me early in the editing process (and came up with the suit symbols)
and Margaret Sullivan was a savior at the end.
Friends and family who provided exemplary support and requisite enthusiasm:
Kym Abernathy, Geraldine Amaral, Arnell Ando, Valerie Antal, Becky Ferrell-Anton, Janet Berres,
Nina Lee Braden, Sergio Carrozzo, Anastasia Cleaver, Lori Cluelow, Adrienne Cooper, Robin Cooper,
Asrianna Dameron, Linda Dunn, Lon Milo DuQuette, Mary and Ken Gemmill, Paula Gibby, Mary Greer,
Jean Hutter, Michele Jackson, Saskia Jansen, JASNA and Jane Austen Book Club Members, Debbie Lake,
Dr. Gillian Lautenbach, Tom Tadfor Little, Luanne Love, Lola Lucas, Adrienne Mendell, Rachel Pollack,
Ellen Lorenzi-Prince, Zoe Matoff, Charlotte Porter, Amy Rogers, Frances Serpico, Valerie Sim, Arielle Smith,
Sally Anne Stephen, Diane Turek, Jane Anne Vanderhoff, Doreen Vitkuske, Alyce Walker, Charlotte Wilkes.
I apologize in advance to anyone I've inadvertently forgotten to mention.
My Bruce Springsteen blood brothers and sisters:
Mike Coy, Diane Evans, Maureen Ford, Tom and Mo Gardner, Mary Genovese, Luanne Love (again),
Michele Nicastro, George Skladany (I owe you my life!), and all my other Laker and Roadie pals.
I thank Riccardo Minetti for his great patience with me.
Thanks to all my students, past and present, for their encouragement and insights.
Lastly, I want to pay tribute to two influences who are no longer here – my aunt, Sophia Wilkes Hirsh,
who taught me to read, among other things, and my friend Brigit Horner, who passed too soon.

Index

Introduction

Tarot of Jane Austen

At first blush, one might think that the writings of Jane Austen would not mesh particularly well the occult nature of the tarot. Jane Austen's books and the tarot do, however, contain one essentially identical message: the vital importance of balance in our everyday lives.

Through her understanding of humanity, illustrated on the canvas of her "little bit of ivory," Jane Austen recognizes that any quality, when non-proportional, can become a negative characteristic. Two of her book titles emphasize that message quite clearly: *Pride and Prejudice* and *Sense and Sensibility*. But all of her books illustrate this point in some fashion: when unchecked, high spirits devolve into dangerous imprudence (as in the case of Lydia Bennet in *Pride and Prejudice*). Vitality can be a positive characteristic, as evidenced by Lizzy in *Pride and Prejudice*, but problematic when used and abused by corrupted individuals like Mary and Henry Crawford in *Mansfield Park*. Sensitivity taken too far can be fatal – Marianne in *Sense and Sensibility* almost dies from the pain of a broken heart given too quickly and completely. Even firmness of character can, in an excessive amount, lead to headstrong riskiness, as Louisa's stubborn leap off the rocks in *Persuasion* illustrates.

The tarot illuminates the necessity of balance by its very structure. There are 22 cards devoted to matters of spirit (the "Major Arcana") and the four suits, 16 cards each, that address the lesser, more mundane matters of life (the "Minor Arcana). The spiritual life takes precedence, but the four suits embody all the elements. In the Jane Austen Tarot, these four suits are Candlesticks, which correlate to passion, energy, and initiative; Teacups, which convey aspects of love and emotion; Swords/Quills, the rational, analytical, and intellectual side of life; and finally, Pentacles/Coins, embodying physical and tangible matters.

If one reads Austen carefully, she provides a template for the way life should be lived. Our moral compass is highly individual, and must be pure, unheralded by egotistical bombast. But if we neglect the other elements of existence, or honor one at the expense of the others, our lives will be out of harmony, putting that compass at risk of being inaccurate or breaking altogether.

The Jane Austen Tarot book and deck are based on the commonality Austen's oeuvre and the tarot share – that of recognizing the benefit of equipoise and equilibrium in our lives. The deck imagery is taken from the characters and situations of Austen's novels. It is loosely based on the iconography and meanings of the Rider-Waite-Smith Tarot, which is the most popular deck in the United States.

The ideal audience for this deck and book is two-fold; tarot enthusiasts and devotees of Jane Austen. The standard interpretations will make it easy for tarot enthusiasts to use the cards with ease, and the tarot novice who is familiar with Austen's characters and stories will find the wisdom of the tarot surprisingly accessible.

Austen Movie Guide

While I can't understand why, if one has read one Austen novel, one hasn't read them all, I recognize that some people have not yet done so. For those individuals who wish to more fully understand the Jane Austen Tarot but have not yet read all of her works, I suggest the following movie versions (hastening to add that they are but poor substitutes for the books themselves).

Pride and Prejudice – the BBC miniseries starring Colin Firth takes the time required to tell the story of the novel. It also includes Colin Firth in the (in)famous water scene. You can't miss with this one – you'll learn the story and get major romantic thrills simultaneously. Avoid the Greer Garson/Laurence Olivier version, as it has little to do with the actual book.

Sense and Sensibility – Emma Thompson's screenplay and Ang Lee's direction are excellent – though the real Elinor would never have lost her Pentacles serenity the way Ms. Thompson does in her portrayal at the end of the movie.

Emma – There are two popular versions of this book. The Knightley character in both of them is not how I imagine him at all. I prefer the one with Kate Beckinsale, but each of these movies has grown on me and they are both quite true to Austen's *Emma*.

Mansfield Park – You can't cut corners here. The Rozema-directed movie has the same title as the book and has characters with the same names, but there the resemblance ends. Sadly, this is Jane's longest and least popular book. Many find the protagonist impossible to like because she is too good to be true, without the vivacity of Lizzy Bennett or the wit of Emma Woodhouse. But it is, in many ways, Austen's richest work. It is also the source of many of the JA Tarot cards, so I urge you to read it.
An alternative is to track down the BBC version of *Mansfield Park*, which is a significant improvement of the more popular, but faux movie version of *Mansfield Park*.

Persuasion – The movie of *Persuasion* starring Ciaran Hinds and Amanda Root is very true to the original text.

Northanger Abbey and *Lady Susan* – These are both such short novels that there is no excuse not to read them. They're even available for free online. You'll love them. Trust me.

Major Arcana

Tarot of Jane Austen

0 – The Fool
Pride and Prejudice

Card Description
Elizabeth Bennett walks in an open field towards a large manor house. She is a slender and somewhat athletic looking young woman; this is not an exhausting walk for her. As she approaches a long rivulet that separates her from the manor in the distance, she seems undaunted in her approach. Her look mixes expectancy and determination, and her cheeks are rosy from expended energy. Even her eyes sparkle, glowing with good health and intelligence renewed from a fine walk in nature – although her sensible shoes are a bit muddied. A small dog accompanies her; he is a faithful friend who seems delighted with life in general.

Storyline
Early in *Pride and Prejudice*, Jane Bennett is invited to Netherfield, the home of the eligible bachelor Charles Bingley, by his sisters. Her mother concocts the scheme of sending Jane on horseback, desiring that the impending rain will compel the Bingleys to invite Jane to spend the evening. Her plan has an unexpected dividend – Jane falls ill with the 'flu, ensuring a stay of several days. Lizzy, Jane's sister, is sincerely concerned for her sister's health when she hears the news. Despite family opposition, her anxiety prompts her to walk the three miles to Netherfield. This shocks and appalls Bingley's sisters, who see the behavior as "almost incredible" and describe Lizzy's appearance as "almost wild".

Card Interpretation
When this card is drawn in a reading, it strongly suggests – nay, insists – that this is a time of independent thought and action on your part. Follow your instincts, not the currently prevalent beliefs of others. Lizzy's decision to walk several miles highlights her independence, compared to her older sister Jane, who is (somewhat unwillingly) complicit in her mother's scheming. Lizzy, in her walk as

The Fool, moves forward against others' advice, spurred on only by the disquiet she feels upon hearing her beloved sister is ill. She has no ulterior motives, nor does she allow herself to be anyone's puppet. Independence is her watchword. Let it be yours, as well.

Others may see you as "almost wild", but you need to have faith in your decision-making skills, regardless of possibly frightening obstacles in your path. The stream that appears in the card symbolizes the murky waters of society in which Lizzy will now be immersing herself. Treachery, intrigue, and the cunning, self-serving behavior of others who travel in that realm will prove more dangerous to her well-being than any three mile walk in the countryside. There may be perils lurking in the depths for you to be aware of, in addition to the obvious risks you are taking. With faithful friends, such as the dog who scampers at Lizzy's side, as well as your core desire to take a leap of faith, you will arrive safely at your chosen destination. Trust in the Universe as you travel steadfastly and surely on your own two feet.

This episode occurs early in the book. Lizzy has much to learn on her Fool's Journey, but without this first leap into the unknown, she would remain in the bosom of her family, possibly forever. The leap you are taking is but the first step into the unknown, but, like Lizzy, you are on the right path.

What Would Jane Do?

"To walk three miles, or four miles, or five miles, or whatever it is, above her ankles in dirt, and alone, quite alone! what could she mean by it? It seems to me to show an abominable sort of conceited independence, a most country town indifference to decorum."
Jane Austen, *Pride and Prejudice*

Jane's Advice: You have looked into your heart, and know its answer. If you follow it in this matter, even if your action(s) seem impetuous to others, you will ineluctably be moving in the right direction. Disregard societal strictures if they thwart you. Your individual path is independent of others' worldviews. Wear those muddied boots proudly!

There is a time to look and a time to leap. This is the time for leaping, for only in movement is there opportunity you could never have foreseen in your rational mind. Just be sure that your motives are pure, or your fall could be most embarrassing.

I – The Magician
Mansfield Park (Henry Crawford)

Card Description
Henry Crawford, a man who is "not handsome" but has "air and countenance", stands at the front of a well-appointed sitting room in Mansfield Park. He stands by a piano, holding a volume of Shakespeare in his hand, but doesn't look at it as he declaims to Fanny Price and Lady Bertram. Both sit with needlepoint in their now idle hands. Their attention is riveted on the orator, who has one hand pointing in the air, the other (with the book) pointing downward. On top of the piano beside him sits a rose in a bud vase, a lit candle, and a pitcher of water.

Storyline
Despite the fact that Henry Crawford is not a particularly handsome man, he enchants the two beautiful Bertram sisters, Maria and Julia, the first time he comes to Mansfield Park. The only one at Mansfield Park who does not fall under Henry's spell is Fanny Price, whose position as the insignificant, penniless cousin allows her to initially escape Henry's notice. Once he realizes that she not only exists, but has no love for him, Henry makes it his mission to ensnare Fanny as well – there is nothing he loves more than a challenge.

Henry soon discovers that Fanny is only too able to withstand his amorous assaults, which causes the contrary man to admire and then fall in love with her. Her strong convictions, her humility, and her wisdom enchant him – and it doesn't hurt that she is quite lovely, physically, as well. He brings his considerable gifts to bear on winning Fanny as his bride.

However, when she continues to reject him, his ego can not bear it. When he encounters the now-married Maria Bertram and she, too, treats him coldly, he determines to reignite her interest. In Maria, Henry finds an easier target. He convinces her to run away with him, despite her married status.

But she can not hold his interest long, and he leaves her, knowing he has ruined Maria's reputation and life.

Card Interpretation
The card shows Henry Crawford enchanting Lady Bertram, and even the unwilling Fanny Price, with his dramatic skills and powers. He brings all the elements together in his reading – intellect, physicality, warmth, and emotional fervor. These are seen in the card's symbols: the book represents air; the rose, earth; the candle, fire; and the pitcher of liquid, water.

In a reading, this card holds many positive – and negative – possibilities. Like Henry, you possess many gifts – great charm, fluidity of communication, and the ability to manifest your goals seemingly without effort. However, you can use your innate talents for good or ill. The key is to recognize what is worth applying your considerable abilities to – choosing your aspirations with good judgment and then working diligently toward attaining them. You must be even more diligent in selecting the appropriate receptacles for your genius – and in forcing yourself to keep an eye on the long view, not immediate gratification.

Diversion is only too easy for you, and you loathe being bored. You may even consider the concept of "diligence" a kind of curse. But steady and consistent application will win you the greatest gifts of all. You shouldn't settle for second-best, because you can achieve anything you truly desire and work for.

You relish a challenge and respond well to any tests. Your will is extremely strong. Ideally, the challenges you choose to spend your energy on will be ones that are truly worthy of you and your highest desires. Sometimes you get involved in a game simply in order to exercise and affirm your own skills, only to discover that the resultant prize is more of a punishment than a reward.

Your particular gift is in the area of oratory – your communication skills are without peer. You are probably excellent at articulating your vision of what should be, as Henry is when he makes architectural suggestions. You are a great "improver".

However, you may also be a bit too gifted in this area, and promise more than you are willing to give. You can fall in love with the ideas in your head and speak of these fantasies as truth – and believe your own words! You love wordplay and innuendo, and your sense of humor simply adds to your ability to magnetize others – but you can also fall into the danger of not taking anything seriously, even your own deepest wishes. You can be self-absorbed, but, ironically, find it difficult to recognize your true self's highest aims.

Occasionally, you begin a task that initially seems impossible, but you know from past experience that you can behave as if you are able to do it – and then the behavior becomes the reality. In *Mansfield Park*, Henry says, "I feel as if I could be anything or everything; as if I could rant and storm, or sigh or cut capers, in any tragedy or comedy in the English language." He is speaking of acting in a play, but the symbolism applies to the play of life, as well.

What Would Jane Do?

"A little difficulty to be overcome was no evil to Henry Crawford. He rather derived spirits from it."

Jane Austen, *Mansfield Park*

Jane's Advice: Your natural spirits are engaging. You recognize your lack of constancy as the weakness it is, but prefer to focus your energy on easier challenges. In your rare self-reflective moments, you know what is best for you on every level. If you don't allow your desires of the moment to misdirect your focus, you can achieve the great things your talents hint at, which are only promised by diligence and constancy. Vexation and self-reproach will be your constant companions if you ignore the information your most noble self provides to you. The low road may beckon, but it can not compel you to follow it. The direction of your strong will is that of your future, for good or ill.

II – The High Priestess

From **Ode to Pity**:
The Moon emerges from behind a Cloud
And darts upon the Myrtle Grove her beam.
　　Jane Austen, *Juvenilia, Volume the First*

Card Description

Jane Austen sits in an elegant chair, with a straight spine and a look of wisdom and mystery on her face. She is dressed in white, and is young, slender, and virginal in appearance. Her clothes are not revealing. She wears a cap on her head that is in the shape of a crescent moon.

She holds an open book in her hands – we can see the title on the spine (*Sense and Sensibility*, since she has both and it's an apt book title for the High Priestess). The book's point of view ranks sense and rational knowledge above unchecked displays of emotion. The floor beneath her consists of a black and white checkerboard pattern. A cat sits poised at the High Priestess' feet in a pose exemplifying refinement, fastidiousness, and detachment.

The High Priestess is flanked by two pillars. The white pillar on the left shows scenes of universal human understanding, the black one on the right depicts societal vignettes. Behind her is an ornate mirror, which symbolizes her role as a Sibyl of longevity – she sees the future because she sees the past and the present so clearly. She fully understands a society to which she has rarely been exposed and mirrors it back to us, offering timeless wisdom hundreds of years beyond her physical death. The shelves behind her hold volumes of classic literature and philosophy.

Storyline

The word "virgin" is often associated with the High Priestess archetype – and Jane Austen, as well. Despite her limited exposure to society, Jane Austen understood it – and human nature – more fully than those who participated in it at the most elite levels. At a time when few women were writing novels, Jane Austen was doing so – not for fame or fortune, but

because her very essence demanded that she commit to ink the visions of humanity she saw so clearly in her mind's eye. Growing up surrounded by books, she began writing at age twelve.

Her earliest words reflect an understanding way beyond her years, and her humor punctured the vanities and silliness of society, but never the truly moral or ethical mores that were its underpinnings. While she had little formal schooling, Jane briefly attended the Abbey School. The headmistress, according to biographer David Nokes, had little to offer in the way of learning, but "what she lacked in scholarly skills, she made up for by the cultivation of solemn mysteries", which sounds like an apt educational agenda for a "High Priestess-in-Training".

Austen was also very private (another word one identifies with the High Priestess) when it came to her writing, obscuring it from the view of others. The Rider-Waite-Smith High

Priestess holds a scroll that is not completely open, indicating that the inherent wisdom is not on the surface. There is more there than meets the eye. This is also true of Austen's novels.

Astrologically speaking, the Golden Dawn attributes the High Priestess card to the Moon, the lunar planet that offers an imperfect light. It is also a feminine planet, and the importance of sisterhood is a theme that runs through all of Austen's novels.

A noted spinster, Jane Austen did have beaux, including at least one man, Harris Bigg-Wither, who asked for her hand in marriage. By that time in her life, she had completed – but not published – three novels. While Austen initially accepted his offer, she rescinded her agreement just 12 hours later. One can only conjecture why she agreed (and then changed her mind). Marriage to Bigg-Wither would have greatly improved her troubled financial status, but the life of a married woman in that time period and social strata would not have allowed her to follow her muse and continue the time-consuming pastime of writing novels. This pure and independent approach to financial and social interests seems particularly suited to the High Priestess archetype.

The humorous author, T.C. Boyle, wrote a short story called "I Dated Jane Austen". In this entertaining tale, Jane Austen is portrayed as the virgin priestess. Boyle twice refers to her "cold hands" and depicts her as quite untouchable. Even Cassandra, her "spinster" sister who chaperones their date, is willing to boogie at the disco and hold his hand – but not the cool, dismissive Jane.

While no one could call Austen's writings unintelligible or obfuscatory, there is much that is hidden from the cursory reader. A conscientious one, however, will divine a great deal from what Jane Austen implies, directly, indirectly or by what she doesn't specifically state, another quality of the High Priestess.

The card number for the High Priestess is two, a number that signifies duality, balance, choice, union, and, of course, wisdom. These qualities form the spine of Austen's work. In fact, two of Jane Austen's most famous books, *Pride and Prejudice* and *Sense and Sensibility*, are titled in a way that specifically underscore and emphasize duality. Austen clearly thought in those terms and balanced her writing accordingly. Can you think of black and white pillars more distinct than the characters of Darcy and Wickham in *Pride and Prejudice* or Willoughby and Colonel Brandon in *Sense and Sensibility*?

Card Interpretation

This card's appearance in a reading indicates a wisdom beyond chronological years and experience. There is an instinctive knowing regarding the situation at hand, an ironic perspective that bespeaks an understanding of both human dreams and foibles. Great clarity and even a sense of the absurd permeates the present situation. You know much more than you give yourself credit for, and others seek your opinions and counsel because they recognize your gifts, despite your humble manner and diffident way of offering your advice. You would be wise not to volunteer guidance unless it is sought.

The works of Jane Austen are an Akashic record of human behavior in miniature. You have the capability to tap into the collective unconscious of the past, present, and future. Listen to your inner voice during this time. It is wiser and truer than any external commentary, even if it goes against the societal grain.

What Would Jane Do?

"We all have a better guide in ourselves, if we would attend to it, than any other person can be."

Jane Austen, *Mansfield Park*

Jane's Advice: Sit back and take in the whole situation as if from a great distance. Imagine you are not personally involved, so as to avoid emotional excess. What do you now see that you missed before? If you must choose now between action and inaction, do nothing. Events will play out in a way that you have always known and understood on an internal level. Try to stay balanced, keep your own counsel, and, above all, your sense of humor.

III – The Empress
Emma

Card Description
A beautiful, pregnant woman, Anne Weston, sits on a bench in a garden, her feet raised on a stone footstool. She beams a fond look upon a young lady, Emma, who is walking down a garden path towards her fiancé, George Knightley.

Storyline
Anne Taylor comes into Emma Woodhouse's life as a governess. Miss Taylor educates and nurtures Emma, encouraging her intellectual growth, and offering unconditional love and support to the motherless girl. As Emma matures in age and the ways of the world, her beloved governess becomes more of a wise older sister to the intellectually bold and active younger woman, and Emma sees that Miss Taylor's greatest opportunity for a rich and full life is to marry – and does what she can to arrange a husband for her.

When *Emma* begins, Miss Taylor has become Mrs. Weston, and Emma is bereft from the loss of her teacher and friend. However, there can be no doubt that Mrs. Weston is very happy in her marriage – and that she is an outstanding wife, trained to indulge will and caprices by her interactions with Emma. One of Anne Weston's fondest hopes is that her stepson Frank Churchill and Emma will fall in love, because she holds them both in high esteem and also because that would make Emma literally part of her family. While Frank has not behaved as well as he could or should towards such a stepmother, she even worries about him.

When Mrs. Weston discovers that Frank is secretly engaged to Jane Fairfax, she is far more concerned about Emma's feelings than Frank's fiancée. She is relieved to find Emma's heart untouched by Frank, and delighted when Emma becomes engaged to Mr. Knightley. All that is left for her happiness is to give birth to a healthy baby girl, which she does in the final chapters of *Emma*.

Card Interpretation
The Empress is the essence of femininity. She is the mate and consort of the Emperor. If we look to their astrological and mythical correspondences, the Empress plays the rôle of Venus to the Emperor's Mars.

If you receive this card in a reading, the feminine principle, in all its variegated forms, is being activated in your life. You could be physically pregnant, or about to give birth to a creation: a plan, a book, a craft project.

One need not be a biological mother to be a true Empress, just a nurturer and caregiver. You may care for a child or children, or your elderly parent. You could be making lavish meals for your unattached friends – or catering a low-carb meal for one who is on a diet.

You are supportive and compassionate, like Anne Weston, who is interested in every detail of her loved ones' existence and worries about their potential aches and pains more than they do. You might be almost too willing to please others – their desires can become yours until you can no longer recognize your own needs. On the other hand, Anne Weston truly comes into her own as a woman and a person upon her marriage – it may that your spouse brings out the best in you.

It is also possible you are too loving and supportive – you tend to see only the good in the people you love and over-indulge them and think they do no wrong. As Anne Weston says to Mr. Knightley, "Since we have parted, I can never remember Emma's omitting to do any thing I wished". When she discovers that her stepson has concealed his romantic responsibilities and led her beloved Emma on, she enumerates reasons to continue to esteem him – once she ascertains Emma's heart is unharmed.

While you may have many accomplishments, you are most interested in how these gifts can serve your loved ones. Love is always of vital interest to you, and you are interested in – and try to cultivate – the romantic affairs of others. When Mrs. Weston was Emma's governess, even the family doctor remarked upon her utter dependability. When it comes to your loved ones, there is nothing you won't do for them and you are as steady as a rock in your commitment to them. You are also very protective of the ones you love and their interests – the Empress has often been compared to a lioness with her cubs. Even Frank Churchill, a fully grown man, becomes a repository for Mrs. Weston's concerns – neither age nor distance lessens the protective love of a true Empress.

What Would Jane Do?
"There is something so motherly and kindhearted about her, that it wins upon one directly…"

Jane Austen, *Emma*

Jane's Advice: Self-denial denotes an unattractive propensity towards martyrdom. This is a time for you to indulge yourself in all the healthy pleasures – and even, perhaps, a few unhealthy ones. Others are drawn to your nurturing warmth, but be careful to lavish an equal amount of energy on self-care. See yourself as a bower of beautiful flowers that gives others pleasure, if that is a necessary goad to cultivate your own garden.

IV – The Emperor
Mansfield Park

Card Description
An older man sits on a very large, throne-like chair. His face is grave and serious and he is dressed conservatively, but expensively. Behind him is his home, a grand estate. The surrounding greenery is perfectly manicured and harmoniously balanced, as befits an English manor.

Storyline
When poor relation Fanny Price comes to Mansfield Park, she is particularly intimidated by her imposing and reserved uncle, Sir Thomas Bertram, despite his attempts "to be all that was conciliating". She is relieved when he leaves the country on business for a long period of time, though her Aunt Norris assumes power and treats her poorly in his stead. By the time Sir Thomas returns home, Fanny has grown into an attractive young lady, but despite his obvious approval, Fanny remains afraid of her authoritative uncle. However, her wishes and values are in line with his: a family theatrical she objected to on moral grounds was cancelled immediately by Sir Thomas on his return.

Therefore, she is distressed when a man she despises, Henry Crawford (see Magician), indicates he wishes to marry her – and her uncle clearly sanctions the match. He is perplexed at Fanny's demurral, because Crawford is so well-established. After failing to convince her to accept the proposal, Sir Thomas ascribes her refusal to modest maidenly fears, and fully expects her to change her mind. He pressures her first with great solicitousness, and then with excommunication from Mansfield Park, the place that has become her only real home. Ultimately, Fanny's distrust of and distaste for Henry Crawford seems prescient and wise when he runs away with Maria, Sir Thomas' married daughter, and then deserts her. Fanny returns to her true home, and Sir Thomas realizes she has all the virtues he could desire in a daughter.

Card Interpretation
Everything about this card indicates power and material success. You may (intentionally or unintentionally) intimidate others with your innate command of your self and your expectation of others accepting your sovereignty. Some might consider you repressive. Conversely, you might project your power onto others, and allow yourself to be cowed unnecessarily. Authority is a defining issue in your life when this card appears in a reading.

You have a strong moral code that you live by, and you expect others to fall in line with your way of thinking. You might not like or trust "newfangled" thinking, placing history and tradition at a premium. You can be so sure that your beliefs are correct that, if "reason" does not convince others, you might resort to bullying as a means of persuasion – especially if you are convinced that it is for the other person's good.

Timing is usually on your side. You always have a battle plan and choose your time of "attack" wisely. You are a master tactician and can adapt as needed. However, you can sometimes underestimate the power of spiritual righteousness and its ability to triumph over worldly power: Fanny ultimately "triumphs" over Henry Crawford, and Sir Thomas realizes he was wrong not to want her to. But, as literary critic Tony Tanner asserts, Fanny would be unable to shine her light of consciousness without Sir Thomas' potent strength.

Like him, you are also likely to be a benign ruler, with true vision and positive intentions. The Emperor often has a strong sense of justice, such as that of Sir Thomas when he realizes that Fanny has been living in colder quarters than the rest of the family; he rectifies that situation immediately. He doesn't countermand these changes even when she displeases him – his word is his bond.

Sir Thomas initially attributes good qualities to his obsequious sister-in-law, only to discover she has infected his family with her malign influence. You may be susceptible to flattery at this time, and you will find no end of people who are willing to praise your virtues to the skies, but you must be careful to evaluate their motives. Often, people with true integrity are the only ones who possess the courage to disagree with you.

An Emperor can be so confident of his right to power that he can convince himself that his morality remains intact even when he is enmeshed in immorality (Sir Thomas is involved in the slave trade). It's not really hypocrisy so much as a tendency to compartmentalize, which can lead to unfair decisions. Be sure that you examine your own motives, ethics, and actions on a regular basis.

In familial matters, you might be pushing your relatives in directions that aren't ones they would choose (or, conversely, you might be having issues with a strong parental figure or employer who is pushing you). Might doesn't make right, and, especially in family matters, it might be wise for you to remember that love and respect don't go hand-in-hand with emotional maltreatment.

Communication from the heart can be a real challenge when the Emperor is involved. In *Mansfield Park*, Sir Thomas' relationship with his sons is often stilted. As Austen writes about Edmund's correspondence with his father: "But if he wrote to his father, no wonder he was concise. Who could write chat to Sir Thomas?".

Your presence is vital in order to maintain order and teach values – don't abrogate your family responsibility by absenting yourself. Your personal domain is as important as your material realm. In fact, you might identify too well with your personal domain. Your home is your castle, but it is not you – you are a human being, not a physical edifice, even if you are as imposing as one.

You may not be the life of the party, but you are the person others turn to when they need concrete advice or help.

What Would Jane Do?

"He has a fine dignified manner, which suits the head of such a house, and keeps everybody in their place."

Jane Austen, *Mansfield Park*

Jane's Advice: This is a time for building your empire and drawing your boundaries with precision and directness. Your values are clear and concise and you have the power to do great good for yourself and others.

Responsibility and power go hand in hand, though, and there are always fools who will praise your every act. Choose your counselors and compatriots with wisdom and good sense, and your triumphs will be many and your mistakes few. However, even Emperors are not impervious to mistakes, and that is also something to remember as you go forth and conquer.

V – The Hierophant
Pride and Prejudice

Card Description
Mr. Collins stands at the altar of his church, one hand raised in offering a blessing. Two very well-dressed church-members sit in the front pew, Lady Catherine de Bourgh and her daughter, Anne.

Storyline
When Mr. Collins comes to call on the Bennetts, his intention is to "extend the olive branch" of peace. Their families have been estranged because he is to inherit the Bennetts' home, since the Bennetts have no male heirs, and Mr. Collins hopes to marry one of their daughters (who are famed for their beauty), keeping the estate in the family. Despite being a clergyman, Mr. Collins is a fatuous fool whose true religion is money and appearances. There is nothing he loves better than hearing himself talk; his wealthy patroness, Lady Catherine de Bourgh, comes in a close second, and it is she who has commanded him to seek a bride in the Bennett family.

At first, Mr. Collins sets his sights on the eldest Bennett daughter, Jane, but he easily turns his attentions to Elizabeth when he is informed Jane is on the verge of becoming engaged. When he proposes, is sure that she is merely displaying maidenly modesty when she refuses his offer. After all, he is offering financial security – what objection could she have to him? His pontifications and self-righteous attempts at instructing all five daughters are met with boredom and disdain.

When Lizzy continues to rebuff him, he turns to her friend Charlotte Lucas, who is delighted to accept him. They make a reasonably good match, despite her superior sense and sensibility.

When the youngest Bennett daughter, Lydia, elopes, Mr. Collins sends a letter to the Bennetts suggesting they cast her off completely, in the name of good Christian charity. However, as soon as the family's fortune rises,

he becomes almost as obsequious to them as he is to Lady Catherine. His God is power, prestige, and the values of society and his advancement in that society. He serves his God in whichever form those things manifest.

Card Interpretation
The tarot originated in Renaissance Italy, a time when the Pope didn't merely dominate the spiritual sphere, but was the most powerful and influential person alive. This card, therefore, has a history of representing great power and, perhaps, the desire for more of it. You might be obsessed with hierarchy and, like Mr. Collins, may be overly impressed by clout, ceding great respect to those whom you consider above you, and patronizing and condescending to those you see as beneath you on a social or spiritual level.

As The Hierophant, you might value the letter of the law over its spirit. No one knows the rules and regulations better than you, and you follow them meticulously. You are a stickler for following accepted practices and expect everyone else to do the same. You might assume that your wishes should be gratified and arrangements made with only your needs and concerns in mind. You are not above manipulating the rules for your own benefit, but you will never break them. Twisting them is a different story.

You have great knowledge which you are more than happy to share with others – on your terms. Some may find your pontifications offensive, and you are not always sensitive to others' less-than-enthusiastic response. When it sinks in that your sermons are unwelcome, you can be petulant and resentful – since you are confident that you know what is best for others.

You may be highly practical and often do know what is best for others, at least on a mundane level. Taurus is the astrological attribution for this card, and like that sign, you are extremely pragmatic. You like your creature comforts and are quite proud of the way in which you manifest them.

You can be harshly censorious of others' pleasures and life-choices if they don't coincide with your own. It may be time to examine your own ethical inconsistencies. When Mr. Collins comes to the Bennets' home, he chooses the two most beautiful sisters, and ignores the studious and moralistic Mary, whose sober mien seems ideal for a clergyman.

The rules of etiquette are important to you. You're never remiss in sending thank you letters or other forms of polite discourse. Informal get-togethers, however, may cause you great discomfort, which others interpret as snobbery or your being socially deficient. It is even possible that you practice what you are going to say in advance, as Mr. Collins is wont to do. The Hierophant prefers knowing everyone's precise place, even in casual situations.

If this card appears in a reading, it indicates the above characteristics. They can belong to you or someone else. This is the time to know and obey the rules and regulations of a situation. Careful study, not innovation is called for now, with chaos to be avoided at all costs. You may also be called upon to teach – or learn – something new. If you don't put yourself on a wobbly pedestal, you have the opportunity to do both successfully.

What Would Jane Do?

"I have often observed how little young ladies are interested by books of a serious stamp, though written solely for their benefit. It amazes me, I confess; – for certainly, there can be nothing so advantageous to them as instruction."

Jane Austen, *Pride and Prejudice*

Jane's Advice: The question you must ask yourself is "What or whom do you serve?". What are your core values? Are your beliefs based on familial values, your religious upbringing, society's mores, or do they derive from your own carefully considered personal truths? While we are all influenced to a greater or lesser extent by our cultural experiences and what we have been taught, deep within us is exists an unique compass, a compass of the soul.

Author's Note: Mr. Collins is not the sole religious figure in Jane Austen's books; others are far more sensible and appealing. However, none exemplifies the archetype as well as Mr. Collins. In no way am I suggesting that the Hierophant is always fatuous, pompous, and self-promoting – merely that Mr. Collins' story best fits certain aspects of this card, even if his character does not.

VI – The Lovers
Pride and Prejudice

Card Description
Mr. Darcy looks longingly at Elizabeth Bennett from his seat behind a desk, where he is writing a letter. The woman diverts him against his will from his writing, while her attention is riveted on the delicate petals of an iris. A lit candle symbolizes the steady flame of his feelings.

He does not "see" Caroline Bingley, the woman behind him, who wants his attention. He holds a mirror toward the object of his desires, and she is reflected as Venus, the idealized goddess of love. The flowers that border her enhance the image of feminine beauty. The bookcases in the background connote his dedication to maintaining the scholarly standards of his past, as well as the pride he feels for them, but there is an air of oppressive insularity. The open window offers a more spacious vista, a release from stultifying and musty rules. The iris the woman holds is a tantalizing component of that world.

Storyline
Murphy's Law is illustrated perfectly in this scene from *Pride and Prejudice*. No sooner does Darcy verbally delineate the many ways in which Elizabeth Bennett is unworthy of his attention than he begins to increasingly discover her numerous qualities. He finds himself increasingly attracted to her, initially to his great chagrin.

In the depicted scene, Caroline Bingley continually interrupts Darcy as he writes a letter to his sister. She feels compelled to compliment his writing, his library, and his sister, while Darcy secretly observes Lizzy as much as he can. Lizzy is totally oblivious to his attentions, though she is aware of and amused by Caroline's incessant, adoring prattling. This moment particularly encapsulates the image of the traditional Lovers: one where a man must make a choice between two women. If Darcy's "pride" in his social standing is the determining factor in his affections, his obvious choice is Caroline Bingley, his best friend's sister and a woman of wealth and lineage. But true value does not always accord with social standing, and if Lizzy is his choice, he must truly put pride aside to win her. Lizzy, meanwhile, must also become aware of the true worth of the man she enjoys needling. Her prejudice towards him is due to a combination of fact and fiction, and she needs to see beyond gossip and her pride in her judgment.

Each person has choices to make. Even Caroline Bingley has to decide how she will behave in her pursuit of Darcy, whether her nasty allusions to Lizzy will ultimately hinder or help her in regards to her competitor. All of these are examples of oppositional behaviors and values, something Austen addresses again and again in her novels.

Card Interpretation
When this card appears in a reading, a love relationship is spotlighted. This love can be

romantic or platonic. You have found someone who aids you in becoming whole. The relationship helps you and the other to achieve self-actualization, someone who supplies you with what you lack, and to whom you supply something lacking as well.

You may have to make a choice between two potential lovers or friends. Make a choice that will help you achieve your highest goals and truest desires.

This card can also indicate numerous dangers, depending on who you "are" in the card. Are you Caroline Bingley, slavishly worshipping someone for the wrong reasons? If love is to grow, you must have your own interests and not shallowly echo the desired person's visions and dreams. That does not mean ignore the object of your desire, but to find a way to synthesize your dual needs within yourself. Depending on a person or a relationship to make you whole weakens you and is not love. Share your visions as a unit, but don't try to be someone else's vision, nor lose your own to enmesh yourself in another's.

You could also be Darcy, too entrenched in matters of class and societal standing to separate the gold from the glitter. You could even be Elizabeth Bennett, who prides herself on her discernment to the point where she blinds herself to the good qualities of a man she has decided to despise. Only you can determine which of the three people in this card you are, and choose your actions accordingly.

In many traditional versions of the Lovers card, the image often depicts Cupid shooting his arrow towards the unsuspecting couple. This represents the seemingly arbitrary and irresistible nature of our desires. As readers, we believe that there is nothing arbitrary about Darcy's attraction to Lizzy, but before he overcomes his early pride, he is convinced that he is the victim of Eros' aim.

When you consider your own amorous feelings, it might behoove you to determine whether your emotions are heaven-sent, or come from another, less celestial domain.

What Would Jane Do?

"Will it not be advisable, before we proceed on this subject, to arrange with rather more precision the degree of importance which is to appertain to this request, as well as the degree of intimacy subsisting between the parties?"

Jane Austen, *Pride and Prejudice*

Jane's Advice: It may not be immediately apparent, but there is a choice to be made here. It is likely a relationship choice, as relationships are often in the forefront of our thoughts and feelings. Such a choice can set in motion consequences that last a lifetime. Discernment is of the utmost importance when making emotional decisions. Examine the evidence of the past and present, and you will likely be able to foresee the future.

VII – The Chariot
Mansfield Park

Card Description
Mary Crawford, a young, rapacious woman, sits astride a cantering horse. She looks forward to riding quickly to a new adventure.

Storyline
When Henry Crawford and his sister Mary enter the lives of the denizens of Mansfield Park, they bring great change in their wake. Henry enchants both Bertram sisters, causing conflicts between the two young women, and Mary sets her sights on the eldest male Bertram, Tom, because he stands to inherit Mansfield Park. She little expects to find herself attracted to Edmund, his younger brother, who intends to become a clergyman.

But Edmund falls in love with her, and Mary can't help wishing he were the heir to the family estate. In comparison to Tom, a self-indulgent wastrel, Edmund is a prince – sensitive, intelligent, eloquent – and utterly honorable. Even as he is entranced by the spirited and strong-willed Mary, he turns a deaf ear to her contempt for his chosen profession. He is unable, however, to resist her wiles on any other subject. He even begins preparations to act in a risqué dramatic performance until his father returns and puts a stop to it. Mary also convinces Edmund that his cousin Fanny should marry Mary's brother, Henry.

It is only when Henry runs off with Edmund's married sister, Maria, that he begins to see the light. Even then, Edmund remains loyal to Mary – until the sophisticated and flippant comments that fall from her beautiful lips show her to be more concerned about societal strictures than the amorality of Henry's behavior. When Edmund sees Mary with clarity, he realizes she is a totally inappropriate choice for him. She, however, never pretends to be anyone but who she is – a woman with a penchant for the fast lane, one who has only contempt for the old-fashioned traditions Mansfield Park represents.

Card Interpretation
Henry and Mary Crawford's arrival in *Mansfield Park* can be likened to the carpetbagger invaders in *Gone With the Wind*. Like them, the Crawfords have only disdain for the simplicity of country living and old-fashioned, traditional values.

One of the first comments we read from Mary Crawford shows her annoyance with the limitations imposed by "housekeeping in a country village". She states outright that her respect is reserved for "those that are honest and rich" as opposed to the "honest and poor". She looks down "upon anything contented with obscurity when it might rise to distinction". The Chariot speaks to upward mobility and movement, movement that will heedlessly trample old ways in its focused drive to success. It also speaks to the complete attention necessary to achieve current goal(s), as well as an "I want it yesterday" mentality. Sometimes words spoken in haste, though, can be regretted at leisure, as Mary learns. The Chariot archetype is one that can verbally resemble an automobile careening out of control, with no way to put on the breaks until the vehicle is wrapped around a tree. This card can suggest moving too quickly in all areas, including speech.

Confidence is the watchword of the Chariot. Mary never recognizes Fanny as a competitor for Edmund's heart and is quite kind and generous to her, a woman whom she feels is no threat at all. This card can suggest over-confidence and underestimating others. While this card augurs success, it is wise to reassess the field of competition when receiving the Chariot in a reading.

Confidence and pride often go hand in hand. When Mary realizes that Edmund is planning to take orders despite her aversion to his choice of profession, she considers it an insult to her powers of persuasion. Even when her heart is at stake, she can't help but seeing love as a game in which to triumph. This card can indicate taking a road that leads not to the heart but to the satisfaction of pride.

Individuals who are living the archetype will do what it takes to win. Sometimes that includes deceit. Mary's most obvious use of artifice comes when she gives Fanny an amber cross that is really a love offering from Henry.

The Chariot archetype is not a particularly romantic one. Mary knows her brother will eventually fall out of love with Fanny, expecting there to always be a time of "moving on" from the first flush of love to disinterest. Mary can't imagine Fanny not marrying to improve her financial and social station, ignoring issues of love. Even her brother Henry (The Magician) is less cynical.

While not romantic, this card's message is never a cold one. Fervency and passion are qualities of the Chariot, even if they are not obvious. Those emotions are the motivators of the rider on the path to success. In addition, the Chariot can symbolize a romantic figure, the ultimate bad girl or boy who "hits and runs".

Patience is not a virtue of the Chariot card. Mary makes fun of Henry, sarcastically suggesting that Fanny might love him "at the end of about ten years' happy marriage". Deliberation is never as attractive to those under the rule of the Chariot's influence as moving full-speed ahead, consequences be damned.

Resiliency is one of the Chariot card's greatest gifts. Sometimes the Chariot can get overturned – and no one is more quick to get "back on the horse" than the Chariot's rider. Mary jokes and holds her head high when Edmund rejects her and her values. When faced with defeat, the Chariot's response is always brave and resolute. If you meet with a temporary setback, this card urges you to keep your eye on the prize and never give up hope – or your indomitable spirit.

An expression that can relate to the Chariot is "The grass is always greener on the other side". Mary never values Edmund more than when they are apart. When this card appears in a reading, it may be a good time to re-evaluate your goals. Are your aspirations heartfelt, or simply a mindless continuation of old objectives that are no longer meaningful?

What Would Jane Do?

"There, I will stake my last like a woman of spirit. No cold prudence for me. I am not born to sit still and do nothing. If I lose the game, it shall not be from not striving for it."

Jane Austen, *Mansfield Park*

Jane's Advice: While there is much to be said for tradition, some individuals are born to break with the tried and true. Wit and spirit are qualities that can move mountains and topple towers – just be sure that the mountains and towers you topple are ones you don't need for protection and stability as time passes.

VIII – Strength
Mansfield Park

Card Description
Fanny (Hanged One) and Henry Crawford (Magician) are sitting on a stone rampart overlooking the river at the Naval shipyard in Portsmouth – it's a bit seedy, but bustling with activity. Fanny is dressed all in maidenly white, and holds her white-gloved hand up, as if to stop Henry from speaking. Henry looks extremely vital and passionate as he reaches out to embrace Fanny, but she clearly shrinks from his advances.

Storyline
When Fanny is exiled to her family of birth in an attempt to make her accept Henry Crawford's proposal, he follows her, hoping to overthrow her misgivings with this proof of his ardor. Despite the financial and familial incentives, Fanny withstands his obsequies.

When Henry leaves her, he still intends to triumph in his love for Fanny, but is diverted by the now-married Maria. He convinces her to run away with him, choosing to steal a moment's fiery passion over the enduring warmth of true love.

Card Interpretation
While titles like *Hierophant* and *High Priestess* might be infrequently used in our 20th century vernacular, the word Strength is one with which we are quite familiar. Fortitude and courage are two synonyms for Strength. And as there are two beings on this card, so there are two kinds of strength, as well. Physical strength, which includes our natural and animal urges is one of them; the other is moral and spiritual strength, which does not demand external might, but an internal power that can withstand the corporeal.

When this card appears in a reading, you might be caught in a struggle between your physical and spiritual desires. Every human being encompasses both urges, often in equal proportions. Fanny may play the rôle of spiritual combatant in this story, but she has as many physical needs as Henry – perhaps more, as she is subject to poverty and a lack of personal autonomy. You may feel weaker in one area or the other, but this card indicates that you possess both strengths within you, if you choose to take hold of them.

On the other hand, you might wish to overpower your physical needs because they are temporal, and your goal is of a more spiritual and eternal nature. If so, this card indicates that you have the ability to be victorious with any such inner struggle.

If you are suffering any doubts about a situation, this card indicates you should trust your gut (although Jane Austen surely wouldn't phrase it this way). Fanny is the only one who sees through Henry's charm, and so can withstand the barrage of his arsenal of enchantments. Her animal senses alert her to the danger Henry presents to her and her family.

Sometimes it is not easy for us to hold on to our convictions – Fanny is certainly put in the "lion's den" for her efforts to reject Henry's hand in marriage. There is a reason for the expression "courage of your convictions", and this card urges you to have that courage. It suggests that valor is your birthright, and all you have to do is own it. Control is another word that may be an issue for you right now. Which do you want to control you – your physical nature or your spiritual one? You always have a choice, and in recognizing that, you control your actions and behaviors. Whether you are wrestling with yourself or another, your inner strength will be the factor that dictates the end result.

What Would Jane Do?

"It was a love which, operating on an active, sanguine spirit, of more warmth than delicacy, made her affection appear of greater consequence because it was withheld, and determined him to have the glory, as well as the felicity, of forcing her to love him."

Jane Austen, *Mansfield Park*

Jane's Advice: There is a reason we call upon the physic's science when we become feverish. Before taking action, reflect not with the warmth of passionate desire but the cool, collected wisdom of your intuition and experience. That which we vociferously feel is worth burning for in the moment often results in worthless embers that can not be swept from the grate too soon.

IX – The Hermit
Pride and Prejudice

Card Description
Mr. Bennett, a distinguished man with intelligent eyes is at his desk in his library, which contains no furbelows or feminine accouterments. He holds a lantern in order to read his book more easily. His room is clearly his fortress, lined with shelves of books – the door to the room is closed and one can see that this space is his place of escape. It is clearly the room of an ascetic.

Storyline
As father of five daughters, Mr. Bennett should devote some thought to getting them married off – at least, that's what his wife, Mrs. Bennett, believes. Unfortunately for her, there is no more of a meeting of minds on this subject than any other. The Bennetts are a poorly matched couple – Austen describes them thus:
"Mr. Bennett was so odd a mixture of quick parts, sarcastic humour, reserve, and caprice, that the experience of three and twenty years had been insufficient to make his wife understand his character. *Her* mind was less difficult to develope. She was a woman of mean understanding, little information, and uncertain temper".

However, Mr. Bennett does visit Netherfield in the hope of establishing relations with the wealthy renter, Charles Bingley. He doesn't eschew all societal responsibilities, but, in general, he prefers the sanctuary of his library to mixing with the public.

He can be too lenient with his children, precisely because he isn't engaged in their lives. However, when Mrs. Bennett tries to coerce Elizabeth into marrying the foolish Mr. Collins, Mr. Bennett intervenes and supports Lizzy with light-hearted, humorous remarks that only underline his steadfast support. When his wife convinces him to allow Lydia, his youngest daughter, to go to Brighton without an appropriate chaperone, he regrets his lenience. Lydia elopes with the unscrupulous Wickham, bringing disgrace to the family name. Even Mr. Bennett is roused to regret and he attempts to be a more responsible father with his other children.

When Elizabeth's suitor, Fitzwilliam Darcy, spends a great deal of time and money to insure that Wickham fulfills his matrimonial obligations to the feckless Lydia, Mr. Bennett is relieved. He can return to the solitude of his library, a bit wiser and more well-balanced from his bitter life lesson.

Card Interpretation
The Hermit is a card of deep introspection. You may be feeling rather philosophical, and prefer your own company to that of others. In fact, "I want to be alone" could be the motto of this card. You need a refuge that is solely your own, and you are more than capable of amusing yourself.

There's a certain degree of cynicism inherent in the Hermit card – the Hermit may love humanity, but not individual human beings. The Hermit has great integrity, but often little understanding of the human heart. His domain is philosophical, not emotional. However, you might find that you can see through social subterfuges to the souls of the people in your environment – and you find them amusing, in a mordant way. Your strong moral center makes those who have none seem alien, almost inhuman to you, hence figures of fun and internal sport.

When this card appears in a reading, it may be that the idea of interpersonal communication is abhorrent to you. As long as this is a temporary respite and not a long-term, escapist behavior, honor your desire for solitude. The Hermit can be rather distant, and is certainly not known for his warmth, despite the fact that he carries a lantern in traditional decks, and often prefers books to people. Books make good friends, and the Hermit notices that, unlike people, they don't have ulterior motives.

The Hermit's priorities are grounded in what is real and authentic, and he mocks pomp and circumstance. Scorn for sacred cows can result in being perceived as a non-conformist, a role in which the Hermit is quite comfortable.

When you receive this card in a reading it can represent an astute observer who sees the human follies and foibles beneath the mask. That observer can be someone you consider wise or cynical, and can certainly include yourself.

This card can also represent an attempt to detach yourself from inconsequential frays, and can even appear lethargic, but when you need to stand your ground, as Mr. Bennett does when he stops his wife from pressuring Lizzy into marriage, you do it instinctively and steadfastly.

Unfortunately, you don't always maintain that strength or instinctual wisdom in romantic relationships. Some people are unsuited for partnerships. All people, however, must be very careful not to enter into a relationship based on physical attraction alone, because age erodes outer appeal. Seek depth on all levels when you receive this card in a reading.

What Would Jane Do?

"In his library he had always been sure of leisure and tranquility; and though prepared… to meet with folly and conceit in every other room in the house he was used to be free from them there…"

Jane Austen, *Pride and Prejudice*

Jane's Advice: While you may be surrounded by folly and conceit, you not only recognize it, you find some amusement in it. However, the light you hold up to the world can illuminate your own flaws, if you are but willing to examine them with the same dry and discerning wit you apply everywhere else. It is wise never to take any thing too seriously, but perhaps your light will shine the brighter if you take yourself a bit more than you do at present.

X – The Wheel of Fortune
Emma

Card Description

A dance in the shape of a circle is taking place. Emma (the Maiden of Quills), dancing with Frank Churchill (Knight of Quills), looks approvingly at her friend Harriet and George Knightley, who are paired together. Also present is Mrs. Weston (the Empress).

Storyline

At a dance, the newly married Mr. Elton publicly snubs and humiliates Emma's friend Harriet, but George Knightley comes to the rescue and asks her to dance, to Emma's great satisfaction. Emma takes pride in Knightley's gallant and upright nature as she watches them, while she dances with Frank Churchill, who is secretly engaged.

Card Interpretation

There are numerous examples in folklore where a seeming stroke of good fortune turns into unmitigated disaster – and what initially seems like a negative turn of events evolves into the best thing that could have happened for all concerned. The Wheel of Fortune goes up and down, over and over again – and not recognizing these ups and downs as the nature of the life cycle is what keeps us dangling precariously from the hub. We do not control the motion of the wheel, merely our responses to its turning.

When this card appears in a reading, you might feel that you are riding a crest of good fortune. If you are wondering whether now is the time to take a bold risk, this card invites you to take part in the dance of life, not remain on the outside looking in. Unexpected opportunities await you, as Knightley's gallant rescue of Harriet awaited her. However, your own worthiness and efforts – and an ability to be realistic even as you dare to dream – will determine whether opportunity leads to ultimate success or becomes a source of disappointment and disillusionment.

But this card doesn't only apply to new opportunities. This card indicates that old dreams that have never really died in your heart can be revisited, and end on a more positive note. Mr. Knightley has sought Emma's heart for many years, yet never expects his love to be returned. However, Mr. Knightley's gallant rescue spurs Harriet's crush, which leads Emma into recognizing her love for him. When he dances with Harriet out of decency and charity, he has no foreknowledge what his reward will be.

As you look at this card, you see couples engaged in a dance, yet none of these couples ultimately end up together. Things are not always as they seem, which is one of the hidden dangers of this card. Emma has no idea that the man she is dancing with is secretly engaged to another. Harriet mistakes Knightley's kindness for attraction. Even as you seize the day (and the dance), you should not forget that as the Wheel goes up, it also goes down. Fluctuations of fortune are inevitable. In the blink of an eye, you may go from feeling confident and positive to despair. Emma travels from pride in Mr. Knightley's gallantry to despair that he might feel a romantic interest for Harriet, then to relief and delight when she learns that he has loved her, Emma, all along. Understanding that such shifts are part of life is the key not only to survival, but success.

In matters of the heart, this card reminds you that your soul mate may not originally look or be like the person in your imagination. On paper, the Maiden and Knight of Quills sound like the perfect couple, but Emma would never be able to tolerate Frank Churchill's disingenuous ways, any more than he would receive the grounding from her that he so desperately needs.

If there is someone you have been discounting as a potential match, it may be time to take another look – and take a chance!

The expression "felix culpa" comes to mind with this card as well. Emma's matchmaking could have resulted in disaster, but her mistakes in that area led her to realize that she did, in fact, love Mr. Knightley.

According to John Wood, an important architect in Jane Austen's day, the circle symbolizes "god's perfection". Never doubt that each turn on the wheel is a divinely planned road on your particular path, even if you don't know where it leads.

In general, this is generally a very positive card to receive in a reading, occasionally offering prospects and prosperity seemingly out of the blue. That said, no cycle lasts forever. We can never know whether our movements in the dance of life will be rewarded or punished – we can only keep dancing as best as we can.

What Would Jane Do?

"I have never been in love; it is not in my way or my nature; and I do not think I ever shall."
Jane Austen, *Emma*

Jane's Advice: The moment a man positively declares who he is invariably leads to events that conclusively prove he has no idea whom he is at all. The fairer sex is hardly exempt from this universal law. Foibles and frailties are what separate us from the Divine. No human being is exempt from that separation. However, we are all endowed with free will – men and women alike – and our actions determine how well we fare under the capricious tides of fortune, as well as how closely we achieve any degree of divinity.

XI – Justice
Pride and Prejudice

Card Description

A fountain pen is placed diagonally across the card from one corner on the top to one corner on the bottom. In the top section, Darcy (Lord of Quills) is writing a letter at his desk; at the bottom, Lizzy (Lady of Candlesticks) is reading said letter. The words in the letter appear in the background of the card.

Storyline

From the moment Elizabeth Bennett meets Fitzwilliam Darcy, she is convinced by his behavior that he is an overbearingly proud man who thinks himself superior to everyone around him. This opinion is reinforced when the charming Wickham.

While Darcy does disdain Elizabeth at their first meeting, he finds himself increasingly attracted to her. When she visits the neighborhood of the aunt with whom he is staying, the close and frequent proximity intensifies his ardor and he proposes.

Darcy's patronizing approach incenses Elizabeth, who rejects him, enumerating his offensive behaviors – his proud manner, his maltreatment of Wickham and his maneuvers regarding his best friend, Charles Bingley, whom he has steered away from Elizabeth's sister, Jane, who loves him.

Darcy writes and delivers to Elizabeth a letter that clarifies his behavior, providing her with details of Wickham's perfidy. Darcy also communicates that Jane's amiability to all led Darcy to think she didn't care much for his friend, Bingley. Over time and with repeated readings, Elizabeth realizes that she has been guilty of unfair prejudice against Darcy. The letter opens her heart a bit toward a man she has always found insufferable.

While Darcy is initially furious with Elizabeth, lengthy reconsideration of her words makes him reflect upon his own behaviors with honest self-criticism. He realizes his pride has interfered with his own clarity of vision.

Card Interpretation

When the Justice card appears in a reading, clarity and resulting fairness are your best and safest guides. It may be that you have been seeing things unclearly, and your behaviors have reflected this astigmatism. Like a road sign, this card alerts you to look not at your feelings, but the facts of a situation, and to pay attention to all of them, not just the ones that are in accordance with your beliefs. Like Elizabeth's resentment of Darcy, you may need to cut away old false thought patterns with relentless determination.

You may have an important decision to make that can affect your entire life, as Elizabeth does when Darcy proposes. You need to weigh the situation judiciously, and ensure that you have all the information you need prior to coming to a final conclusion.

In the tarot, the Sword symbolizes air and thought. A modern symbol for the Sword is the pen, which is said to be mightier than the sword because the power of communication can prevent wars and augment peace. In *Pride and Prejudice*, Elizabeth's eloquent and specific rejection of Darcy's proposal, as well as Darcy's written response, serve to illuminate both parties. Perhaps you need to put your thoughts on paper in order to clarify things for yourself, or to shed light on a situation for another. Your initial words may be muddied and muddled with emotion, so be sure to write a rough draft before sending something in writing that you'll later regret.

Another traditional symbol of Justice is a scale, which is simulated by the positioning of Elizabeth and Darcy in the Jane Austen Tarot version of this card. Justice signifies that you need to weigh your options carefully at this time. Balance should be a priority in your life now, and if you see that your scales are tipping dangerously in one direction, you need to shift your priorities to create equipoise and personal harmony. Cards surrounding the Justice card might give you an indication as to the areas in which you need to make changes.

Often, our lives are decorated in shades of grey. Nuances abound. When you receive the Justice card in a reading, subtleties are mere dross. The choice on the table is in black and white. Use your Sword-Pen to distinguish between the two, then cut away what does not serve you.

What Would Jane Do?
"Pleased with the preference of one, and offended by the neglect of the other, on the very beginning of our acquaintance, I have courted prepossession and ignorance, and driven reason away, where either were concerned. Till this moment, I never knew myself."

Jane Austen, *Pride and Prejudice*

Jane's Advice: It is easy to take pride in our own discernment when we are so very rarely wrong. Even the most observant of us, however, can err when our hearts – and vanity – are involved. Yet that is precisely the time when we most need all our wits about us – and when we need to be our most careful that our vision is not blinded by pride or prejudice.

Strong emotional displays may make for entertaining scenes. However, the truest and best hearts are not found clamoring in a parade of red velvet, but are frequently hidden beneath suits of a more sober colour. Hence, you may need to look a little wider and deeper before making a choice that could have lingering effects.

XII – The Hanged One
Mansfield Park

Card Description
A mock stage set (with piano and sofa) in a family library is given the addition of new green baize curtains, in order to increase the similarity to a professional play. Fanny Price stands on the top of a ladder in a bent-over position, sewing something onto the curtains. The ceiling above has two wooden planks crossing one another in the shape of a cross.

Storyline
Fanny Price lives at Mansfield Park, but is not really of it. The quintessential poor relation who has been taken in at a young age by her well-off relatives, she is treated with conde-scension by all but her cousin Edmund, for whom she feels a love bordering on worship. She is expected to serve her aunts – one of whom is dilatory and the other, demanding. Her uncle, Sir Thomas Bertram, means well, but he frightens her with his rigidity and stern demeanor.

When the young people decide to put on a worldly play, the only dissenters are Edmund (who is in the process of becoming a clergy-man) and Fanny. Eventually, Edmund gives in against his better judgment, but Fanny stands firm, the lone holdout for the Mansfield Park way of life. When Sir Thomas returns and puts an end to the proposed plans for the play, Fanny is relieved, yet her sufferings are just beginning. Henry Crawford decides to make Fanny fall in love with him and pursues her. Ironically, Henry is the one who falls in love and proposes.

Fanny recognizes Henry as the charming rogue he is. Because she is also in love with Edmund, Fanny refuses him. Sir Thomas exiles her from Mansfield Park in order to make her see reason. While Fanny is in despair at returning to the coarseness of her birth home, she hangs on to her principles. When Henry persuades Maria, Fanny's married cousin, to run away with him, Fanny returns to Mansfield Park at her uncle's behest. The Bertrams finally recognize her value, and Edmund eventually recognizes her as his soul mate.

Card Interpretation
When the Hanged One appears in a reading, you may literally be hung up or feel as if you are suspended in time. Like Fanny, you may be sacrificing yourself for a higher purpose, or even for something that doesn't personally resonate for you. In the card image, Fanny is sewing curtains for a play that she disap-proves of, but she represses her own needs in order to serve others' desires. Fanny is the embodiment of sacrifice for those she loves and the morality to which she ascribes. If you are feeling "hung up", you may want to examine what you are waiting for – and deter-mine if it is worth the costs: financial, emo-tional, physical, and spiritual.

Fanny never likes to speak of her own good qualities and doesn't even recognize them.

This may be a time when you are hiding your gifts from the world and/or yourself. While humility is a virtue, taken too far it can be detrimental. Just as Fanny's vision is sorely missed when she leaves Mansfield Park, you may have things to contribute that are unique, yet you hold back out of modesty or a lack of self-esteem. What are you withholding from the world?

Sometimes it may seem like you see things differently from others, and question yourself. Don't allow peer pressure to sway you from your vision, even if you are the only one who has it. You will ultimately be proven right, as Fanny is about the play:

"Fanny is the only one who has judged rightly throughout; who has been consistent. *Her* feelings have been steadily against it from first to last. She never ceased to think of what was due to you. You will find Fanny everything you could wish".

Edmund says these words to his father, but they could fit any religious devotee.

Throughout most of *Mansfield Park*, Fanny watches and suffers as the man she loves becomes more and more infatuated with a woman she believes isn't good enough for him. You may be attracted to someone who is unavailable on some level, yet you feel it is worthwhile to wait patiently for a return of your feelings. You may eventually be rewarded for your persistence, as Fanny is, but you also may be prolonging heartache. When this card appears in a reading, you must determine if you are sacrificing time and emotion for a true soul mate, or surrendering your power to a fantasy that will (shall) never be realized.

Fanny is not physically strong, and her sensitivity to others and their needs might be a contributing factor of her weak constitution. At the very least, too much self-sacrifice will result in a loss of energy and vitality. This card indicates that you might be physically impacted because of your own sensitivity to others, and you may want to think about whom or what is negatively impacting your well-being. Fanny Price, for all her virtues, is disliked by many Austen fans – she seems too good to be true, a humorless prig. The scent of sanctimony is not alluring to many people, and the line between sacrifice and martyrdom is a fine one. If you find yourself feeling morally superior to all whom surround you, you may be exuding that unappealing aroma. Real humility does not feel like superiority.

Fanny's upbringing is one of not-so-benign neglect, wherein she is always treated like the poor relation. She sleeps in a small, unheated room while the rest of the family stays warm and cosseted. You could feel unable to move forward in life because, as a child, you were given the message (directly or indirectly) that you deserved less than others. If this is the case, you might wish to try and "reverse" your point of view about yourself and your worth.

When Fanny receives the summons to return to Mansfield Park, Austen writes, "Never had Fanny more wanted a cordial". Sensitive people can be more susceptible to substances that dull or calm the senses, such as alcohol and drugs. This card can occasionally be an indicator of such a weakness.

What Would Jane Do?
"Fanny found herself obliged to yield, that she might not be accused of pride or indifference, or some other littleness…"

Jane Austen, *Mansfield Park*

Jane's Advice: Living in an upright manner seems to come easier for some people than others. Often, this does not emanate from innate virtue, but is molded by circumstances and environment. Structured, peaceful and traditional surroundings are the optimum soil for goodness to flourish in the garden of life, but challenges and sacrifice are also needed to ensure the blossoming of morality.

XIII – Death
Sense and Sensibility

Card Description

An old man, looking rather agitated as he lies on a bed in his well-appointed bedroom, is clearly at Death's door. His worried wife and two daughters stand at the doorway. His son kneels at his bedside, holding his hand, agreeing to something the older man is asking as a deathbed request.

Storyline

Carol Shields, among others, remarks in her biography of Jane Austen on how very rarely Austen mentions death in her novels. However, the first chapter of *Sense and Sensibility* begins with the death of Henry Dashwood, and the entire novel builds on how his death transforms the life of his family.

Henry Dashwood has a son, John, from a previous marriage, and a wife and three daughters when he dies. Knowing that his son John will inherit his estate, Henry asks John to take care of the women who will now be bereft of their home and financial security.

John promises to do so, and Henry dies, comfortable in the knowledge that his family will be protected. Yet even deathbed promises can be broken, and once we pass away, we have no control over the lives of the living. It can be argued that Henry's romantic daughter, Marianne, would never have learned to value Colonel Brandon's sterling qualities if her brother John had protected her from the machinations of the dashing, but sybaritic Willoughby, and Elinor, her practical, refined sister, might not have wed the man she loves if she were more financially secure. Perhaps it is better that we don't completely control the events of our lives, as the unexpected can transform us in positive ways we can't even anticipate.

Card Interpretation

While it is exceedingly rare that the Death card will refer to physical death in a reading, this card depicts one. The reality is that every

living being dies, even if their spirit lives on in the hearts of those who remain. But the message of the card goes far beyond this mortal coil, addressing the many repercussions and transformations that a single ending can engender, and that is borne out by the story in *Sense and Sensibility*, in terms of the impact that death has on Henry Dashwood's family. Irrevocable change always involves loss, but it can also bring unexpected rewards. In addition to the true and complete sorrow that Henry Dashwood's untimely passing engenders, it also initially seems like a literal death blow to his daughters' opportunities for marriage. Their resulting move to Barton Valley from their beloved Norland, which never would have happened had he lived, leads Marianne to meet her future husband. In turn, that husband is able to ensure that Elinor and her beloved can marry, as well.

When this card appears in a reading, metamorphosis is inevitable. The change may per-

tain to external circumstances or inner transformation, but whether or not you would like
the status quo to remain, it will not. The life
force demands change, and death is part of
that two-sided coin.

Whether the alteration is desired or not, most
of us fear change. The stark finality of the
Death card reminds us that we can never go
back. That can be a scary thing to contemplate. Nothing is permanent – death forces us
to realize any thought of physical eternity is
delusion and attempts to resist inevitable
change will make your life more, not less, difficult. Occasionally someone receives this
card in a reading when he or she is emerging
from a period of immobility – a new life is
beginning. It can be a harbinger of hope for
those who seek change in their lives.

Another thing to remember about death is
that it is a natural transit in human evolution.
It's the last stage in a life that consists of phas-
es. This card can suggest that something in
your life is coming to a natural end – you may
feel it has arrived before its time, but we don't
control the world's revolutions. Sometimes
we seek the transformation of Death and
sometimes it is thrust upon us. Either way,
this card signifies an end, an end that usually
does not reflect our wishes or regrets.

We generally think of immortality in terms of
gods and goddesses, powerful rulers throughout history, and those famed individuals
whom we continue to remember as years pass.

But all of us leave a legacy for good or ill.
Henry Dashwood, though well-meaning, dies
at a surprisingly early age, and his unintended
legacy is that the vulnerable members of his
family are left in want and need. Are there any
legacies you wish to leave? If so, it's never too
early to plan for unexpected exigencies. They
are as much a part of life… as death.

What Would Jane Do?

"The old gentleman died: his will was read,
and like almost every other will, gave as
much disappointment as pleasure."

Jane Austen, *Sense and Sensibility*

Jane's Advice: While death is not a subject one
enjoys discussing, it's a subject that employs –
and enjoys – the final word. Death is an aggra-
vating reminder that preparation for the
future must be both thorough and far-sighted,
that our legacies are uncertain, and that none
of us are immune from its bony fingers. Those
immutable facts are precisely why the subject
is not particularly favored in any sphere of
society.

Unalterable change may seem a bitter pill on
initial ingestion, yet as the stages of the meal
of life are placed upon our table, we may find
the resultant foodstuffs unexpectedly to our
taste. Bitter or sweet, we must continue to
consume the fare we are served, in the order
in which it is served. Digestion is, of course,
another matter entirely.

XIV – Temperance

Emma

Card Description

Jane Fairfax reaches out to Emma Woodhouse in a room with a small, elegant pianoforte. The two women look at each other with understanding and esteem. They stand beneath a fine and capable drawing of an angel, who looks as if she is beaming down upon them.

Storyline

Wealthy and indulged Emma Woodhouse is the same age as Jane Fairfax, a poor, but accomplished young lady who lives in her community. They do not bond as children, and the more Jane is held up to Emma as a role model, the more she resents this paragon of perfection.

As the novel begins, Emma chooses to befriend Harriet, whose ancestry is mysterious and whose intelligence and accomplishments are clearly inferior to her own. When Emma sees Jane, she admires her elegance and resolves to be friendlier, but her superior accomplishments, combined with her cautious and cool demeanor, convince Emma to be no more than civil. Jane is equally disinterested in forming a friendship with her, though both women are polite – too polite – to one another. When Frank Churchill arrives in the neighborhood, he seems eager to attach himself to Emma, and they bond over a shared rumor about Jane. Over time, Jane Fairfax is discussed and dissected by both of them. In public, Frank teases Jane, and Emma takes pleasure in Frank's asides. She finds him attractive, and wonders if she is in love with him.

At a gathering in Box Hill, Frank is particularly attentive – and while Emma flirts back, she has decided that their relationship will remain platonic. Jane removes herself from the situation after remarking that relationships born in haste are easily dissolved if the two people involved realize they have made a mistake.

Frank and Jane have been secretly engaged, but Frank's demands, coupled with his inability to marry her without risking his future inheritance, have persuaded Jane to take a position as a gov-erness rather than rely on Frank's honoring his promise of matrimony. She is heartbroken, but determined to do what she feels is the right thing for herself and her family. She is determined to make a clean break from any and all of society's pleasures and returns Frank's personal letters.

Soon thereafter, Frank's aunt suddenly dies. He is now able to marry Jane. Meanwhile, Harriet confides to Emma that she has feelings for George Knightley and suspects he returns them. This causes Emma to realize she has loved Knightley all along; she fears that her past encouragement of Harriet's romantic ambitions forces her to support the union. When Knightley proposes to Emma, she is a wiser woman. Her "judgment was as strong as her feelings, and as strong as it had ever been before", because she has learned to recognize and own her emotions.

Card Interpretation

Vitality as opposed to delicacy is but one of the contrasts between Emma Woodhouse and Jane

Fairfax, though Austen alludes to Jane's healthier aspect once her future plans are established in the quotation cited below. Emma exudes confidence and graciousness, an outgrowth of the comfort and wealth she has always known; Jane possesses application and perseverance born from the knowledge that she may well have to earn her living. When this card appears in a reading, we need to look at our own qualities and personality traits. Are we in balance or do we need to temper ourselves in some way? What qualities or traits in a friend (or a rival) do you wish to emulate and make your own? Emma's intelligence makes her overconfident of her own abilities. Which of your talents has become so emphasized that they are now your weakness? Emma's belief that she has a gift for making matches causes no end of mischief. Yet she is well-intentioned; she wishes those around her to be happy and successful in love. If she focused on understanding herself, instead of toying with the lives and hearts of those around her, she might have comprehended the secrets of her own heart sooner. Knowing one's self is the first step to being able to help others, and Emma gains that wisdom – the hard way – by the end of the novel. If your actions are focused on helping others at this time, it may be wise to examine your motives. Are you balancing your needs with others' or are you neglecting your own growth or inner harmony in the name of charity or friendship? At first it might appear that Jane Fairfax embodies the qualities we attribute to the Temperance card. She is temperate, modest, beautiful, and accomplished and she even looks like an angel. But Jane is also an enigma; she has dark secrets and a mind that is not at rest. She is also not moderate – once she turns 21, she vows she will shun all of the former pleasures in her life "for ever" in order to earn her living as a governess. Few things in life are black and white – Jane's intended self-mortification gives way to a prosperous marriage. The Temperance card reminds us to eschew an all-or-nothing mentality.

Emma fears George Knightley, the man she loves, is attached to another; Jane wonders if she will be forced to renounce her plans to marry Frank Churchill. In a sense, both women's beliefs must die in order for them to be trans-muted through the magic of Temperance.

Unlike the more seemingly perfect Jane Fairfax, Emma is somewhat transparent, an open book. She makes numerous mistakes, but the only thing she attempts to hide is her ego. Emma's errors come from her belief that she can control the lives and feelings of others, but her actions are overt and she is quick to acknowledge her mistakes to herself and those whom she wrongs. If Emma is yang, all vitality and openness in her feelings and opinions, Jane is yin; all her emotions and intentions simmer beneath the surface.

When the Temperance card appears in a reading, it is time to note where we need to be more expressive and open like Emma – or areas in which, like Jane, it would behoove us to be more languid or discreet. The Angel that appears on this (and most) Temperance cards reminds us that we humans can invoke the heavenly realms by virtuous actions. Tempering our selves with concerted effort and a devotion to inner and outer balance brings us one step closer to that angelic being.

What Would Jane Do?

"Emma had never seen her look so well, so lovely, so engaging. There was consciousness, animation, and warmth; there was every thing which her countenance or manner could ever have wanted."

Jane Austen, *Emma*

Jane's Advice: Candor and discretion must go hand in hand. While there are times when concealment is necessary, it is not a virtue. On the other hand, one need not advertise every fleeting inner thought; many times they are fleeting because they are meant to flee quickly from our minds.

Paragons of virtue are not attractive even in fiction, and we rarely become them in fact. Were we to continually attempt to be models of temperance, we would find ourselves veering endlessly from one side of a virtue to another, like a boat on stormy seas. Occasionally we find ourselves suffering from that kind of queasy seasickness. When we do, nautical tradition reminds us that an even keel will get us through even the most querulous waters.

XV – The Devil

Lady Susan

Card Description

Lady Susan, a beautiful woman past her prime ("delicately fair, with fine grey eyes and dark eyelashes") is an "uncommon union of symmetry, brilliance and grace". On her left, she holds her daughter Frederica's neck down, forcefully cupping her neck. Frederica is pretty, but, from her stance, she seems reluctant to be in the picture.

On the other side of Lady Susan is the fatuous James Martin. He is on his knees, staring adoringly at Lady Susan. He resembles a human lapdog, silly, not-too-bright, and utterly subservient. Unlike Frederica, he doesn't have to be forced to be a part of the tableau. At the doorway stands an angry onlooker, Catherine Vernon.

Storyline

Lady Susan Vernon is, like de Laclos' Marquise de Merteuil, a character of great charm and great wit – and amoral. The widow of a wealthy man, Lady Susan is also the mother of Frederica, a 16 year old innocent whom she paints as a rebellious, headstrong teenager to her sister-in-law, Catherine Vernon. Lady Susan is paying her sister-in-law a visit only because her last hosts, the Mainwarings, the married couple with whom she was previously staying, have kicked her out of their home. The husband wouldn't have minded if she remained, as they are having an affair, but his wife and daughter force her to depart immediately. The daughter is put out not just for her mother's sake, but her own – Lady Susan has captivated her suitor, James Martin, as well.

Initially, Catherine Vernon doesn't trust Lady Susan. Catherine remembers all too well how Lady Susan tried to prevent her from marrying into the family, but Lady Susan charms her, too – in the beginning. However, when Catherine sees her once-cynical brother falling under Lady Susan's romantic enchantments, and observes that Frederica is nothing like her mother's description of her, she recognizes Lady Susan as the dangerous entity she is.

Catherine tries to protect Frederica, but Lady Susan forbids her daughter from confiding in her aunt her negative feelings about marrying James Martin, the rich fool Lady Susan is attempting to force her daughter to wed. Lady Susan is such an outstanding manipulator that she can convince a man she has bewitched to transfer his affections to her daughter!

Lady Susan costs Catherine Vernon her serenity in another area, as she worries that her brother will become ensnared by Lady Susan's clever machinations and marry her.

Catherine realizes that the only person Lady Susan truly cares for is herself (though she finds Mainwaring quite attractive, because he is as conscienceless a sybarite as she is). She is not only willing to lie and scheme to achieve her means, she takes great pride and pleasure in her manipulations. Finally, after causing others infinite hours of heartache, Lady Susan is unmasked for her licentious behaviors. She must marry the foolish James Martin herself.

Card Interpretation

When this card appears in a reading, it is tempting to look elsewhere for the clever manipulator trying to bend you to his or her will. However, it is often more edifying (and infinitely more productive) to examine one's own motivations.

You may possess an impeccable understanding of human nature – and an ability to manipulate others into carrying out your wishes. In addition, you may take what you consider justifiable pride in your knack for "handling" others. In the business world, especially, this aptitude can serve you well. However, in personal transactions, this behavior can cross the line into deceitfulness.

You may be so convinced that you know what is right for others that you feel it is appropriate to direct their movements in whatever manner you find effective. "The end justifies the means" could be your motto, and you even sometimes find it mystifying that others could object to your actions. You may respond to objections with an extremity completely out of proportion to the situation. You hate to be thwarted, and feel honor-bound to complete whatever you set out to do, by any means necessary.

Your self-pride can be considerable. It is possible that you think your opinion is the only meritorious one and that others should accede to your will without contest or complaint, as Lady Susan exhibits in attempting to yoke her daughter to James Martin. Your great charm and charismatic nature assist you in manifesting your will more often than you reasonably should. You also possess unusual vitality and wit, as well as an excellent sense of humor, though you might use that as yet another method of manipulation. Often, though, if you can laugh at yourself, you will maintain a healthy sense of perspective that mitigates a great deal of the boundless hunger for power that this card can indicate.

Sexual confidence can walk hand-in-hand with the belief that you are entitled to do what you want, when you want. This can lead to disapproval from others who are more strait-laced or, in your opinion, repressive. You may even have contempt for conventional morality. If you so choose, though, you might present a demure face to the world and indulge your habits in secret – you are skilled in obscuring what you wish to conceal.

There is also a tendency to hold others in contempt for behaviors you yourself have frequently displayed – and even, perhaps, have taught by example. You expect complete loyalty, but feel it would be a mistake to bestow that kind of allegiance to others.

You may have some dark secrets that you not only conceal from the world, but that you hide from yourself. If you are willing to examine them with perspective and your vaunted sense of humor, you might discover that the light of day makes them less horrific and threatening.

If the above description doesn't ring true to you as an accurate portrayal of your self, but you recognize another in it, you must ask yourself why are you releasing your power to someone whom you know doesn't have your best interests at heart.

What Would Jane Do?

"There is exquisite pleasure in subduing an insolent spirit, in making a person predetermined to dislike acknowledge one's superiority."

Jane Austen, *Lady Susan*

Jane's Advice: There is always a temptation, when one is cleverer than one's associates, to reap the benefits of that intellectual disparity. However, the expression "too smart for your own good" can prove the sagacity of that time-honored phrase. Honorable intent and a deep understanding of your truest needs and desires will garner rewards greater than any machinations will ever ultimately provide, though temporary success can not be doubted. You must decide in advance which will give you the greater satisfaction.

Major Arcana

XVI – The Tower
Persuasion

Card Description
The image on this card is a little different from traditional tarot Tower cards. A high brick stairwell is placed amidst a wall of cliffs overlooking the sea, and directly below the stairwell is a cement walkway. Louisa Musgrove lies crumpled on the cement walkway, surrounded by young people who look on in horror. One is a distraught handsome man in uniform (Captain Wentworth). Only Louisa's sister-in-law, the slightly older-but-still-beautiful Anne Elliot, kneels over her to ascertain the extent of her injuries.

Storyline
It hurts sensitive, sensible Anne Elliot to her core when Captain Wentworth, whom she rejected in her youth, and is now wealthy, successful, and eminently eligible, re-enters her life as the potential suitor of her younger, privileged sister-in-law, Louisa. Louisa, filled with a zest for life which some might deem incautiousness, has gotten into the habit of jumping into Wentworth's arms from high places, no doubt as a way to physically become close to him in a relatively socially-acceptable way. Though he warns her not to leap from this particularly dangerous spot, she does it twice, but only once successfully.

Louisa does not fall to her death, but her intemperate leap leads to great physical changes. She receives a major head contusion from which she recovers, but she also falls in love with another man during her lengthy recuperation.

Wentworth, whose perception of Anne's betrayal has long fired and fed his ambition, is filled with resentment towards her, resentment that blinds him to her worth and his feelings for her, which are inextricably mixed with the taste of distrust. He has determined that the time has come for him to marry, and he seeks a partner who will be all admiration and adoration, someone younger and more appealing than the now considerably older Anne Elliot.

He flirts with several women and seems to have settled upon Louisa, only to be exposed anew to Anne's substantive superiority. This is borne resolutely home to him when Louisa jumps off the cliff stairs, and it is only Anne's coolness of head and ability to act quickly in the face of disaster that saves Louisa's life. He realizes that a marriage to Louisa would be a house built on an ill-designed foundation that could never stand, yet he feels that he is now morally obligated to her.

Card Interpretation
An unexpected tragedy is always shocking, and Louisa's hot-headed behavior initially leads to distraught feelings on all sides. Yet her foolhardy leap results in happy – and fitting – consequences for all concerned. Sometimes disaster seems to come out of nowhere, yet if we inspect the past carefully, we often see that we have sown the seeds that have led us to a less-than-pretty pass.

Anne's decision to listen to her godmother over her heart has caused her years of sorrow. Wentworth's refusal to recognize Anne's virtues because of his pique and anger lead him to give Louisa and the rest of their friends and acquaintances the belief that his interest in her is serious. When she almost falls to her death, he feels so guilty that he allows the myth of that serious interest to stand. Louisa's impetuousness is nearly the cause of her death. Yet this disaster eventually leads to the promise of breakthrough and the construction of several solid and happy lives.

When you receive the Tower card, you need to examine what "disaster" is occurring in your life and how you might have contributed to it. You may find that recovery is a matter of recognizing and changing old beliefs that no longer serve you, not a simple matter, but a necessary one if you wish to avoid repeat "disasters".

The Golden Dawn's astrological attribution for The Tower is Mars, the planet of action and aggression. Mars can be beneficial, such as when Wentworth's anger at Anne's lack of trust fires his ambitions and energizes him to be successful in his career. It can also be harmful, as in the case of Louisa's rash behavior, or when Wentworth's anger blinds him to Anne's good qualities. When this card appears in a reading, it is a warning against rash behavior of any kind.

Sometimes, a Tower experience does truly come as a bolt from the blue. An example of this is the re-emergence of Frederick Wentworth into Anne's life, which she has done nothing to precipitate. Just as in *Persuasion*, what seems like a guaranteed prescription for renewed heartache and pain can lead to a blossoming of new life and love.

If something shocking and seemingly unpleasant has happened to you, try to see what opportunities to grow and evolve exist within the situation. Almost every hardship inevitably presents us with the possibility of renewing positive thoughts and strengthening already-developed qualities, although this insight doesn't necessarily make a Tower event any easier to bear when we're experiencing it.

Life serves us difficult experiences that we simply must live through, and sometimes it seems as if our particular cloud utterly lacks a silver lining. But we need to realize that while we may be powerless in the face of external events, the one thing we have complete control of is the attitude we take toward them. Our power lies in our ability to perceive and create rainbows from the clouds of life's downpours.

What Would Jane Do?

"They set forward, treading back with feelings unutterable, the ground, which so lately, so very lately, and so light of heart, they had passed along."

Jane Austen – *Persuasion*

Jane's Advice: Oft-times, what initially seems to be most unpleasant becomes what we most embrace, just as what we most look forward to can become abhorrent. We have no way of knowing our Divine plan. Trust in providence, but also learn to meet all occurrences with trust in yourself, trust earned by logic and compassion, spirit and sense. These behaviors, not fortune or beauty, are what ultimately define a lady and a gentleman.

XVII – The Star
Persuasion

Card Description

Louisa (The Tower) lies on a bed, a doctor in attendance. In another room, the handsome 31-year-old Captain Wentworth (Lord of Candlesticks), Anne Elliot (Lady of Quills), and Captain and Mrs. Harville all sit, looking up hopefully towards the large picture window that dominates the room. Through that window, we see the night sky, with one star burning particularly large and bright.

Storyline

When Louisa, through her own impetuousness, falls from a steep stairwell, she loses consciousness. Her rescue is managed by cool-headed, efficient Anne Elliot, who takes command and organizes the situation.

Until Louisa regains consciousness, her friends and family wait anxiously to discover if she will live or die. Even though she immediately goes back into unconsciousness, she does open her eyes, offering "proof of life" and calming those who now sit in vigil upon the doctor's verdict. The "proof of life" is, indeed, a prognosticator that Louisa's health is likely to return and the anxious family and friends must begin to make plans. Life goes on.

Captain Wentworth, impressed anew with Anne's calm, capable nature, remembers why he originally fell in love with her. Anne's love for him has always remained steady, but her observational skills lead her to see that Captain Wentworth's feelings for her are markedly improving. But at this point, she doesn't dare hope that these feelings will lead to marriage.

Card Interpretation

The star is a symbol of hope and wish fulfillment in many cultures. We "wish upon a star" and see the glowing lights in the night sky as something beautiful, yet ineffable. Stars fill us with awe, a sense of something greater than ourselves.

When this card appears in a reading, it is a beacon illuminating your truest self. You have either reached beyond what you thought you were capable of, possibly dazzling others during your shining moment, or you are about to take such an action. But this feat is not motivated by any potential impression you might make on anyone else; you are simply tapping into your core nature, your innate self, and acting upon that true self's ethos. The resulting glory is nice, but better still is the realization that you are capable of so much more than you ever dreamed. Your future path is considerably brighter due to the newfound self-confidence that you've obtained by your instinctive act.

The Star, which A.E. Waite refers to as "Truth unveiled". follows The Tower, a card of great and dramatic upheaval. Sometimes it takes an intense occurrence for our own truths to be unveiled to us. It is only when Captain Wentworth juxtaposes Louisa's foolhardy behavior with Anne's courage under fire that he finally has the clarity to recognize whom he truly loves. This card can represent an insight born of recent upheaval or from the aftermath of a personal drama.

Waite also speaks of this card as "interior light". Any reader of *Persuasion* can see that Anne Elliot's light is "hidden under a bushel", but it burns all the brighter when compared to her shallow and selfish family. Sometimes this card simply serves as a reminder of your own inner luminescence. Is it currently flickering from lack of recognition? If so, it may be time to tend the flame and remember that you possess a powerful internal light.

Another way of interpreting this card is as an indication of your hopes being fulfilled. Louisa's recovery is much-wished for by Anne – and unexpectedly, Louisa completely recovers from her life-threatening fall. Yet this could have ultimately had an adverse impact on Anne, had Frederick been in love with Louisa. Sometimes we can't imagine the consequences of our wishes, yet when we have noble hopes, the rewards can stretch beyond the boundaries of our highest expectations.

What Would Jane Do?

"That he did not regard it as a desperate case, that he did not say a few hours must end it, was at first felt, beyond the hope of most; and the ecstasy of such a reprieve, the rejoicing, deep and silent, after a few fervent ejaculations of gratitude to Heaven had been offered, may be conceived."

Jane Austen, *Persuasion*

Jane's Advice: In Psalms: "Weeping endureth for a night, but joy cometh in the morning". That does not mean, of course, that we cannot rejoice and feel gratitude at any time of the day – or night. It is always timely to recognize and appreciate our blessings. When a star shoots across the sky it's a rather definite and literal signal that there really is a divine plan…and we are part of it.

XVIII – The Moon
Emma

Card Description

An attractive young woman (Emma) is in her nightgown, looking into a water basin that she is clearly using to wash her face. The disturbing vision she sees is that of George Knightley with Harriet Smith. She sees this image via the light of the full moon, which is streaming through a large window in her bedroom.

Storyline

Self-avowed spinster Emma Woodhouse has long encouraged her young friend, Harriet Smith, to find a mate to whom she can "look up". When Harriet considers the suit of a local farmer, Robert Martin, Emma persuades her that he is not good enough for her. She convinces her to set her sights on Mr. Elton, the town clergyman, instead. Mr. Elton proposes marriage not to Harriet, but Emma herself, causing Emma to feel foolish – and guilty for instilling false hopes in an impressionable young woman.

Emma then attempts to nurture feelings of romance for Frank Churchill in her friend, despite his superior social status, but soon realizes this is also a dead end. Emma is horrified to discover that Harriet has indeed taken her advice and set her sights quite high – on George Knightley, Emma's neighbor and best friend. Her horror increases when she learns from Harriet that she has reason to believe her feelings are returned.

As a result, Emma has "a dark night of the soul". Harriet can not marry Mr. Knightley because Emma she loves him. Knowing that Harriet would not claim an interest Mr. Knightey had not evinced, Emma tortures herself all night with feverish imaginings of their inevitable nuptials. The most painful fact of all is one Emma can not hide from herself: she is the one who nurtured Harriet's ego to the extent that she could believe herself worthy of a man of Mr. Knightley's qualities and status.

Card Interpretation

Much as the Empress is to the Emperor, the Moon card serves as the yin to the Sun card's yang. When the Moon appears in a reading, it represents mysteries and their unfolding, This can include the enigma of your own truest, deepest feelings – Emma has no clue as to her feelings for Knightley until she fears he might be lost to her forever.

This card also signifies delusions and fears of the unknown. Emma is wrongfully persuaded that Knightley might well be planning his marriage to Harriet, making poor Emma toss and turn sleeplessly in her bed of thorns. When you draw this card in a reading, focus on the facts, not fiction. You might risk potentially positive opportunities because of baseless fears. If you are feeling pessimistic (or panicking), this card is a reflection of your emotions, not necessarily the actuality of a situation.

There may be something tangibly problematic going on in your life, but you need to be an unbiased and wise judge, not an impressionable and foolish animal blinded by fear.

On the other hand, you may instinctively sense something is wrong, despite a situation looking "good on paper." You may have to delve more deeply to discover the facts. This card can represent psychic undercurrents and understandings, as well as visions that can change your life. This paradox demands of you a rather delicate balancing act. Trust and investigate your instincts, yet don't allow them to override your rational and intelligent side to the point where you feel like you're drowning in them.

Another aspect of this card is illusion. Emma, for all her initial belief in her own intuitive powers, is proven throughout the novel to be wrong about almost everyone. Be careful not to imagine you know more than you do, or to think you can't miss obvious and important facts that have the potential to rock your world. The Moon is never a card of superficiality. When you receive The Moon, your feelings run deep and true. They are likely to be com-plicated, complex, and, occasionally, over-whelming. On the other hand, they – and you – will never be accused of being boring.

What Would Jane Do?

"How inconsiderate, how indelicate, how irrational, how unfeeling had been her conduct! What blindness, what madness, had led her on!"

Jane Austen, *Emma*

Jane's Advice: The point where our emotions are most engaged is often the precise intersection wherein our follies are most pronounced. Rationality is a quality to be striven for, but it is hardly the domain of those in love – or those who believe themselves to be in love. For who can determine true love from false affection at the pinnacle of attraction? It would be wise to refrain from making decisions of the mind when enmeshed in the tangled landscape of the heart. Protect me from paragons who are capable of that kind of rationality .

XIX – The Sun
Emma

Card Description

Emma Woodhouse is in a sun-drenched garden. She looks up at a man (George Knightley, who also appears in The Moon) with blissful joy, and he beams down at her with equal delight. Large flowers bloom around them.

Storyline

The passing of the night's Moon flows into the rising of the Sun. And when day dawns, Emma Woodhouse knows she will have to see and speak with George Knightley, the man she has always regarded as an older brother, but whom she now knows she loves romantically. She must keep her fears that he wishes to marry her silly friend Harriet Smith to herself. The only thing worse than fearing Mr. Knightley loves Harriet will be hearing from his lips of this love.

When Emma and her beloved go for a walk, we learn Emma is not the only one with fears. Mr. Knightley is convinced that Emma is heartbroken at the news that another man, Frank Churchill, has been secretly engaged to Jane Fairfax. Mr. Knightley wishes to comfort Emma (and throttle Frank for leading her on). In the course of their walk, Mr. Knightley discovers that she is not remotely heartbroken, and in the heated joy of the moment, is inspired to ask Emma, the woman he has loved for years, to marry him. However, Emma is so sure that he is about to bring up his hopes of marrying Harriet Smith that she asks him not to speak. After a moment of reflection, she decides this is unfair, and she assures him that, as his friend, she will hear whatever he has to say.

Mr. Knightley then bares his soul, telling Emma that he asks only for the hope that one day she will look upon his love for her with favor and marry him. Emma realizes her Moon-based fears of the night before were for naught. The two once-deluded lovers stand before each other, finally able and willing to openly acknowledge their true feelings.

Card Interpretation

When you receive The Sun card in a reading, all is clear and out in the open. What has been dark and confused is now bright and unambiguous. You feel protected and vulnerable simultaneously (as opposed to the fearful vulnerability of the Moon), because you are able to glory in your true feelings without the need for any defenses. You have literally "seen the light".

Instead of the pessimism and fear often associated with the Moon, this card indicates optimism and delight towards any new venture. Even an old project that had previously been written off as unpromising could take on new life.

This card is often depicted in more traditional tarot cards with an image of two naked and joyous children standing in the bright sunshine; the expression "childlike optimism" is often associated with The Sun. If you have been considering trying something new, or taking a chance, this card suggests that all systems are go. There is a literal sense of tangible joy and triumph when you receive this card in a reading.

This card can also specifically refer to marriage. This is not, however, necessarily a marriage of two individuals. You could be wedding together two disparate sides of yourself, or separate strands of a puzzle that need to be united in order to achieve success.

Occasionally, your joy comes at the price of someone else's happiness. Emma's bliss necessarily decimates Harriet Smith's fantasy of being Mr. Knightley's wife – yet never once does Emma consider sacrificing her joy on the altar of friendship. This is a card of selfhood, not selflessness.

It is not your fault if others resent your joy because they feel badly about their own lives. However, if there is a downside to this card, it is that it can indicate overconfidence, a quality that is only a step away from arrogance or smugness. Both of those qualities lead to unpleasantness for Emma before the book's denouement. Let her errors serve as a lesson to you so that your pleasure can remain undiluted.

What Would Jane Do?
"The sun appeared; it was summer again...He had passed from a thoroughly distressed state of mind, to something so like perfect happiness, that it could bear no other name."

Jane Austen, *Emma*

Jane's Advice: Perfect happiness is an exalted state that is as intense as it is infrequent. When you attain it, relish it, because with it comes a statute of limitations. For women in particular, it is a tenuous condition, one that is not supported by anyone but the newly smitten lover, and even there, longevity is not indicated. Ecstasy will always be followed by a gnat in the ointment, so soak up the Sun as long as you are able.

XX – Judgment
Emma

Card Description
The image on this card shows several of the cast of characters in *Emma* placed in a garden, all of them reaching up to what they want in the sky. Emma reaches for the hand of George Knightley, and vice-versa. Mr. Woodhouse reaches for his home, and you can see a big lock on the door. Harriet Smith reaches for herself in a wedding dress, and Mrs. Weston reaches for her baby.

Storyline
In most books, once the protagonist and his or her beloved have declared their love for one another, the words "The End" follow rather quickly. In *Emma*, there is still one more obstacle for the loving couple to overcome. Mr. Woodhouse, Emma's father, has an aversion to even minor changes in his lifestyle, and the idea of his daughter marrying anyone – even Mr. Knightley, whom he considers a son – is abhorrent to him. Emma's frequent assurances to her father and anyone else who would listen that she never planned to marry are now fetters of guilt; they restrain her from upsetting her adored father.

Fortunately for the young couple, robberies in the neighborhood unnerve Mr. Woodhouse enough that he consents to the marriage – so that Mr. Knightley can move into the house and protect them all. Mrs. Weston, Emma's former governess, gives birth to a beautiful baby girl and Harriet Smith agrees to marry Robert Martin, her first suitor.

Card Interpretation
Each of the characters pictured in this card is yearning to ascend to another level, another phase in their lives. Emma and Mr. Knightley are reaching towards one another, a symbol of their mutual longing to unite in wedlock. The conscientious and warm-hearted Mrs. Weston is less obvious in her aspirations, but can anyone doubt her desire to be an even better mother to her newborn baby than she was to Emma? Harriet Smith has longed from the beginning of the story to marry, although the identity of her wished-for mate oscillates with unusual speed. Mr. Woodhouse never seeks change, but his need for security may supersede his aversion to his daughter's impending marriage.

With which character do you most identify? Are you, like Emma and Mr. Knightley, seeking to take your love life to another level or are you, perhaps, desirous of self-growth, either in an interpersonal rôle or in your career, à la Mrs. Weston? Perhaps what you are seeking is still amorphous and unknown, like Harriet's fluctuating amorousness. Or, like Mr. Woodhouse, are you simply deliberating upon whether to accept a major change in your life in order to retain what you most value?

Whichever individual issue pertains to you, this card heralds a new and major life phase. In many decks, this card has religious overtones – it depicts the Last Judgment or ascension, now known as "the Rapture" in Fundamentalist Christian jargon. This is not an indicator of minor change, but dramatic and, yes, fundamental transformation. But unlike the Death card, it always indicates a higher calling, a more evolved perspective.

This card sometimes literally demands "judgment". When you receive this card in a reading, it could indicate the necessity for evaluation and assessment of a current situation, as Mr. Woodhouse must evolve in his wishes for Emma never to marry. This is not the time for a cursory inspection, but a serious and even visionary perspective that takes into account past, present, and future conditions.

If recent circumstances have been confining, consider this card an indicator that you can choose to free yourself. However, salvation isn't free – you have to be willing to expend some effort in order to achieve it. If you simply lie back and wait to be emancipated because this card indicates liberation, you could literally lie in wait for an eternity.

What Would Jane Do?
"What totally different feelings did Emma take back into the house from what she had brought out! – she had then been only daring to hope for a little respite of suffering; – she was now in an exquisite flutter of happiness, and such happiness moreover as she believed must still be greater when the flutter should have passed away."

Jane Austen, *Emma*

Jane's Advice: We cannot depend that people will remain consistent in every area of their lives. In fact, we should become quite depressed if we were to rely on a perennial lack of advancement in the people we most esteem. If soulless flowers can blossom and grow, certainly one should be able to expect at least as much of our friends and lovers. Those who refuse to flourish in their particular patch of earth, despite the constant nurturing of well-meaning gardeners, and those who refuse to look upwards to the sun, might just as well be left to languish. That way, the garden can continue to grow in beauty and harmony.

XXI – The World
Emma

Card Description
Dressed in their wedding finery, Emma and George Knightley reach towards each other to embrace. The image is of a traditional World card, in that they stand within a wreath of several flowering bushes. The four elements are in the four corners of the card, water symbolized by a baby; fire, a wand; air, a pen; and earth, a flowering bush like the one in the main image.

Storyline
The World is the last card in the Major Arcana,* so it is fitting that this card is based on the ending of one of Jane Austen's novels. In Judgment, the card that precedes Trump XXI, several characters in *Emma* are depicted reaching towards their ideas of personal salvation. In The World, two of them, Emma and Mr. Knightley, achieve it.

Despite the fact that Emma and Mr. Knightley wish to wed, Mr. Woodhouse expresses reservations regarding his daughter marrying, and Emma does not wish to distress him. When several robberies occur in the neighborhood, Mr. Woodhouse considers how much safer the family will be with a younger and healthier man in the house to watch over things, and he agrees to the match.

The scene depicted in this card is the wedding of two souls who have grown in harmony with themselves and one another. The flowering bush symbolizes not just their love, but also the garden of lives in bloom, despite and because of the travails of the world.

Card Interpretation
Usually, an androgyne dances alone in the center of this card, but that would not be Jane Austen's concept of an ideal World card, so it shall not be ours, either. Austen knew only too well the perils of dancing alone in 19th century England.

When you receive this card in a reading, peril is not an issue for you. Through your own efforts, you have achieved worldly success, in the form you have chosen.

The four elements are depicted in the corners of this card, showing that your success can take the form of love and/or marriage, a particular initiative or aspiration, intellectual achievement, or significant financial expansion – or some combination thereof.

This is also a card of great harmony and balance and is an indicator that you are progressing as you should. Any present undertaking will benefit from your current state of grace. Although the future is not often given us to know – even in fiction – Austen promises Emma and Mr. Knightley the reward of a long and fulfilling union. It is a benediction that applies to you as well, though it may not refer specifically to marriage.

While this card is an augury of great attainment, it is not a blessing showered upon you from above, but one that you have earned. The bushes that surround the happy couple represent the physical world – and the constrictions and limitations of that world. Every rosebush contains thorns. Success does not equate to an absence of contention and struggle, but an acceptance of worldly boundaries and an embrace of the fullness of all that life offers, both the rose and the thorns.

Even in the midst of perfect attainment, there are always those who will find something with which to find fault (wedding attendee Mrs. Elton is appalled by the lack of finery). It can be difficult to deal with the petty envy – and even, occasionally, malevolence – that is engendered when you achieve your heart's desire. You are still living in the world of human frailty, after all, with all its physical and spiritual limitations. To complain about minor grievances would be small indeed – and not in keeping with the glory of the World card.

What Would Jane Do?
"The wishes, the hopes, the confidence, the predictions of the small band of true friends who witnessed the ceremony, were fully answered in the perfect happiness of the union."

Jane Austen, *Emma*

Jane's Advice: Wedded bliss, or indeed, any form of bliss, is dependent upon fortune and discernment. Fortune is indiscriminate and pours down Her blessings upon the deserving almost as frequently as she does upon fools. Discernment allows us to recognize benedictions when we receive them, which is why it sometimes seems Fortune favors the intelligent. Fools are simply more likely to drown when showered with Fortune's bounty – or to complain about the rain.

---

* The Fool is both beginning and end, Alpha and Omega… and anywhere else he/she wants to appear in the order.

Minor Arcana

Tarot of Jane Austen

Ace of Candlesticks
Pride and Prejudice

Card Description
A single, long lit red candle burns at the center of the card. It is in a crystal candleholder. The flame is almost as large as the candle itself.

Card Interpretation
The Aces are the elementals in the tarot, and so don't represent a part of a story, per se, but are instead, the essence of the suit. *Pride and Prejudice*, with Elizabeth Bennett at its center, is the essence of fiery vitality. The story itself speaks of a spiritual journey, a journey of self-understanding, of growth and expansion on the part of the principals (Elizabeth and Darcy) – and the rewards of that growth, of that light.

When you receive this card in a reading, it reminds you of your own inner candlestick, the fire that burns within you. When you look at your life in the present moment, is it fulfilling you? Are you in a growth period, or are you stagnant? What initiative do you need to take in order to feel more alive, more deeply fulfilled? In order to achieve a desire, you first must recognize it – and continue to fan its flame. This card is that first spark.

What Would Jane Do?
"A lady's imagination is very rapid; it jumps from admiration to love, from love to matrimony, in a moment."

Jane Austen, *Pride and Prejudice*

Jane's Advice: The spark of love is not limited to relationship, but the initiating principle remains the same. Matrimony is an institution, but is rooted in the flicker of attraction. The road to any destination must begin with a first step. The key is to choose a destination that is truly representative of your core being. The quality of the journey will be in direct proportion to how well – or ill – it reflects your essential self.

Two of Candlesticks
Mansfield Park

Card Description
Susan Price, Fanny's younger sister, holds an old end of a lit candle in her hands. She stares, slightly angrily, into the flickering flame. Fanny, standing behind her, holds out a full-length taper in a candlestick. This candle is not yet lit. A silver knife lies at Susan's side on the bed, in a room that has unmatched, old, and battered furniture and is rather unkempt.

Storyline
Unlike her more fortunate sister Fanny, Susan Price has grown to adulthood in their financially and spiritually impoverished Portsmouth home and family of origin. Susan is unlike Fanny in other ways as well – she is healthier and far more spirited. When Fanny is exiled to Portsmouth, her renewed acquaintance with her sister allows her to see the

injustice Susan has suffered by being in such an uncivilized environment.

Despite these deprivations, Fanny is impressed with her 14 year old sister's "natural light of mind" that "could so early distinguish justly... the faults of conduct to which it led". Fanny works with Susan to improve her mind and manners. Ultimately, Susan is inserted into Fanny's position at Mansfield Park, a place of opportunity. Susan's spirit and good health will ensure that she does not suffer in the same ways as Fanny.

Card Interpretation

When you receive the Two of Wands in a reading, your first reaction might be to ask, "Is this a good card – or a bad one?". It is more subtle than cards such as The Sun or The Devil.

Our first glimpse of Susan Price in the book *Mansfield Park* is of her responding to her mother in a "fearless, self-defending tone." This tone surprises her sister, Fanny, who is inclined toward timidity, but soon she recognizes Susan as courageous and remarkably desirous of growth and self-improvement. The astrological attribution for this card is Mars in Aries, and both planet and sign are known for their bravery – and an inclination for self-orientation. This card is a reminder of your own inner fire and bravery, particularly if you are currently feeling that your rights or spirit are being infringed upon in some way. Your environment may be one of negativity, but illumination is there for you, if you actively seek it.

Drawing this card indicates you are becoming more of who you are or who you are meant to be. While this sounds good, it's often a time in your life which can be tremendously uncomfortable. Susan is a "diamond in the rough". and while one is always delighted to be compared to a jewel, one would prefer to be placed on a velvet pillow more than forced to travel a rugged terrain. Consider yourself a "diamond in the making". if that makes this challenging time less onerous. Adding new facets to old strengths is not always easy, yet it prepares you to approach your future with self-confidence, much as Fanny's lessons

groom Susan for her next position in life. While you may be discouraged by an initial awkwardness, it is a necessary process for ultimate grace. Few achievements are automatic. Don't allow frustration to metamorphose into anger and aggression – it will only lengthen your apprenticeship.

This is also a card of potential and possibilities. Susan's inhospitable environment, while unpleasant, has not doused her inner spirit; she continues to dream and hope for a better life. She has a vision for herself. Fanny is astounded that her sister's spirit has been strong enough to withstand the relentlessly negative influences of a boorish father and a slatternly mother, yet Susan's essential self is unspoiled – she possesses grit, integrity, and strong principles. It seems unlikely that she will ever escape her coarse family, yet she ultimately ascends to the civility and amenities that Mansfield Park affords. Receiving this card in a reading is a powerful message of hope – along with a bracing dose of reality. You are not where you want to be now, but you can get there – by utilizing your innate spirit and resolve And, like Susan, you have someone who can assist you on your journey. You might want to consider who in your life can help you move forward at this time.

What Would Jane Do?

"Susan, who had an innate taste for the genteel and well-appointed, was eager to hear, and Fanny could not but indulge herself in dwelling on so beloved a theme. She hoped it was not wrong; though, after a time, Susan's very great admiration of everything said or done in her uncle's house, and earnest longing to go into Northamptonshire, seemed almost to blame her for exciting feelings which could not be gratified."

Jane Austen, *Mansfield Park*

Jane's Advice: It is certainly odd that some of the most innately principled souls are born in unpromising surroundings, whereas some of the most depraved are given every advantage at birth. A special few are born with a spark that can develop into a pure and healing fire of spirit – or ignite into an unmanageable blaze that burns and destroys. A civilized atmosphere can channel that fire more easily than a barbaric one, but you will find the flame exists in hovels as well as the grandest estates. Direct your warmth accordingly.

Three of Candlesticks
Mansfield Park

Card Description

Overlooking Portsmouth Harbor stands a young man, William Price, in his naval lieutenant's uniform. The *Thrush*, a British Navy frigate, is in his sights. He holds a globe in his hands as he looks ahead at the ship that is to make his fortune, and remove him from poverty. He is average-looking, but tall, vital, and proud as he envisions his future successes.

Storyline

The Two of Candlesticks addresses one of Fanny Price's siblings, the Three, another: her brother, William. Like his sister Susan (and unlike Fanny), he is high-spirited and energetic, brimming with aspirations and ambition. While his background is underprivileged, he has set his sights on the Navy, the military being the one field in Great Britain at the time where a commoner could rise to great heights.

William and Fanny have always been close and supportive of one another – he is one of the few members of her family of origin that engenders pride, not shame. It is to her he confides his greatest dreams and enterprises. When he comes to visit Fanny at Mansfield Park, their uncle treats him well, orchestrating a dance to honor his presence. Henry Crawford, Fanny's would-be suitor, assists William in getting a promotion to lieutenant as a calculated move to sway her affections, but this brings about a beneficial outcome for William nonetheless.

Card Interpretation

The card image reflects William in a scene that is somewhat imaginary – it is based on Austen's description of him and his expressed comments in *Mansfield Park*, yet some accouterments are added to reflect its Rider-Waite-Smith counterpart.

In this card, we see the assertive spirit of the Two of Wands channeled and progressed in the more focused Three. Where Susan is undergoing "growing pains" in the Two, William has made strides towards his dreams and aspirations. He hasn't reached his ultimate goal, but he's figuratively and literally on his way.

When you receive this card in a reading, you have progressed beyond the realm of contemplation and into the sphere of action. Like William, you have achieved some success in your chosen profession (or area of inspiration), and the world you wish to create is literally in your hands.

This card's attribution is Sun in Aries, which is an easier, more harmonious placement than Mars in Aries (the Two of Candlesticks). Even if your situation has not progressed to the extent you are currently aiming for, you feel more positive about your present and future. Your understanding of your needs and desires is clearer and more defined. This may be a time when you specifically plan the next phase needed to reach your goals, and begin to enact them.

William's "open, pleasant countenance, and frank, unstudied, but feeling and respectful manners" make him quite well-liked. It may well be that your warmth is contagious, and helps to ease your progress. This is not a time for diffidence, but an open display of your optimism and enthusiasm.

The tarot frowns on extremism. It would be wise to temper your optimism with effort, and focus more on the journey, rather than spend your time in fantasies about a dreamed-for destination. It is one thing to have aspirations of rising in the Navy, as

William does; it is quite another to expect to leapfrog from the rank of Sailor to the position of Admiral.

What Would Jane Do?

"He was full of frolic and joke in the intervals of their higher-toned subjects, all of which ended, if they did not begin, in praise of the Thrush, conjectures how she would be employed, schemes for an action with some superior force, which (supposing the first lieutenant out of the way, and William was not very merciful to the first lieutenant) was to give himself the next step as soon as possible."

Jane Austen, *Mansfield Park*

Jane's Advice: A man without ambition is not likely to win admirers. Aspiration costs nothing and yet must be the core foundation of any successful endeavor. Without planning and consistent and clever effort, however, the roots will twist and turn in on themselves, creating an in-dwelling of foul resentment and bitter dreams.

Four of Candlesticks
Pride and Prejudice

Card Description

Elizabeth and Jane Bennett are in bridal finery. Fitzwilliam Darcy and Charles Bingley are also dressed for their wedding. They are also dressed in wedding finery. They stand beneath a canopy of flowers held up by four wands. In the distance is Pemberley, an elegant old English estate. This is a double wedding, and the scene is both sacred and celebratory.

Storyline

The lovely and good-hearted Jane Bennett falls in love with Charles Bingley the moment they meet at a dance. Despite having his pick of the county maidens, he is also smitten, but his sisters and best friend, Fitzwilliam Darcy, conspire to keep them apart. When Darcy falls in love with Jane's sister, Lizzy, he realizes keeping Jane and Charles apart might not have been as clever as he initially thought – especially since Lizzy has discovered his culpability in that affair and rejects his suit in large part because of it.

After overcoming various obstacles and misunderstandings, both couples unite in holy matrimony, as seen on this card. They have earned their partners' love and trust, and there is every indication that their marriages will be long and prosperous.

Card Interpretation

Two cards that are largely seen as celebratory in the tarot are the Three of Teacups and the Four of Candlesticks. There are subtle distinctions to be made between them, differences that can be explained by their numbers and suits. Three is an odd, precarious number, whereas four is even and stable. Think of a four-sided box or square – there's something solid and firm about the number four. So, the three is a more temporal celebration; the four, a more solid and lasting one. Teacups, like the water that is the element of the suit, are fluid and emotional. Fire is the element of the suit of Candlesticks, and is reflective of spiritual expression. The Three of Teacups speaks to giddy fun or emotional support; the Four of Candlesticks is more of an earned commemoration, a pleasurable, but formal acknowledgment of a newly established phase, like a graduation – or a wedding.

When you receive this card in a reading, it can indicate a celebratory event, including a marriage – but that does not mean that this card promises marriage. If you are inquiring about a tall, dark, and handsome figure whom you recently met, it might well indicate that your relationship is going to reach a different, more stable, level – but don't order the wedding bouquet just yet. Like Bingley and Jane (and/or Darcy and Elizabeth), you need to recognize that an initial spark does not a fire make without a lot of serious flame-fanning.

On the other hand, the astrological attribution of this card is Venus, the planet of love, in Aries. Jane almost loses Bingley because she has not overtly shown that he has won her

heart, and, in his humility, he is persuaded by others that she does not return his affections. "Carpe diem" should be your motto when this card comes up in questions regarding matters of the heart.

The stability of the four heralds completion – and a new beginning. In this card, we see these young people transitioning from being unmarried to a commitment that will likely entail the responsibilities of children, as well as maintaining a home and a particular rôle in society. Perhaps you, too, are ending one cycle and beginning another. You may wish to think about what you are losing, as well as gaining. Each couple in this card has a particular dynamic. In the case of Bingley and Jane, like marries like: they are talked about as both being so good-natured that they will be taken advantage of by the rest of the world. Lizzy and Darcy, on the other hand, are quite different; Lizzy is fiery and engaged, Darcy, cool and detached. Yet both couples harmonize very well – the first because their good humor is tempered with good sense, and the second because, while opposites attract, they are united in their core integrity and moral values. What or who are you meshing or harmonizing with in order to establish a "more perfect union"?

Interestingly, A.E. Waite offers words like "country life" and "a haven of refuge" when defining the Four of Wands, and Jane Austen favors the conservative values and customs embodied by country living over that of the fast-paced, more modern city lifestyle (this bias is emphasized particularly in *Mansfield Park*). This card may be a reminder to slow down, savor and appreciate your surroundings. This may be time to ruminate over what you have accomplished up until now, as opposed to focusing on the next rung of the ladder.

What Would Jane Do?

"The feelings of the person who wrote, and the person who received it, are now so widely different from what they were then, that every unpleasant circumstance attending it ought to be forgotten."

Jane Austen, *Pride and Prejudice*

Jane's Advice: Rash decisions do not often result in prudent results, and success and achievement are rarely achieved without effort. Yet people continue to insist that prosperity and happiness are worth the expenditure – especially in retrospect. With humans being the malleable creatures that they are, present happiness always trumps past pain.

Five of Candlesticks
Northanger Abbey

Card Description

Four young people are disagreeing on the streets of Bath. Isabella Thorpe, pouting as prettily as possible, holds the hand of her younger, less fashionable friend, Catherine Morland. Isabella is trying to stop her from leaving. Isabella's brother, John Thorpe, assists her by holding onto Catherine's hand. Catherine's brother John does not physically try to hold his sister back, but he is clearly remonstrating with her and has a hand out as if he, too, would like to stop her progress, yet his gaze is fixed on the prettily pouting Isabella.

Storyline

When country miss Catherine Morland first arrives in Bath, she is delighted with her new friend, the more worldly and beautiful Isabella Thorpe. Isabella holds the incorrect belief that Catherine – and her elder brother James – are exceedingly well-to-do. As a result, she wishes to ensnare James for herself, and, to an almost equal degree, she is desirous of Catherine and her brother, John Thorpe, becoming romantically involved.

Catherine, however, has no interest Isabel's boorish brother. She is falling in love with Henry Tilney, and has made a new friend in his sister, Eleanor. When she makes plans to walk with the two of them, John Thorpe dishonestly claims he has seen them going in another direction, almost ruining the burgeoning relationships Catherine so wishes to develop. Fortunately, the situation gets resolved and they schedule a reprise of their plans.

However, the naïve James is now entranced by the self-promoting Isabella and is spending all of his available time with her. They, along with the ubiquitous John Thorpe, try to persuade her into going with them to Clifton; he has taken it upon himself to cancel her plans with the Tilneys.

Poor Catherine is prodded and pressured into going along with their wishes. Isabella uses her wiles, John attempts to bully her into going, and even her brother, James, applies pressure. Yet the once-trusting Catherine has learned from her previous experience. She feels torn, but fights back in order to honor her personal integrity. Her most pervasive wish is to spend time with the Tilneys, and this is what allows her to stand firm, despite her desire to please her friends and her brother.

Card Interpretation

This card indicates struggle and conflict, though it differs significantly in spirit from the other yang five, the Five of Quills. You could be feeling deeply conflicted about a situation, as Catherine feels while being unfairly pressured to violate both her own wishes and her knowledge of what constitutes appropriate behavior. The argument could be of a physical or verbal nature. The matter itself is often rather trivial, but the conflict may be importuning you disproportionately because it reflects a spiritual discordance that needs to be put into balance. With Saturn in Leo as the astrological underpinning of this card, there is a constriction on your self-expression that may cause you to feel limited or frustrated in some way, which can sometimes lead to aggressive behavior.

Sometimes ideas or opinions need to be tested before they are firmly set. Isabella had previously displayed her self-absorption in a number of ways to Catherine, but until she is crossed in a matter of principle, she is unable to recognize her friend's true nature. It is only when Catherine's purpose is firm that she finally recognizes Isabella as being "unkind…ungenerous and selfish".

If you see this card and immediately recognize yourself within, it may indicate you are not only aware of the situation, but are preparing to defuse it in some way. Forewarned is forearmed.

Occasionally, this card reflects a situation where interpersonal dynamics are being played (or replayed) out in a family squabble. It does not indicate toxicity, but if the roughhousing becomes too rough, you may wish to clear the air and set some boundaries.

What Would Jane Do?

"Catherine was distressed, but not subdued…The three others still continued together, walking in a most uncomfortable manner to poor Catherine; sometimes not a word was said, sometimes she was again attacked with supplications or reproaches, and her arm was still linked within Isabella's, though their hearts were at war."

Jane Austen, *Northanger Abbey*

Jane's Advice: Rude and uncontrolled displays of expression can often teach what years of polite exchanges at tea will not – if you don't allow yourself to become too engaged a participant in them.

Boisterousness is barely acceptable in children – and even then, it is particularly unattractive. When adults express themselves intemperately, it is a sign of their advanced state of juvenilia. There is nothing wrong with childish behavior, per se; it is merely a question of determining the amount of time you wish to inhabit the playroom. In small doses, freedom from adult companionship is more stimulating and certainly less stultifying.

Six of Candlesticks
Pride and Prejudice

Card Description
Two men, Fitzwilliam Darcy (Lord of Quills) and Charles Bingley (Lord of Teacups) ride on horseback towards a small English manor, Longbourn, home of their future brides. Jane and Elizabeth Bennett (Lady of Teacups and the Lady of Candlesticks) are seen looking out the window at the riders. The Lord of Quills is in the lead. Both men look extremely triumphant. A small dog follows at their heels.

Storyline
Jane Bennett falls in love with Charles Bingley the moment they meet at a dance, and he feels much the same. On that same occasion, his best friend, Fitzwilliam Darcy, is less impressed with Jane's sister, Lizzy, but upon further contact with her, he finds himself captivated by her wit and individuality, much against his will and his strong feelings of social superiority.

Darcy manipulates Bingley into thinking that Jane doesn't return his affections.

When Lizzy discovers Darcy's part in removing Charles Bingley from her sister's life, her previous dislike of him becomes even stronger. When Darcy seeks her hand in marriage, Lizzy is shocked, but quick to let him know that one of the reasons for her refusal is his brutal and unwarranted interference in her sister's love life.

Darcy is humbled by Lizzy's enumeration of his flaws and seeks to make amends for the wrongs he has done by behaving in a more gentlemanly manner to Lizzy and her family, and he also encourages Bingley to renew his attentions to Jane. He also discovers through his interfering aunt that Lizzy has refused to promise that she will never marry him, which gives him hope that he might yet have a chance to win her affections. He even acts as a "knight in shining armor" by arranging a marriage between his mortal enemy, Wickham, and Lydia, Lizzy's disgraced sister whom Wickham has seduced.

The scene on the card shows Darcy and Bingley riding on horseback to Longbourn, the home of the Bennett sisters. Bingley, newly engaged to Jane Bennett, is already triumphant, but Darcy seeks his reward with optimism. He knows he has finally earned the right to propose to – and be accepted by – the woman he loves, a woman he recognizes as more than worthy to be his wife.

Card Interpretation
The constriction of the Five expands and seeks to triumph in the Six of Candlesticks, where the astrological correspondence moves from Saturn to Jupiter in Leo. The character of Darcy has undergone significant spiritual expansion – this card shows a literal movement, but his transition from a figure of constrained arrogance to gracious humility has been every bit as much a progression. When you receive this card in a reading, you have been tempered by meeting and exceeding some of life's more

fiery challenges – and have grown spiritually as a result. You are ready to receive your earthly reward, as well as reap the spiritual benefits of such action.

You may feel newly confident and vibrant, as both Bingley and Darcy do in this image. There is a sense of a battle won, a victory achieved, and this reinforces your self-assurance.

The fact that your triumph is spiritual at its core makes the victory pure and sweet.

The book this card is based on is called *Pride and Prejudice*, and pride is a defining characteristic of Mr. Darcy. Pride is not, in and of itself, a flaw, but a positive and deserved quality if procured with noble effort. Self-esteem is a synonym for pride. Hauteur based on social standing is unearned arrogance, but any kind of overweening assurance can be off-putting. The tarot emphasizes balance in all things. If you are feeling cocky instead of confident, you may want to tone down your ego a bit. It did wonders for Mr. Darcy.

What Would Jane Do?

"There is a gentleman with him...who can it be?...It looks just like that man that used to be with him before...That tall, proud man."

Jane Austen, *Pride and Prejudice*

Jane's Advice: There is nothing more attractive than a man with a dashing manner – provided he is also amiable and physically appealing. As soon as an individual struts about, insisting that he is the finest at anything – or slinks about, insisting he is the worst – our natural inclination is to disbelieve the first, and completely trust the second. The more rational individuals of our acquaintance recognize their values as well as their foibles. Needless to say, we don't know many who qualify, and never enough of them to round out a table.

Seven of Candlesticks
Pride and Prejudice

Card Description

Elizabeth Bennett stands at a white picket fence in a country garden, pointing to the

gated door. We see six painted white planks. In the garden, an angry older woman, Lady Catherine de Bourgh, stands with her cane slightly raised towards Lizzy. The cane isn't about to strike her – Lady Catherine is using it to make her point, and her point is displeasure with Lizzy. Lady Catherine has an imperious demeanor and looks quite angry.

Storyline

Lizzy has captured the heart of Fitzwilliam Darcy – but has rejected his proposal of marriage, in part because of his aloof and prideful manner, but also because of her own prejudices. When she meets him again, he's at Pemberley, his magnificent home, where he's shown to best advantage. Lizzy can't help but feel honored at being the object of his affections when she realizes how great the disparity of their circumstances really is – and when his housekeeper regales her with example after example of his many fine qualities, she sees him in a more favorable light.

When Lizzy learns that her sister, Lydia, has run away with Wickham, disgracing the entire family, she realizes that there is no chance of she and Darcy reconciling.

Lydia's elopement turns into a wedding, so the Bennett sisters don't have to shrink in shame before anyone, but Lizzy is still convinced that there will never be a renewal of Darcy's suit when his officious and snobbish aunt, Lady Catherine de Bourgh, surprises her with a visit. Rumors have come to Lady Catherine's ears that Lizzy and Darcy are engaged, and she wants to ascertain that there is no truth to those words. Her high-handed, meddlesome approach annoys Lizzy and she refuses with equal measures of politeness and determination to answer her questions. Lady Catherine assails her with the superior firepower of her status and will, but Lizzy parries her every display of rudeness with cleverness and spirit. Lizzy acknowledges that she and Darcy are not engaged, but when Lady Catherine insists she will not leave without a promise that they never will become so, Lizzy refuses to give her that comfort.

Lady Catherine must take her leave with an unfamiliar and unpleasant sensation – that of being bested in verbal battle. Her annoyance leads her to confront Darcy, which has the unexpected and undesired effect of providing him encouragement to ask Lizzy again to marry him.

Card Interpretation

When you receive this card in a reading, you may be feeling outmatched or fighting a losing proposition. Your disadvantage could take the form of youth or inexperience or you might be combating an entrenched and powerful opponent – or it could be a matter of the odds being against you. The Seven of Candlesticks reminds you that, though you might be standing alone against a crowd, you have right on your side, and that evens the battlefield.

Those words might seem more wishful than realistic, yet it is your fears that make them so. This is not the time for pessimism or negativity, but one of purpose and courage. With Mars in Leo, the biggest battle you must fight is against the fragility of your own ego-strength. Lizzy is only too aware that she is beneath Lady Catherine in social status, and that Lydia's behavior has stained her entire family in the eyes of Mr. Darcy, yet she draws on an inner strength to assert her own merits without stooping to the level of Lady Catherine's discourtesy. Virtues are powerful allies – wield them wisely and you can never really lose.

Though it may not be easily seen on the surface, this card is also about taking responsibility for your actions. Lizzy knows she is making a dangerous enemy by standing up to Lady Catherine, yet she does so because her self-worth will not allow her to kow-tow to a woman whose power is all external and whose values are so foreign to her own. Elizabeth Bennett's spiritual understanding allows her to reject society's false pillars of rectitude, and adhere to her personal ethos – but it comes at a cost. She must fight for it. You may also have to engage in a similar battle, and sacrifice ease for integrity.

This is not to say that you should perpetually gird yourself for battle. You may be too combative, too quick to see challenges or enemies that only exist in your mind, or continue fighting long after your struggles are no longer necessary. If you find yourself engaged in disputes more often than you'd like, you may want to meditate on whether you are waging new crusades or simply defending yourself against old, dead shadows.

What Would Jane Do?

"Angry people are not always wise."
    Jane Austen, *Pride and Prejudice*

Jane's Advice: Courage is an easy quality to assert when the playing field is distinctly to your advantage, but valor can only be claimed when you are truly challenged by your circumstances. A weak position stems not only from an inequitable distribution of weaponry, but a more dangerous defect: a failure to recognize your own worth. Once you realize your strength comes from your inner value and not your valuables, your opposition's superiority begins to dissipate.

Eight of Candlesticks
Pride and Prejudice

Card Description
Lydia Bennett and George Wickham are traveling in the back of a carriage that is moving at a very fast pace. They are in a laughing embrace that would have been considered quite improper in England in Jane Austen's day.

Storyline
Sixteen-year-old Lydia Bennett (Maiden of Candlesticks) is feckless and imprudent, like most sixteen-year-olds. In her fantasies, she imagines herself dressed boldly and "tenderly flirting with at least six officers at once."
When she is permitted by her equally injudicious mother and disengaged father to go to Brighton unsupervised, she is easy prey for any unscrupulous – and physically attractive – man who wishes to take advantage of her.
Opportunist George Wickham fits that description and convinces her to elope with him. Elopement has a different meaning in Regency England than it does today – their alleged plans to eventually marry are nebulous at best and Lydia and her sisters are all socially damaged by her actions. Eventually, Mr. Darcy uses money and other methods of coercion on Wickham, who weds the blithely unconcerned Lydia.

Card Interpretation
When the Eight of Candlesticks appears in a reading, expect a whirlwind of activity and growth. Things may be moving so quickly that, if your inclination is to control every

aspect of your life, you will feel considerably unnerved. More flexible individuals might perceive this as an exciting time period. For those who never consider the future, this card might reflect your day-to-day lifestyle, for good or ill.
Mercury in Sagittarius is the astrological attribution of the Eight of Candlesticks; it is a combination that emphasizes overt and incautious movement or communication. Lydia frequently communicates in a tactless way, and her imprudent behavior is foreshadowed by the mentality we have come to understand through her words. This card serves as a reminder to think before you speak.
Lydia's elopement is the essence of impetuous action. Lizzy warns her father of the injudiciousness of sending the volatile Lydia to Brighton. He doesn't take her warnings seriously, to his later chagrin. Lizzy even learns of Lydia's elopement via a letter, echoing the traditional interpretation of receiving a message

when you receive this card. The message of this card can be to consider your actions and communications – both speaking and listening – carefully. You might make an imprudent decision or a rash and regrettable comment and have no Mr. Darcy to come to your rescue.

At the same time, living a completely controlled life is no life at all. Sagittarius is ruled by the Great Benefic, Jupiter, and urges you to take a leap of faith – unless your entire life is that of one who leaps without looking as a modus operandi.

Another way to interpret this card in a reading is as a sudden occurrence that leads to an unrelated, but usually fortunate, event. Had Wickham and Lydia not run away together, Darcy could not have come to Elizabeth's rescue and shown himself as the true hero he is. Austen even alludes to this when Lizzy remarks:

"My resolution of thanking you for your kindness to Lydia had certainly great effect. *Too much*, I am afraid; for what becomes of the moral, if our comfort springs from a breach of promise?".

Still, she is being humorous – she would not trade her future with Darcy in order to go back in time and have Lydia return home from Brighton her unmarried, feckless self. It would just have delayed the inevitable act of heedlessness Lydia was born to make.

What Would Jane Do?
"It seems but a fortnight I declare; and yet there have been things enough happened in the time. Good gracious! when I went away, I am sure I had no more idea of being married till I came back again! though I thought it would be very good fun if I was."

Jane Austen, *Pride and Prejudice*

Jane's Advice: Velocity is not necessarily progress, though many mistake action for the vibrant and exciting picture it paints. Haste is only really advisable when there's a burning building or an oncoming chaise. Discernment speeds up the decision-making process, yet, oddly enough, it seems the least discerning are the speediest at resolving matters. This sometimes earns them the reputation of being quick-thinking, when thinking, in reality, does not enter the equation.

Nine of Candlesticks
Lady Susan

Card Description
Frederica Vernon (daughter of Lady Susan, The Devil) kneels in a darkened hall, holding a candle in one hand, which illuminates her in the darkness. She pushes an envelope addressed to Mr. Reginald de Courcy under a closed door. As she does, she looks over her shoulder, with a panicked look on her face. Clearly, she does not wish to be discovered.

Storyline
Master manipulator Lady Susan Vernon has convinced one of her swains, James Martin, to transfer his affections to her daughter, Frederica. Frederica's affections are engaged to another of her mother's suitors, Reginald de Courcy, who sees her much as her mother does – a difficult and unmanageable child. When Lady Susan applies pressure to her daughter to marry Mr. Martin, she also cleverly forbids her to confide in her aunt or uncle, who might take Frederica's side.

Frederica is, in fact, a shy, frightened and honorable young woman who is nothing like the malcontent her mother paints her as. However, Frederica is more afraid of entering into a loveless marriage than she is of asking for assistance – and as her mother has forbidden her to confide in her aunt and uncle, Frederica has no one to turn to except Reginald de Courcy. She writes him a letter alerting him to her plight and places it under his bedroom door. Despite her fears of retaliation from her powerful mother, she dares to act.

Her daring is rewarded. Reginald de Courcy not only takes her part, he convinces Lady Susan to give her daughter time. Time is Frederica's friend: soon thereafter de

Courcy realizes how duplicitous and immoral Lady Susan really is and, in due time, he falls in love with Frederica. But, had she not acted bravely during her time of desperation, the ending might not have been a happy one for her.

Card Interpretation

When this card appears in a reading, you may be feeling your situation is as desperate as Frederica's. You might feel overpowered and outgunned. Despite appearances however, you can triumph, if you dare to act with the courage of your convictions.

You cannot allow yourself to be cowed. This card suggests that you are feeling fearful, but the fear is larger than the situation warrants. You are not without weapons of your own – you have spiritual and moral clarity on your side. You have truth and vision. These may not be the weapons of your opponent, so it would be wise for you to choose the battlefield or the terms of engagement. Play to your strengths, and override your awareness of your weaknesses. Even if your victory is incomplete, that result is superior to utter loss and devastation.

Moon in Sagittarius is the astrological correspondence for this card, which suggests that, at your core, you feel the courage of your convictions. Sagittarius is forthright and direct, and though the Moon addresses our deepest fears, it is the essence of our innermost desires. Let your spirit give you the strength you need to act in accordance with your moral surety.

This might be a good time to do some creative visualization. What is the worst thing about confronting your opposition? What is the most deleterious potential outcome? What responses should you make? Imagine the situation in your mind until you can see yourself as the victor – and then take the plunge.

You may be concerned about the timing of the situation. Be assured when you receive this card in a reading that this is the time to engage – waiting is only another barrier created by your fears. You will grow in strength from bravely taking action – what you've

done once, you will know you can repeat again and again.

What Would Jane Do?

"I am equally confounded at HER impudence and HIS credulity."
Jane Austen, *Lady Susan*

Jane's Advice: It is said that Fortune favors the brave. I suspect that bravery is not the only attribute favored by Fortune, but this does not mean that bravery goes unrewarded. We sometimes view courage as something practiced only on the battlefield, but we have the potential to display it daily in our lives. These occurrences take place not when we are assured of triumph, but when we are convinced of defeat – and yet act as if victory is assured.

This does not mean, of course, to engage in battle simply to evince courage. One would be foolish to fight meaningless battles, even if victory were assured. But when our mettle is truly tested, responding with boldness and valor is the soundest course of action.

Ten of Candlesticks
Persuasion

Card Description
Anne Elliot sits at the pianoforte, her capped head down. Though the face we see is downcast, she is totally focused on her playing. Her clothes are drab and her face looks somewhat ravaged by time and pain. In the lighted room, well-dressed dancers are more festively attired – and are enjoying themselves immensely, dancing to the music that is born of Anne's labor.

Storyline
In the bloom of youth, Anne is persuaded to break her engagement to Frederick Wentworth. Her family and friends believe he is socially and financially unworthy of her, but she thinks she is doing what is best for him. When he leaves town, her heart quietly breaks and she regrets having heeded their advice.

Seven years later, Captain Wentworth has made his fortune, and now seeks a wife. He has not forgiven Anne, and she suffers, watching him court her younger sisters-in-law. She feels as if her youth has passed her by, and now must pay the price of her once-too-tractable nature. This scene depicts her playing the piano for their dancing – she is contributing to the pleasantries and courtship that so wound her.

Card Interpretation
Saturn, the planet of limitations, in Sagittarius is the astrological association for the Ten of Candlesticks. You may yearn to dance with your spiritual partner, as Anne does with Captain Wentworth, yet you have put yourself in a position of servitude and self-denial. For reasons of circumstance or misguided notions of nobility and correctness, you may find yourself yoking your will and energies to

fulfill the desires of others, often in direct contrast to your own wishes.

This card urges you to perform a serious self-appraisal: Where, how, and why are your energies currently being spent? If you feel overwhelmed or pressured, how much of that duress is self-imposed? Which duties are necessary life burdens and which could you delegate? Most importantly, what are your deepest desires? Are the activities you currently perform in service to those desires, or are they misdirected? You are the one who determines your actions – or inactions. If they are not in alignment with the life you want to live, you must make the changes you want your life to express.

All fire signs, of which Sagittarius is one, are highly expressive. Note how Anne, by playing the piano, is creatively channeling her energy, even though it is in an opposite direction from her desires. You may wish to find an artistic outlet for your energies, as this is a card with tremendous potential for innovation and creativity – a potential that will remain latent if your occupations do not include time for yourself.

What Would Jane Do?

"Anne offered her services, as usual; and though her eyes would sometimes fill with tears as she sat at the instrument, she was extremely glad to be employed, and desired nothing in return but to be unobserved…"
Jane Austen, *Persuasion*

Jane's Advice: If nature abhors a vacuum, you are not required to be the one to fill it. The more you rush to assist others, the more they will be assured that it is their right to receive your assistance. In no time, you will be apologizing for attending to any of your own needs, and exciting great indignance in those to whom you seek pardon. It is far more difficult to carve away time for your own pursuits if you begin by giving that time away. You may not feel time spent on artistic pursuits will amount to much, but it is as necessary as breathing – or tea.

Maiden of Candlesticks

Lydia Bennett (Pride and Prejudice)

Card Description

A young, dark-haired girl of 16 is flirting with her reflection in an old-fashioned mirror. She is not pretty, but she is filled with vitality and life – she will never appear more attractive than she does now, in the full bloom of youth. She is wearing simple garb, but the mirror shows a different picture – a young girl bedecked with jewels, admirers, and fine clothes, surrounded by swains in redcoat (military men). On a bed in the background, her sister watches her every move admiringly.

Storyline

Sixteen year old Lydia Bennett is silly, irresponsible, and self-absorbed – much like most teenagers. However, in contrast to her elder sisters Jane and Elizabeth, she seems particularly shallow and imprudent. Lydia thinks only of clothes and flirting and gratifying her own desires, not necessarily in that order. She does have some good qualities – she is warm and vivacious, and, in her determination not to be bored or inconvenienced, is quite in touch with her inner child. While every Bennett is wishing their visiting cousin, Mr. Collins, will stop his ponderous reading of a dull book, Lydia is the only one to express her boredom. She is undoubtedly rude, but her method is effective – he stops reading and everyone but Mr. Collins is gratified by that particular result.

When Lydia is permitted to go to Brighton with a friend in an unsupervised capacity, she succumbs to the charms of George Wickham, and runs away with him, assuming they will marry – eventually, if not immediately. Her cavalier morality in this area carries over to others; she does not spare a moment concerning herself with the detrimental effect this will have on her sisters' status in society or the impact it will have on her parents.

She is saved from herself by the intervention of Mr. Darcy, who arranges a wedding between Wickham and Lydia at great inconvenience and humiliation to himself, yet her airs at being newly married and therefore "superior" to her sisters are as dramatic as any grande dame's. Instead of being humbled by her actions, she continues throughout her life as brazenly as she has behaved in her youth. We know this from Austen's report that Lydia and her equally self-serving husband never cease to importune her sisters for money and other perquisites.

Card Interpretation

The Maiden of Candlesticks, elementally speaking, is a card of great fire and passion. When that fire and passion is tempered with rationality and emotional maturity, the potential for a vital and brilliant spirituality is unlimited. Lydia's intelligent but disengaged father has neglected her upbringing, leaving Lydia to be primarily influenced by her rapacious, fatuous mother. The result is a young girl with an enormous store of energy and no focus to direct it.

When you receive this card in a reading, it may be that you are brimming with passion and a creative urge to do something, but are unsure how to go about doing it. You may be dissipating your drive into unproductive, or even dangerous, channels. Conversely, you may have a single-minded focus and are fervently applying yourself to your goal. Like Lydia with Wickham, you will not rest until you get what you go after, so be sure the prize is worthy of its seeker.

This card is one of not just taking, but seeking, risks. You may feel the need to spice up your life by taking a chance on something or someone. Feeling vital and alive is your birthright and, if you have been feeling listless, the Maiden of Candlesticks reminds you of the need to self-rejuvenate. While selfishness is not a virtue, self-care is, and if you've been imposing constraints on your joie de vivre, this may be the time to cut loose some of the reins.

Clearly, though, there is a balance between putting yourself at risk and repressing yourself. For each person, that balance is determined differently. Trust yourself to know if this card urges you to run with the wolves – or put a small, protective chain on the door.

What Would Jane Do?

"Lydia was Lydia still; untamed, unabashed, wild, noisy, and fearless."
Jane Austen, *Pride and Prejudice*

Jane's Advice: Any quality, however attractive, can become a detriment if it is not tempered. This is particularly true of the spirit, which has the power to kill or cure. Unfortunately, a wild and untamed spirit damages not only itself, but all who come in contact with it, and the greatest victims are often the ones who make the most valiant attempts to help. Vitality in combination with good sense creates an Elizabeth Bennett; without it, one is left with self-absorbed, feckless Lydia.

Knight of Candlesticks
Henry Tilney (Northanger Abbey)

Card Description

Jane Austen describes Henry Tilney as "rather tall" with a "pleasing countenance, a very intelligent and lively eye, and, if not quite handsome, was very near it". He is suntanned, "with dark eyes and rather dark hair". In this image, he is at the reins of a curricle. He appears to be dashing, but not reckless, in his top hat and red cravat. Next to him is Catherine Morland, looking at him with adoring eyes.

Storyline

The gothic hero has been described as an old soul, burdened with the weight of a secret sorrow. He is strong and sensitive, but his burden generally demands a level of dramatic self-absorption that would not be much fun to live with in real life. Austen turns the concept of the gothic hero on its head with her depiction of Henry Tilney, the warm, engaging male protagonist of the satirical *Northanger Abbey*. Catherine Morland, a small town girl from Fullerton, loves gothic novels and takes them to heart, despite being urged to read more wholesome literature. When she goes to Bath, she falls head over heels for the unconventional Henry Tilney, a clergyman with a great sense of humor and an engaging personality. He finds her attraction to him to have considerable allure, as well.

When another man, John Thorpe, attempts to win Catherine over, Henry finds his actions annoying, but is pleased to note that Catherine rejects these attempts. However, Thorpe has presented a false picture to Henry's avaricious father, General Tilney, who now believes Catherine to be richer than she is – so the General spends time and effort promoting a match between her and his son. The General even invites her to spend time at Northanger Abbey, the home he shares with his daughter, Eleanor, who has also become friendly with Catherine.

Henry does not mind his father's encouragements, because he enjoys teaching Catherine about the ways of the world and finds her unique combination of naïveté and integrity charming and refreshing. They both also share a penchant for gothic novels. When Catherine's gothic novel-influenced imagination runs wild and she becomes convinced that General Tilney has killed his wife, Henry must reprove her. He does so with characteristic humor and kindness, and Catherine is embarrassed, but grateful that he doesn't allude to her mistake afterwards. He treats her even more kindly than he has always done, which increases her already great love and respect for him.

When Henry is away from the Abbey, General Tilney returns home and insists that Catherine leave their home immediately, offering no explanation. We later learn that Thorpe has informed the General that Catherine is virtually penniless, which is no more true than his first assertion about her wealth. The General is furious; he now forbids his son to marry her. However, Henry is a man of integrity and

knows what is right. Catherine has captured his heart and he will not have her treated shabbily simply because she isn't rich. When he returns to find how his father has treated her, Henry goes to Fullerton to ask Catherine to marry him – and after a short time, they wed.

Card Description

The Knight of Candlesticks seems lighthearted, but he has the courage of his convictions. If you receive this card in a reading, you may be – or are attracted to – a Knight of Candlesticks. You may, like Henry Tilney, be drawn to a person whose character you can help to form – or a clever and idealistic person like Henry Tilney. Candlesticks are a suit of creative energy and what could be a more creative act than transforming another person? Being transformed by one can be a different form of creativity – adaptation, as opposed to innovation. If you are the one being transformed, be sure the transformer is worthy of the rôle.

How can you know this? All Knights of Candlesticks have enormous personal magnetism and charm, but Henry Tilney shows "astonishing generosity and nobleness of conduct in never alluding in the slightest way to what had passed", when Catherine mistakenly believes his father has killed his mother. A fiery knight doesn't continue to bludgeon someone after making his point, but treats you with respect. (If you are a Knight of Candlesticks, try to remember that!)

The Knight of Candlesticks demands honesty. He finds coquettish behavior abhorrent and expects above-board behavior at all times. While he is refreshingly unconventional and doesn't seem to take very much seriously, he is not cynical, but operates from a personal code of ethics that is idealistic and straightforward. He doesn't play mind games and hurt someone because she hurt him first. Once his heart is won, he is loyal. He is, however, quite open-hearted and willing to be pleased; he is not a one-woman man (or vice versa) in the beginning of an infatuation. His own gregarious ways don't equate to a lack of jealousy – but if it is baseless, he is easily persuaded of that fact.

There are actually two Knights of Candlesticks in *Northanger Abbey*. In some ways, Henry's dashing brother, Captain Frederick Tilney, is the shadow side of the Knight of Candlesticks, with his "florid complexion and dark eyes." Frederick Tilney oozes flirtatious charm and enjoys making conquests, but idealism takes second place to the cozening of his ego. He goes after the heart of Isabella Thorpe, an engaged woman, simply for the thrill of the pursuit. Yet he is too wily a practitioner of the arts to become captured by his intended prey – and he removes himself from her sphere with his rakish heart intact and her engagement in ruins.

The more upright Henry Tilney is very appealing. He is high-spirited, but he is not reckless (unlike John Thorpe). Comparisons to the boorish Mr. Thorpe also abound – Thorpe is obsessed with money and his equipage, but Mr. Tilney is more person-centered and idealistic, valuing love and honor over riches and material possessions. Thorpe abuses his horses, but Henry Tilney loves his dogs and treats his horses well. Mr. Thorpe says one thing and changes it to another in the next minute and will generally lie in order to make himself look better (but he's not swift enough to do it well). Mr. Tilney, on the other hand, is as good as his word. Thorpe is a bore; one particular gift of the Knight of Candlesticks is that, like Henry Tilney, he is a mesmerizing conversationalist. Catherine may be a naïve girl, but she recognizes insincerity and boorishness, even if she isn't sophisticated. When you receive this card in a reading, you may need to examine your (or another's) motivations – what is the basis of your attraction or attractiveness? Are you in thrall to spiritual vitality or personal magnetism?

As a clergyman, Henry Tilney is a voice of spirit, actively eliciting others to be in touch with the divine. There is an instinctive reverence in idealistic fire (Candlesticks) that combines with lightheartedness – and a propensity to want to make – or at least, teach – history, instead of writing about it or (worst of all) bore anyone with it. This card can be a reminder of that.

The Knight of Candlesticks is also proud (sometimes overly so) of his talents and skills. Henry twits Catherine (and his sister) about their word usage – he is a clergyman, after all, and makes his living by words – as such, he is careful about them and teasingly ensures that others are equally so. You may justly be proud of your accomplishments, but be sure to use humor in order to remind others of them, so that, like Henry Tilney, you will be more charming than obnoxious.

What Would Jane Do?

"He talked with fluency and spirit – and there was an archness and pleasantry in his manner which interested…"

Jane Austen, *Northanger Abbey*

Jane's Advice: There is nothing more appealing than someone who recognizes your gifts and values them higher than you do. Yet it is crucial to determine what lies behind that esteem – if it based on the same degree of integrity that you harbor, all will be well, but a lifetime of misery can ensue if you choose admiration in a prettily wrapped package, only to discover it is an inferior muslin that can easily be twisted beyond repair. However, a life of the spirit need not be garbed in drab material – in fact, when it is, it's generally the dress of masquerade.

Lady of Candlesticks
Elizabeth Bennett (Pride and Prejudice)

Card Description
Elizabeth Bennett is seated in an elegant chair. One hand is lifted in the act of holding a candle or lantern to a letter, which she is reading. She is in an elegant, well-appointed room, and an orange cat sits at her feet. An open window offers us a glimpse of a flower-filled garden.

Storyline
While Elizabeth begins the book more as a Maiden, she is burnished by experience into a Lady of Candlesticks by the end of the novel. Her potential is hinted at in the first chapter via her father's preference for her; Elizabeth has a "quickness" her sisters lack. Lizzy's sense of humor includes herself, as well as others. She is utterly loyal to her worthy sister, Jane, even as she notes the flaws and foibles of her other relatives. When she meets the wealthy, refined Fitzwilliam Darcy, the man who ultimately becomes her husband, she makes light of his snobbery, when he pointedly disparages her charms.

Only the aforementioned loyalty to Jane induces her to visit Netherfield, which puts her in closer proximity to Darcy. In this case, familiarity breeds contempt only on her side – Darcy can't help being attracted to both her "fine eyes" and "a mixture of sweetness and archness in her manner which made it difficult for her to affront anybody". He fights this attraction because of the relative unworthiness of Lizzy's familial connections, while she remains blithely unaware of his feelings for her. She is more interested in Wickham, a charming officer whose low opinion of Darcy bolsters her own.

When Lizzy discovers that Darcy has interfered with Jane's marital hopes, it merely adds fuel to her fire. She blasts him with its full force when he proposes marriage. She comes to learn that Wickham is a cad and that Darcy's good qualities are just the ones she most wants in a partner.

Fortunately, one of those good qualities is his unswerving devotion to Lizzy. When his interfering aunt, Lady Catherine de Bourgh, discovers that Darcy might have proposed to societally-inferior Lizzy, Lady Catherine visits Lizzy to command her not to marry him. Lizzy does not deign to respond to such importunate demands, so Lady Catherine turns to threaten Darcy of the perils of marrying so far beneath himself. Darcy, encouraged to discover that Lizzy hadn't rejected him outright, now has hopes that his second proposal, a much more respectful and humble supplication, will be accepted. Lizzy, who has grasped that her initial observations can be tainted by willful prejudice, is delighted to accept this proposal from the man she has come to love.

Card Interpretation
When the Lady of Candlesticks is drawn in a reading, she represents an aspect of yourself or a querent who is vibrant, candid, friendly, and energetic. This card embodies an individual with great inner integrity who speaks her truth. This card describes someone mature, but who is in close touch with her inner child, and her good qualities include honesty, humor, and leadership abilities, as well as warmth and wit.

You may be both strong-willed and decisive, as Lizzy shows so clearly she is in the Seven of Candlesticks. You might occasionally think too highly of yourself or your opinions, and can lack detachment, as Lizzy does in her relationship with Darcy, causing her to be prejudiced against him. Some more timid souls may find it difficult to be in your company, because your directness can wound, but you rarely speak with the intent to harm. In *Pride and Prejudice*, Austen cleverly uses the clever but vitriolic Caroline Bingley as a foil for the arch but never cruel Lizzy Bennett. By comparing and contrasting these characters, you see why Darcy rejects one in favor of the other. Both women are witty, but Caroline is poisonous, caustic, and unkind, while Lizzy's humor is tangy, gentle, and humane. Is it any wonder Darcy found Lizzy so enchanting after such up-close and personal intimacy with the toxic Caroline Bingley?

Like all Court cards, the Lady of Candlesticks can represent an aspect of yourself or the querent, but she can also describe a loyal friend who can be counted on completely, someone who is vitally attractive and generally offers excellent advice. This individual may, however, be too loyal, and not see your flaws, and/or urge you to believe you are always in the right. She can also be overpowering. You may be living vicariously through this person's energetic vitality rather than displaying some of these qualities yourself.

What Would Jane Do?
"Whatever bears affinity to cunning is despicable."

Jane Austen, *Pride and Prejudice*

Jane's Advice: While circumspection is ofttimes the wisest approach, if you have researched the facts thoroughly, speak and act with confidence. Candid and open ways delight all worthwhile candidates for your attention and affection. Observant, witty, and brave women are rare and valued. Openness is an essential quality of your vitality. Just be sure that you have, indeed, researched your facts before announcing your conclusions to all and sundry. That will spare you the embarrassment that is sure to follow if you mistake your candor and good sense for omniscience.

Lord of Candlesticks
Persuasion

Card Description
Captain Frederick Wentworth, a dark haired man, is meticulously dressed in his military uniform. He strides triumphantly towards town, wearing a look of strength and determination about him. He has a commanding presence.

Storyline
When Anne Elliot breaks her engagement with Frederick Wentworth, it is not that she doesn't think he will make something of himself in the Navy. She correctly senses his fire, purpose, and determination, but she is convinced by a woman who is like a second mother to her to be prudent.

When Captain Wentworth returns, he is still the dashing man Anne fell in love with, but the tables have turned. He is the eligible, sought-after bachelor and Anne is perceived as an on-the-shelf spinster. He treats Anne coldly, but shows interest in her two sisters-in-law, Louisa and Henrietta Musgrove, who are both quite interested in the dashing captain.

He is very clear as to what he is looking for in a woman: "a strong mind, with sweetness of manner". He considers Anne weak for breaking their engagement at the behest of Lady Russell, and will not have his heart broken again by someone who can be turned against him.

Though they are thrown together at social events, Anne and Captain Wentworth barely exchange words. However, when one of Anne's young nephews jumps on her back and won't get off, Captain Wentworth comes quickly to her rescue. When, in conversation with Louisa, Captain Wentworth discovers that Anne had turned down the wealthy Charles Musgrove (Louisa's brother), he begins to understand that Anne's breaking of their proposal was not motivated by avarice.

When the family and Captain Wentworth go to Lyme, it seems that he and Louisa will become betrothed, but her rash leap off of steep stairs almost causes her death. Only Anne's cool head saves the day, and Captain Wentworth can't help admiring her intelligence and rational decisiveness.

Unfortunately, he now feels that if Louisa recovers from her fall, he is honor-bound to marry her – and he isn't happy about the prospect. He realizes he has been in love with Anne all along.

When Louisa becomes engaged to someone else, Captain Wentworth goes to Bath seeking Anne. When he overhears Anne say that women's love lasts longer than men's, he writes her a passionate letter asking for her hand in marriage. Captain Wentworth realizes it was his stubborn pride that stopped them from being united years before, as once he had begun to make his way in the world, Anne would have gladly married him.

Card Interpretation

When he and Anne first become engaged, Frederick Wentworth is a Knight. Romantic and confident, he has no doubt he will make

his way in the world. We meet him when he has aged a few years and has been very successful in his naval career, but he has lost none of his dash and fiery spirit. He has matured into the Lord of Candlesticks: assured, but not brash; brave, but not foolhardy; energetic, but hardly impetuous.

Astrologically, the Lord of Candlesticks is the Fiery part of Fire. That is a very hot combination, and explains why, even though Captain Wentworth never stops loving Anne, his pride will not allow him to forgive her at first. Fiery types have a temper, as you know if you are a Lord of Candlesticks, or even have a passing acquaintance with one. The King of Candlesticks is very passionate (Frederick Wentworth's letter to Anne burns) and he blazes with any emotion, be it love or hate.

In a reading, this card represents someone whose impulsiveness has been tempered with time, but is still ardent and tempestuous for all that. This person has great personal charisma, and draws people in with his or her confident, enthusiastic nature. A natural leader (Frederick Wentworth works his way up to the title of Captain), this card signifies someone to whom people are proud to give their trust, loyalty, and allegiance.

This card also suggests achievement and self-expression. It is the card of someone who is creative and expressive, filled with motivation and enthusiasms. If the Lord of Candlesticks appears in a position regarding a situation, it signifies a positive, high energy response. There is no "die" in this card, only "do". Optimism and honesty are your allies.

What Would Jane Do?

"The years which had destroyed her youth and bloom had only given him a more glowing, manly, open look, in no respect lessening his personal advantages."

Jane Austen, *Persuasion*

Jane's Advice: Carpe diem! Boldness and ebullience serve you well, as long as honesty underpins your great enthusiasms, and experience guides your actions. Others might find you overly blunt, but only if they fear truth and hide their own intentions from others or themselves. This is not something you can understand, because guile and chicanery are foreign to you. May they always remain so.

Ace of Teacups

Emma

Card Description

A teacup of bone china sits at the center of the card. It is filled with fragrant clear liquid with steam rising above the cup.

Card Interpretation

The Aces are the elementals in the tarot, and so don't represent a part of a story, per se, but are instead, the essence of the suit. The story of *Emma* encapsulates many characteristics, but it can be said to be the story of one human being opening to the power of love.

Almost from the moment we first encounter

Emma, she extols the benefits of remaining a single woman. Love doesn't enter into her calculations at all. Poorer, less fortunate women might benefit from marriage, but not the rational Emma Woodhouse, who is blessed with wealth and societal status and a father who adores her. What else could she possibly need?

As for others, Emma believes she can control their love lives better than they, and her matchmaking attempts are evidence of that philosophy. She analyzes and plots for her quarry with the foresight of a general. Yet she does not reckon on the ways of the heart, so her accountings miss the most important factor of marriage, for others and for herself.

When Emma realizes that she is in love with Mr. Knightley, it comes as quite a surprise to her. Her intelligent and acute observations of others don't protect her from her own feelings, or her own irrationality on the subject. If you receive this card in a reading, it signals a new love of some kind. While this is often a romantic indicator, love is far too vast to be limited to romance alone. The Ace of Teacups presages an opening of the heart, and that can be for a new friend, a new pet, or a renewed affection for a relative or spouse.

Like Emma, this new love may take you by surprise, or this card could merely validate feelings you have recently begun to recognize. Teacups are vessels, and if Candlesticks are representative of the male will, then Teacups betoken feminine receptivity. This Ace is not about activity so much as it is accepting, opening, flowering. When you receive the Ace of Teacups in a reading, your heart blossoms. It means also that you are currently open and, therefore, vulnerable. You may feel that you are a bottomless well of good feeling, which is a desirable, if temporary state. This card urges you to ride the tidal wave of love.

What Would Jane Do?

"Her mind was in a state of flutter and wonder, which made it impossible for her to be collected. She was in dancing, singing, exclaiming spirits; and till she had moved about, and talked to herself, and laughed and reflected, she could be fit for nothing rational."

Jane Austen, *Emma*

Jane's Advice: Rationality and sense are fine qualities, but poets and pragmatists alike must admit they pall in the face of love. Wisdom and reason have their place, but it is not in the quick fluttering of a young person's heart. When one finds his or her beloved, it is a special, magical time. Sanity can – and must – return eventually, but there's no reason to speed it along when you are in the midst of mad joy.

Two of Teacups
Northanger Abbey

Card Description

Henry Tilney and Catherine Morland are at a dance, but they are seated at a table. They are

gazing into one another's eyes; Catherine's gaze is adoring, Henry's amused and interested. Others are dancing but they seem blurry, indistinct. Henry and Catherine could be the only two people in the world, as far as the two are concerned.

Storyline

Country naive Catherine Morland is, at the age of 17, treated to a vacation in Bath, a much more socially active milieu than her usual environs. She is dazzled by everything around her, but mostly by Henry Tilney, an attractive young clergyman eight years her senior, whose wit and charm would appeal to a far more sophisticated woman.

For his part, Henry is first attracted to her obvious admiration for him – adoration has universal appeal even today. Their attraction at this point has no basis in anything solid on which one can or should build future plans. As the couple gets to know each other, they find they have much on which to build a future relationship. Henry's unconventional humorous tone is not the voice of a cynic, but a wise-for-his-years man whose own nobility and grace is proven in his treatment of Catherine. For all her naiveté, Catherine shows integrity and good sense. She is willing to stand up for herself, even though it pains her to hurt others, and is most willing to be taught by Henry in the ways of the world.

Despite his father's objections, Henry remains loyal to Catherine and, at the end of the book, they wed. Since he loves teaching her and she loves learning from him, they are a couple who will likely have a long and happy marriage.

Card Interpretation

Even a complete novice to the tarot can see this is a card of incipient romance. We see the initial flush of mutual attraction, which promises nothing, but suggests love and, to the person whose head is in the clouds, potential marriage. While the potential is unlimited and the moment is magic, this card shows the initial sizzle, not the steak. Only time will tell if the first frisson of passion is a momentary spark or a lifelong flame.

This card urges you to focus on the other person and the present, as opposed to fantasizing about the future. It is important to see the other as a human being, not the perfect and idealized answer to a maiden's (or bachelor's) prayer. Catherine feels Henry is a paragon of perfection, but she glimpses his messy room when she ventures to Northanger Abbey. Catherine's more easily perceived lack of sophistication is not unattractive to Henry, because he takes great pleasure in showing and teaching her how much he knows – especially since her lack of guile doesn't equate to a lack of perception.

When you receive this card in a reading, you need to stay balanced, no matter how infatuated you may feel at present. The astrological correspondence of this card is Venus in emotional Cancer, and this indicates that love and emotions are in abundance and at the forefront of your mind. However, two is an even number, and evenness is called for now. You need to communicate your feelings by listening and responding in equal measure, always staying in touch with your core emotions.

Please note that Henry and Catherine are quite different, yet each person's needs and desires meshes nicely with the other's. True and lasting love is not based on finding your identical twin, but in the interweaving and blending of qualities in a pleasing and harmonious way.

If this card comes up in a position or question not related to relationships, the principles of the Two of Teacups remain the same: focus on the present, not an idealized future; maintain your emotional equilibrium; and communicate in a level manner: talk and listen in equal measure.

What Would Jane Do?

"We have entered into a contract of mutual agreeableness for the space of an evening, and all our agreeableness belongs solely to each other for that time."

Jane Austen, *Northanger Abbey*

Jane's Advice: Fidelity and complaisance may be the principal duties of both marriage and dancing (Henry Tilney says as much in *Northanger Abbey*), and yet one dance does not necessarily encompass our understanding of either. This is not to say that that first impressions can teach us nothing, especially if we are discerning and possess neither pride, nor prejudice. However, as most of us are vessels of frailty, time and experience are invaluable predictors of long-lasting love. These principles in no way diminish, of course, the pleasurable memories provided by that first glance across a crowded dance floor.

Three of Teacups
Mansfield Park

Card Description

Mary Crawford, Maria Bertram, and Julia Bertram are grouped charmingly about a pianoforte, singing. Their arms are about one another's waists and they look very pleasant and pleased with themselves and each other.

Storyline

Once Sir Thomas leaves Mansfield Park to attend to his business in Antigua and the Crawfords arrive with their city ways, there is more of an emphasis on social interaction and the pursuit of creative diversions in the household. Henry Crawford has engaged the interest of both Bertram sisters, the "belles of the neighbourhood" who "joined to beauty and brilliant acquirements a manner naturally easy". Mary Crawford is also a beauty, but the Bertram sisters don't mind because they don't consider her in their league – and they think she'd make a fine sister-in-law. As a social unit, the three women form an attractive triumvirate. In this card, we see them singing together. Later on, their desire to express themselves creatively takes the form of putting on a somewhat risqué play. Sir Thomas Bertram immediately puts a stop to that outlet of artistic expression when he returns home.

Card Interpretation

By contemporary standards, creative expression is something to be lauded and encouraged in all its manifest forms, but in Jane Austen's day, there were stricter limits and a concern that overemphasis of the arts in general society could easily move into hedonism. The three women pictured in this card, while attractive and generally pleasing, are less upright than the moral center of the novel, Fanny Price, and the comparison is drawn in their pursuit of attention via artistic means, which is in direct opposition to Fanny's retiring behavior and her love of nature. When you receive this card in a reading, you may be seeking camaraderie and pleasure over more serious pursuits. You may be emphasizing looks and fun over more productive and/or serious activities. In life, there is a balance, and Jane Austen would not frown upon the occasional "glee" – yet she would also remind us that, in nature, we can find a more calming "harmony and repose". Only you can decide if you are indulging or overindulging in your socializing.

While Maria and Julia Bertram are sisters who have always gotten along well, their desire to each be the object of Henry Crawford's attention creates a rift between them. The sisters "do not have affection or principle enough to make them merciful or just, to give them honour or compassion". It is important to choose your sisters (or brothers) of the heart wisely, and act with justness, mercy, honor and compassion in your friendships. If their treatment of you lacks those qualities, you may need to re-examine your friendship. Someone you thought was an acquaintance can turn out to be a friend, and sometimes someone you think is a friend only deserves the title of acquaintance. This doesn't mean you can't have fun – this card is often an indication of revelry, pure and simple – but don't mistake a friend for an acquaintance and vice-versa.

The three women pictured in this card could be said to each represent one of the water signs. Mary Crawford is the character assigned earlier to the Chariot, whose astrological attribution is Cancer according to the Golden Dawn. The Cardinal aspect of water is one of leadership (even if the crab walks a crooked path, it always has a goal in mind). Her goal not to marry a country parson supersedes her emotional attachment to one (Edmund Bertram). Maria Bertram, whose passions overwhelm her to run from the protection of her safe but stupid husband into the waiting arms of the rakish Henry Crawford, exemplifies the fervent emotions of the sign of Scorpio. Julia Bertram is a bit more wishy-washy, but chooses a creative man, ignoring the importance of money and status completely. This seems like the behavior of a dreamy Piscean.

Yet the actual astrological attribution of this card is Mercury in Cancer, and that combination of planet in sign focuses on emotional communication. Here the three women in combination create beautiful music that moves the audience, and this card can indicate an artistic collaboration. Be sure that each voice is heard if this meaning resonates for you.

What Would Jane Do?

"Being earnestly invited by the Miss Bertrams to join in a glee, she tripped off to the instrument, leaving Edmund looking after her in an ecstasy of admiration of all her many virtues, from her obliging manners down to her light and graceful tread."

Jane Austen, *Mansfield Park*

Jane's Advice: 'Pretty is as pretty does' is the last thing a young woman wants to hear – or a young man believes. However, with age, one recognizes that true grace is not in the turn of a heel, but of a heel being turned into something better, something finer, than seems possible. Of course, no young person will believe one word of that. "Follies and nonsense, whims and inconsistencies, do divert me, I own, and I laugh at them whenever I can."

Four of Teacups
Mansfield Park

Card Description
An elderly woman, Lady Bertram, sits comfortably on a chair with a hassock. She is doing needlepoint, and you get a sense that she is in no rush. The room around her is elegant and extremely well-appointed.

Storyline
When Lady Bertram takes her impoverished niece, Fanny Price, into her home at Mansfield Park, she does so in her usual lethargic, blasé manner. She is kind to Fanny, but exerts no effort in making her feel at home, or empathizing with the frightened young girl who must acclimatize herself to a new home. As Fanny gets older, Lady Bertram begins to count on her assistance and gentle company more and more. Instead of feeling gratitude, Lady Bertram feels her dependence on Fanny supersedes any rights Fanny might have to any pleasures that might interfere with her raison d'etre: serving Lady Bertram.

When Lady Bertram's husband leaves for Antigua, she is sad because she'll miss him, but she doesn't worry about him being in danger or feel concern for any deprivations he might feel. She doesn't often stir from her home, and sees no reason why anyone else should either. This narcissism does not mean she is unfeeling; when he returns to Mansfield Park, she is so excited that it causes her to feel "nearer agitation than she had been for the last twenty years".

When Mary and Henry Crawford come to Mansfield Park, Lady Bertram welcomes them diffidently, never concerning herself as to whether they will be bad or good influences on her children and Fanny. In fact, when they play cards, Lady Bertram allows Henry Crawford to advise her on what cards to play – she is quick to allow others to make decisions for her, as long as it causes her no real discomfort.

When Fanny's brother William comes to visit, Lady Bertram is generous to him, because money isn't very important to her. Her creature comforts are what matter. She commissions William to get her a shawl when he goes to the East Indies; the fact that he could be at risk is completely irrelevant and doesn't occur to her.

Despite Lady Bertram's reliance on Fanny, Lady Bertram urges Fanny to accept Henry Crawford's proposal of marriage; it's her "duty". This is "almost the only rule of conduct, the only piece of advice, which Fanny had ever received from her aunt in the course of eight years and a half". A woman's role is to be subservient to men, according to Lady Bertram's philosophy and practice – so when Sir Thomas banishes Fanny from Mansfield Park to punish her for refusing Henry, Lady Bertram never offers a word of dissent.

However, when disaster strikes, Lady Bertram is glad indeed to get "her Fanny" back. When Fanny marries her son, Susan takes her place with Lady Bertram and Susan is more vital and energetic than Fanny ever was. This works out best for all concerned.

Card Interpretation

When this card shows up in a reading, it can suggest a strong inclination for not disturbing the status quo. Moon in Cancer is the attribution for this card, indicating that the domicile is a place of comfort and nurturance – and a risk-averse mentality that can be carried to the extreme of inertia. Like Lady Bertram, you may rarely leave your comfort zone and restrict your activities to reflect only ease and familiarity.

You might be holing up in your personal refuge because of past pain, and believe that your creature comforts are a priority that supersedes any other. You might even desire that others take on your wishes as their own. If this is a temporary phase, you may need a degree of respite and indulgence, but if this is a chronic condition, there may be a degree of depression that needs further scrutiny and outside assistance. This is not an unfeeling card, but occasionally your own needs loom so large that you can be selfish and narcissistic. A temporary menu of petits-fours and peeled grapes is fine for the temporarily wounded soul, but as a regular diet, it needs a serious overhaul.

Another aspect of this card involves luxury and lavish living. There is nothing inherently wrong with enjoying all the perquisites that wealth has to offer, but if your life no longer holds any charms for you, it may be time to proactively seek changes that invigorate you on every level. If you are feeling malaise, more of the same is not a good prescription for change. Other perspectives might be of service at this time.

If you are currently involved in a creative project, this might be a time where you feel stuck or blocked – the Muse simply won't come. If you have waited a long time, you might want to try moving forward without her. Sometimes the simple act of moving forward will bring her silently and stealthily to your door.

Fours are stable, but Cups/Emotions are extremely fluid; you can be easily influenced at this time, as Lady Bertram is when Henry plays her cards and Sir Thomas decides whether or not Fanny can be spared. If you want to control your own life, the only person who can take charge of it is you.

If the idea of counting your blessings repels you, this card clearly reflects your state of mind. Try and count them anyway.

What Would Jane Do?
"Lady Bertram did not at all like to have her husband leave her; but she was not disturbed by any alarm for his safety, or solicitude for his comfort, being one of those persons who think nothing can be dangerous, or difficult, or fatiguing to anybody but themselves."
Jane Austen, *Mansfield Park*

Jane's Advice: If one has just returned from a visit to the city, a time of reflection and refreshment is vital to one's feelings and spirit. However, the beauty of nature affords replenishment to those who observe it. Those who willingly entomb themselves in their homes – no matter how well-appointed they are – do themselves a disservice. The rest of us, however, should not grieve overlong at their absence, as they frequently have but little to add to the harmony of our surroundings.

Five of Teacups
Pride and Prejudice

Card Description
George Wickham stands in his dashing red military uniform, talking to Elizabeth Bennett. His pose is one of great and dramatic sadness, he looks away from her to the river as if he is imagining "what might have been". He even has his hand raised to his forehead in the traditional Five of Cups "Oh woe is me" pose. Elizabeth looks appropriately sympathetic.

Storyline
Elizabeth Bennett finds the charming, attractive militiaman, George Wickham quite appealing. She observes Mr. Darcy snub him and questions Wickham about it at a dinner party. Despite claiming he will never say a word against Mr. Darcy out of loyalty to Darcy's father, Wickham is quick to enumerate the afflictions he has suffered at the cruel hand of Mr. Darcy. Wickham claims that Mr. Darcy's father had promised him a "living" through the church, but after his father dies and he inherits the estate, Mr. Darcy's jealous nature supersedes his sense of duty. He ignores his father's express wishes and turns poor Wickham off the estate without a cent, for no real reason except jealousy. Wickham expresses regret at the loss of a clergyman's life, but now he must literally "soldier" on.

Elizabeth is sympathetic; this tale of Wickham's makes Darcy more odious to her. Darcy, oblivious of this, falls deeply in love with her. When Darcy proposes, Elizabeth rejects him, giving his maltreatment of Wickham as a reason.

She is horrified to learn via a letter from Darcy that Wickham's accounting is not remotely accurate. While Darcy never liked Wickham's profligate and immoral behavior, his dislike reaches its peak when Wickham attempts to elope with Georgina, Darcy's sixteen year old sister and heiress to a fortune that Wickham covets. Darcy foils the plot in time.

Lizzy doesn't want to believe it, but when Wickham next runs away – without benefit of marriage – with her sister, Lydia, she realizes to her great chagrin that Wickham's attractive façade is just that. His great protestations of sorrow are a dramatic and false display of emotion, nothing more.

Card Interpretation
This card is typically a picture of great grief, and we can certainly recognize that overwhelming feeling in this version of the Five of Teacups. However, excessive displays of emotion benefit neither the performer of such histrionics nor the often uncomfortable audience. Mars in Scorpio is the astrological attribute for this card, and involves the principles of action and assertion awash in deep, intense emotion. George Wickham may sincerely believe him-

self to be wronged, but the facts do not bear him out. When this card appears in a reading, you might well feel yourself to be in the throes of the greatest sufferings known to man and womankind. Joy and pain are heightened for those with emotional depth, but unfortunately, neither emotion often comes paired with detachment or perspective. Like Wickham's red coat, this card serves as a red flag to introduce both those qualities into a reappraisal of your circumstances

Life, by its very nature, contains disappoints both minor and severe. A sensitive person is likely to exaggerate the former and wallow in the latter. Look at your current situation and determine if you are truly giving yourself an appropriate and necessary time to grieve – or if your response is out of proportion to the specific situation in question. It may even be necessary to examine your own role in your current state of unhappiness; unless you wish to make bewailing your state of affairs your modus operandi, you may want to break patterns of behavior that have kept you in less than sanguine circumstances.

Conversely, if you look at this card and can not relate to it at all, you may wish to do a different kind of examination. It may be that you have not given yourself time to grieve a wound that opens at inopportune times and in covert ways. If you are acting in a way that is out of alignment with your stated desires and goals, it may be that you have glossed over a serious injury to your spirit, and you need to acknowledge that sadness before you can move on.

What Would Jane Do?

"But what," said she after a pause, "can have been his motive? – what can have induced him to behave so cruelly?"

Jane Austen, *Pride and Prejudice*

Jane's Advice: Those who spend the majority of your time enumerating the wrongs that have been done them are holding you and your actions in reserve to add to their number. If they used their accounting skills to assess the nature of their torment, they would bene-

fit themselves, not to mention their equally afflicted listeners. Suffering silently is a virtue done too rarely by too few. The more glorious the display of anguish, the more it is shared, but the less it is healed.

Six of Teacups
Mansfield Park

Card Description
Teenager Edmund Bertram holds out paper and pen to Fanny Price, an eleven year old girl. With his other hand, he wipes a tear from the young girl's eye. They are sitting in an elegant room in Mansfield Park, and a portrait of Sir Thomas Bertram (The Emperor) hangs above the young people.

Storyline
When the young and timid Fanny Price first arrives at Mansfield Park, she is intimidated

not only by the wealth and elegance of her new residence, but also at being forced to develop new relationships. Her older female cousins are too snobbish and self-involved to reach out a hand of friendship and her oldest male cousin, Tom, is not only much older, but completely self-absorbed. It is only her cousin Edmund who is considerate of her situation and her needs.

When Fanny expresses that she misses her brother, William, Edmund provides her with pen and paper and sends the letters for her. More than that, he is "always true to her interests, and considerate of her feelings, trying to make her good qualities understood, and to conquer the diffidence which prevented their being more apparent; giving her advice, consolation, and encouragement".

When Fanny expresses her indebtedness, Edmund assures Fanny that her "grateful heart" makes her an excellent "friend and companion". As Fanny and Edmund grow older, his solicitude does not ebb. He even gives her a horse to provide Fanny a healthful outlet, and continues to encourage and protect her from the less thoughtful members of the family who use her for their own ends.

Little wonder that the young Fanny's esteem grows into a romantic love, though it is not initially returned. Eventually, he sees how perfect a spouse Fanny will be to him in every way and they wed.

Card Interpretation

Even though we see portrayed in this card a young man giving and a younger woman receiving an object, the Six of Teacups intimates emotional reciprocity. Edmund gives Fanny both concrete and emotional support; in return, he values her loyalty and sincere and affectionate heart. When you receive this card in a reading, consider the emotional bonds in your own life – are they on an even keel or are they lopsided in some way? Is someone offering you a generous gift that you have previously ignored, or is that generosity tempered with cunning, a present that has strings attached?

Another thing this card suggests is a friendship that can become the foundation of a romantic love, as seen in the example of Fanny and Edmund's altered relationship. If so, the partnership has the potential to be stronger because of that initial honest intimacy that is untainted by romantic pretensions, but it may also lack the excitement of unadulterated passion.

It is somewhat telling that not only does Edmund never imagine Fanny's true feelings for him, he allows his father undue influence in terms of Henry's pursuit of Fanny's hand in marriage. Another aspect of this card can indicate a certain innocent or childish way of viewing a situation. Both Edmund and Fanny are almost hypersensitive to the others' feelings, and sometimes this card can indicate a childlike dependence on one or both parties.

However, this card is primarily a positive one. The astrological assignment is Sun in

Scorpio, and speaks of a natural ease, pleasure, and loving-kindness in partnerships of all kinds.

What Would Jane Do?
"I have no pleasure in the world superior to that of contributing to yours. No, I can safely say, I have no pleasure so complete, so unalloyed. It is without a drawback."
Jane Austen, *Mansfield Park*

Jane's Advice: Words of kindness can provide balm in the worse of times, deeds of kindness stir the soul, but a combination of the two are an ideal foundation for any relationship. Emotional support without the practical resources to relish them can be but empty comfort. On the other hand, practical assistance without kindness tastes as bitter as bread without jam. Even if your tea is truly sparse, however, it is better to share it with an amiable companion.

Seven of Teacups
Emma

Card Description
A young woman sits in dreamy reverie at a table holding a cup of tea to her lips. Six cups, each filled with attractive male heads float in the sky.

Storyline
Harriet Martin is an emotional young woman who is delighted when Emma Fairfax takes her under her wing. As their friendship grows, Harriet confides that Robert Martin, a farmer, has taken an interest in her, and she returns his affections. While she is hopeful that he will make her an offer of marriage, Harriet discovers Emma is not nearly as delighted with the idea of the match – she considers him Harriet's inferior.
Emma encourages Harriet to set her sights on Mr. Elton, the local clergyman. Harriet's malleable emotions are easily redirected to the unctuous and affable Mr. Elton. When Robert Martin proposes, Harriet turns him down.

However, it turns out that Mr. Elton's attentions are focused not on Harriet, but Emma. Harriet is deeply disappointed, and, when Emma rejects Mr. Elton, he quickly woos and weds another woman.
As Emma watches Harriet sadly destroy some trinkets that belonged to Mr. Elton, she recognizes that Harriet's sentimentality could lead her to return her attentions to Robert Martin. However, it seems that Emma's pep talks have given Harriet the confidence to think herself worthy of George Knightley, a man Emma realizes she herself loves.
Fortunately, Knightley loves her, not Harriet, which makes Emma quite happy. Harriet does not suffer for long, however. Robert Martin proposes again, and this time she accepts him – he is the one she truly loves.

Card Interpretation
While Harriet's imagination runs wholly to the subject of love and lovers, and this card

alludes to far more, the importance of discernment and discrimination in all of the things that most move our heart is reflected in her story. Things are quite different than they were in Jane Austen's day, when almost every marriage was permanent. Even today, if we play the field romantically, we make a choice by not making a choice – and that is not to be in a fully committed relationship with one person, with all the treasures and tribulations that can bring. If we select one love at the age of 18, we either grow and change together with our partner, or we must go through the pain of an unhappy marriage or an inevitably hurtful divorce.

But there is another aspect of Harriet's emotional malleability and imagination that also applies more universally to the Seven of Teacups, and that involves the issue of fantasy vs. reality. While Austen does not, thankfully, offer the reader a detailed accounting of Harriet's schoolgirl daydreams about Robert Martin (or any of her other imaginary swains), Harriet's constant allusions to her attachment du jour in the midst of unrelated conversation (combined with her destruction of her once-precious Elton-related souvenirs) convinces us that they exist and form a large part of her existence. When this card appears in a reading, it can serve as a warning that you might be indulging in fantasies that have no basis in reality, like Harriet's misplaced confidence that Mr. Knightley is in love with her. If you are thinking romantically about someone in your life who has not given you specific and tangible proofs of his or her commitment, do not start planning the wedding just yet. If you are looking for a real relationship, you need to act in the real world instead of spinning fantasies that have no basis in reality.

However, it may be that you prefer the world of imaginary, idealized love over actual human interaction, which necessitates scripts you can neither write nor direct. There's nothing wrong with that choice – as long as you are aware that you are making it, and not waiting for your real life to resemble your fevered or feathery reveries.

Individuals who dwell in the land of fantasy are particularly susceptible to romantic manipulation when they emerge into the real world, and can be easy prey for hustlers. Austen writes that Harriet's marriage would protect her:

"She would be placed in the midst of those who loved her, and who had better sense than herself; retired enough for safety, and occupied enough for cheerfulness. She would be never led into temptation, nor left for it to find her out".

Someone under the spell of the Seven of Teacups is in love with love, and may respond to any indication of interest with impetuous and unwise assent. Jane Austen reminds us that the dreamy romantics need protection. There are only happy endings in fantasyland. Reality, however, demands both discernment and action.

Astrologically speaking, the attribution for this card is Venus (the Goddess of Love) in the emotional sign of Scorpio. This combination can be overly focused on beautiful fantasies that are based in water, not earth; in other words, the reveries this card suggests are built on uncertain seas, not solid ground.

What Would Jane Do?

"Harriet, tempted by every thing and swayed by half a word, was always very long at a purchase…"

Jane Austen, *Emma*

Jane's Advice: Our imagination is a pet creature of our constitution. It reflects its master – or its servant – well. Those with far-seeking, curious minds have visions which can neither be contained nor predicted, and frequently give birth to inventions and devices that those with more limited minds will use with relish while they contemplate their next bonnet or beau. Notice how many more bonnets and beaus exist than innovations, and you will grasp the composition of the populace. A good imagination is a fine quality – in a mind that is equipped to use it well.

Eight of Teacups
Mansfield Park

Card Description
A carriage rides away from Mansfield Park. Inside, we can see an unhappy Fanny Price crying despite the open book on her lap. In the far distance, we see a rundown town with water and ships.

Storyline
When Fanny Price refuses the hand of wealthy suitor, Henry Crawford, her uncle Sir Thomas Bertram does everything he can to convince her to accept him. Though Fanny is a timid, gentle soul, she remains intractable, in part because she has seen through Henry Crawford's charm, recognizing his amoral nature. Her love for her cousin Edmund strengthens her resolve.

Finally, Sir Thomas decides to banish Fanny temporarily from Mansfield Park, where she has been his ward for many years, and return her to the bosom of her poor family in Portsmouth. He is confident that, once Fanny is re-exposed to the depths to which a poor woman can sink, and suffers sufficient privation, she will quickly change her mind about refusing Henry Crawford, a man who can give her a financially secure life.

Card Interpretation
When you receive this card in a reading, it is time to leave behind what is familiar to face the unknown. This is necessarily an emotional time, where you may possess mixed feelings about the change to come, as Fanny does when she returns to Portsmouth. While she is sad to leave the people she has come to consider her family behind, she also looks forward to her journey. Fanny's mother has written her a kind welcoming note which Fanny hopes signals a maternal bond, one she never had when she was young.

The astrological correspondence for this card is Saturn in Pisces, which fits Fanny's situation aptly. You recall that Fanny's character embodies the Hanged One, which is ruled by

Neptune – Neptune is the planet that rules the watery, emotional sign of Pisces. Saturn is the planet of limits and structure, and Fanny quickly discovers that her home in Portsmouth has none of the physical order or conveniences of Mansfield Park. Yet, physical ease or formalities are not what she seeks, but the love and connection with her birth family that Fanny so desires is equally constrained, both by her family's impoverished and disorganized circumstances and the fact that her mother prefers her sons to her daughters – not that her mother has much energy to give even to her male children.

Fanny's relationship with her father – a drunken lout – is even more disappointing. The only new emotional connection Fanny makes is with her younger sister, Susan, whose rough edges do not long hide a loving heart and an individual who desperately wants to improve herself. Fanny is just as eager to teach Susan as she is to learn, and in this process, Fanny gains as much as Susan, in terms of newfound confidence in herself and her own internal resources. Even in a disordered milieu, Fanny develops self-sufficiency and grows a great deal in understanding.

The new path that lies ahead for you might well contain challenges, particularly in the way of initial emotional dissatisfaction. However, we often learn more from the difficulties we encounter on unknown terrain than we do from treading a recognized, smooth road.

The growth you will experience on every level is necessary for your development now, even if it includes sacrifice and loss. We can not forget that *Mansfield Park* begins with Fanny's first journey to Mansfield Park. Life is a series of paths and transitions. Each choice we make, each new path we take, involves giving up at least one thing in order to create room for something else, something greater, something that will expand our worldview.

When we have achieved that necessary and new knowledge, it will be time to take another journey, forge a new path. Sometimes, as in the case of Fanny, it seems a return to the known; Fanny does make her way back to Mansfield Park. But she is not the same girl; the new Fanny has gained much in the way of self-confidence and self-understanding. She is more appreciated than she had been before, and, when she marries Edmund Bertram, she becomes a permanent and true denizen of Mansfield Park.

What Would Jane Do?

"The next morning saw them off again at an early hour; and with no events, and no delays, they regularly advanced, and were in the environs of Portsmouth while there was yet daylight for Fanny to look around her, and wonder at the new buildings… Fanny was all agitation and flutter; all hope and apprehension."

Jane Austen, *Mansfield Park*

Life is a series of planned and unplanned journeys. Many times the expected destination is never reached, and, if it is, the arrival often brings with it unexpected outcomes. It is in our responses to these unanticipated happenstances that we show our mettle. If our aim is to travel in body, but not spirit, we can not be surprised if our ultimate destination is a stultifying sameness.

Nine of Teacups
Emma

Card Description

Mr. Weston sits at the head of a table. His goblet is lifted in a toast and he is smiling. At his right is his son, Frank Churchill, and next to him is Emma. Across from Frank sits Jane Fairfax. Mr. Weston is the picture of a happy host who clearly sees the world with an optimistic gaze.

Storyline

Emma begins with the marriage of Emma's governess, Miss Taylor, to Mr. Weston, whose convivial and expansive nature make him a particularly good match. Because Miss Taylor has no money to speak of, she is considered truly fortunate, except by Emma's father, who feels anyone who "must" leave his household – even for the blessed state of matrimony – is a figure to be pitied.

Mr. Weston had previously been married to a Miss Churchill, who came from a wealthy family that had cast her off when she wed him, a man of inferior connections and wealth. While his exemplary qualities made him an excellent partner, his spoiled wife "did not cease to love her husband, but she wanted at once to be the wife of Captain Weston, and Miss Churchill of Enscombe." They had one child together, Frank, who was taken in by her family when she died. At the time, Captain Weston was not in a position to raise a child, and the Churchills' wealth provided a comfortable and secure berth for Frank.

Soon after Mr. Weston remarries, Frank contacts him after a long absence; he wishes to visit and pay his respects to his new stepmother. The Westons hope Frank and Emma will fall in love and do what they can to promote the match, but Frank's heart is already engaged, as is he, to Jane Fairfax, though he keeps that fact a secret until it is expedient to for him to disclose the information.

When the Westons learn of this, they worry about Emma; Frank has flirted shamelessly with her, but her heart is thankfully untouched by him. At the end of the book, Mr. Weston happily welcomes two new additions to his family: his new daughter-in-law, Jane Fairfax, and a brand new baby daughter, Anna.

Card Interpretation

The image on this card is one of expressive joy and pleasure. Jupiter in Pisces is the astrological correspondence for the Nine of Teacups; Jupiter is the planet of expansion and Pisces is a sign of great compassion and a desire to remove all personal barriers. Mr. Weston is the embodiment of this astrological aspect. He is good to his first wife, despite her being less-than-adaptable to his needs. He sacrifices the pleasure of raising his son in order for Frank to be more financially secure than himself – and when his son finally contacts him after an overlong period of neglect, he doesn't hold a grudge, but welcomes him into his life with open arms. His choice of a wife is one where he is happy and proud to provide for her, as opposed to choosing a woman of means who could bring money into the household.

When you receive this card in a reading, it indicates that you, too, have an open, welcoming and happy heart. You literally abound with affability and cordiality. You are a gracious host or hostess who loves company and pleasant interactions with other. Others love to be in your company because of your warmth and good humor. You are likely content with your lot in life whether your finances are exactly where you want them to be – or not. Like Mr. Weston, your self-esteem and happiness are not dependent on the status of your bank account.

In tarot lore, the Nine of Teacups is known as the "wish" card; when you receive this card in a reading, your heart's wishes are guaranteed to be gratified. Think of Mr. Weston welcom-

ing two beautiful new daughters into his home and you get a picture of a man whose cup literally overflows with joy.

However, Mr. Weston, while a man of means, is hardly the richest man in the neighborhood. This card focuses on emotional gratification, not material success.

If, as in Mr. Weston's first marriage, you are not fully valued and appreciated, do whatever you must to ensure that your loved one(s) understand that you have needs, too. While you are far too generous to measure your emotional giving, you should be treated as lovingly and cared for as unstintingly as you deserve. Even a vast emotional well can run dry, if it is not occasionally refilled by others. Mr. Weston's second marriage provides him with an abundance of refills.

Indiscriminate amiability is one of the few downsides of this card. You may choose to confide in unworthy recipients of your trust, or assume good-will where it does not exist.

Occasionally, this card can also indicate emotional self-absorption, wherein one is only interested in his or her admittedly wide sphere of loved ones.

Being the recipient of this card does not promise that you will be as rich in love as Mr. Weston, merely that you deserve and yearn to be. You need to take the necessary actions to achieve his state of great contentment.

What Would Jane Do?

"Mr. Weston is rather an easy, cheerful-tempered man…he takes things as he finds them, and makes enjoyment of them somehow or other…"

Jane Austen, *Emma*

Jane's Advice: A healthy diet of love and affection – combined with a lack of financial worry – is the best guarantee of longevity. Add to that regime a healthy appreciation of society and the means to indulge it and you add an additional decade to your life. Finally, remove tension by becoming the quintessence of affability and you might well live forever.

Ten of Teacups
Pride and Prejudice

Card Description

The Darcys (Fitzwilliam and Elizabeth) and the Bingleys (Charles and Jane) stand in front of a large home. Everyone looks beatifically happy, and the rainbow in the sky indicates that the sun is now shining on the two couples.

Storyline

The lovely and good-hearted Jane Bennett falls in love with Charles Bingley the moment they meet at a dance. Despite having his pick of the county maidens, he is also smitten, but his sisters and best friend, Fitzwilliam Darcy, conspire to keep them apart. When Darcy falls in love with Jane's sister, Lizzy, he realizes keeping Jane and Charles apart might not have been as clever as he initially thought – especially since

Lizzy has discovered his culpability in that affair and rejects his suit in large part because of it.

After overcoming various obstacles and misunderstandings, both couples unite in holy matrimony, as seen on the Four of Wands. This card is the continuation of that union, two couples who are committed to one another, standing on solid ground. Unlike the four, a first solid step (matrimony), this is a card of a felicitous home life that includes strong familial bonds. At the end of *Pride and Prejudice*, the Jane and Charles Bingley move near the Darcys, so they can maintain their closeness all their lives.

Card Interpretation

When you receive this card in a reading, it is an augury of love and happiness, but with the astrological assignment of this card being Mars in Pisces, it generally signifies that you've been tested through the fire before being able to merge in peace and harmony. The ten, being the last number, indicates completion, and, in general, nothing good is completed without hard work. In some ways, you can see this as the "payoff" card for the good faith efforts you have expended, much as the Bennett girls' marriages are a culmination of an emotionally-challenged journey. This card is an indicator of domestic happiness, both present and future.

If your issue or question does not concern love or a romantic relationship, this card has other relevant meanings. It can represent emotional growth: Lizzy has learned to be less judgmental and Jane has learned to be more so; Darcy has become more open and Charles has learned to set boundaries with his sisters.

This card can also represent becoming more emotionally confident of yourself, with new-found (and hard-won) recognition of your qualities and strengths. This confidence radiates from you, and is a source of pleasure and happiness for others, as well as yourself. This is a card of unstinting and limitless joy.

When this card is less positively placed, it might indicate some small and uneven waves in what remains a solid and loving relationship. Before the waves get larger and cause more serious quakes, clear the "deck" of any emotional debris.

What Would Jane Do?

"Jane and Elizabeth, in addition to every other source of happiness, were within thirty miles of each other."

Jane Austen, *Pride and Prejudice*

Jane's Advice: A happy and loving marriage does not form in a vacuum, but is enhanced by the support of loving family and friends. If two people have the emotional and spiritual wherewithal to create a harmonious life for themselves, as well as the financial capability in which to live that harmonious life, their future is destined to follow that pattern, unless fate takes a malign hand.

Maiden of Teacups
Marianne Dashwood (Sense and Sensibility)

Card Description

A young woman of 16 is seated at a pianoforte. Her head is thrown back and her expression is rapturous as she plays with passionate intensity. The room is decorated in a romantic style, a fitting repository for this romantic girl. Her hair falls in curly, dark blonde tendrils about her face and her skin is tanned. A goblet sits atop the piano, and inside it sits a single red heart. Underneath it is a fancy lace doily.

Storyline

Marianne Dashwood is the younger sister of Elinor, Lady of Coins in the Jane Austen Tarot. Austen introduces Marianne in the very first chapter as "eager in everything: her sorrows, her joys, could have no moderation". If Elinor embodies the "Sense" in the book's title, Marianne personifies the "Sensibility". She is all feeling, and disdainful of anyone who lacks her level of sensitivity, even her beloved sister.

When the Dashwood sisters' father dies, their now-widowed mother and Marianne give "themselves up wholly to their sorrow," as Elinor, no less saddened by the loss, takes charge of all the practical matters that present themselves when a family death occurs. Their mother is, in many ways, Marianne's role model, as they both take pride in their emotional self-indulgence. They are disapproving of and mystified by Elinor's restraint.

Marianne is full of romantic notions, especially in terms of love. She believes a woman of 27 is too old to feel passion, so one might be an appropriate match for a dessicated old man of 35, such as Colonel Brandon. Marianne describes Colonel Brandon, a wealthy man who finds her attractive, as "infirm". She certainly does not consider him, even remotely, as a potential suitor, despite her less-than-comfortable financial status.

When Marianne trips as she races down a hill, seemingly as if from nowhere, a handsome, dashing young man sweeps her up in his arms and carries her into her home. Such a romantic meeting clearly portends love to Marianne, and she willingly rushes into its thrall. She enters into a full-blown romance, giving Willoughby all of her considerable attention. She imprudently spends time alone with him in his quarters and gives him a lock of her hair, even though these are actions appropriate only to an engaged woman. She is sure of his affections and in her own good taste in bestowing her love on him.

When he goes off to London, she is desolate, and thinks of nothing but him. She and Elinor are given the opportunity to go to London, invited by Mrs. Jennings, a warm, but common woman who lacks Marianne's finer sensibilities. Marianne, who has heretofore ignored Mrs. Jennings as beneath her notice, immediately acquiesces. Once in London, she contacts Willoughby immediately, but he fails to respond to her letters. At a party, he openly cuts her and spends time with a wealthy woman, to whom he is said to be affianced. Shortly thereafter, Marianne receives by post her letters and the lock of hair, once imparted with such innocent love, along with a cold letter from Willoughby announcing his engagement to the heiress.

Marianne gives into her heartbreak fully, not hiding it from her sister nor Mrs. Jennings. She refuses to go out and eats sparingly – her broken heart immobilizes her. All she is able to do for many days is weep.

Marianne, however, is in for more disappointment. She learns that Willoughby has impregnated another, less fortunate woman. The man she thought so perfect is a cad. This reflects on her judgment, in which she once took so much pride. She finally recovers enough to return home, but before she arrives, she develops a dangerous fever. This is partially due to the poor self-care she has employed. Colonel Brandon fetches her mother and does everything he can to assist her. When Marianne revives, she returns home chastened, determined to dedicate herself to self-improvement with the same assiduity she brought to her relationship with Willoughby.

Through her tri-fold trial by fire (her heartbreak, her sister's good example, and her illness), Marianne transforms, becoming a woman able to value Colonel Brandon's qualities, despite his ancient and infirm age of 35, and they marry.

Card Interpretation

Early in the novel, when Marianne first meets Willoughby, she wants to know more of him. She asks the gregarious Sir John Middleton about Willoughby's "pursuits, talents, and genius". Sir John has inquired about Willoughby's hunting dog. Austen writes, "But Marianne could no more satisfy him as to the colour of Mr. Willoughby's pointer, than he could describe to her the shades of his mind". The Maiden of Cups knows much about feelings, but she is not a reliable source for mundane information. It's a matter of desiring knowledge born only of interest, not self-improvement or necessity.

Marianne sees what she wants to see, not reality. When she is hoping for Willoughby to come visit, she is sure it is he walking up the path, even though it's clearly Edward Ferrars, who looks nothing like her beloved. Later in London, despite Willoughby's complete disinterest in seeing her, she is in complete denial, unlike her very realistic sister, Elinor. When this card appears in a reading, it reminds you to look hard at the facts, not the pretty fictions you prefer, about your present situation.

With the innocence – or is that ignorance? – of youth, Marianne thinks her emotions are unchangeable. From the lofty purview of her sixteen years, she declares, "At my time of life opinions are tolerably fixed. It is not likely that I should now see or hear any thing to change them". Of course, they do change considerably as events unfold, which is how and why Marianne finally grows from maidenhood to ladyhood. Is there an area of your life that you have long held strong opinions about, regardless of facts that disprove your personal theories?

The Maiden of Teacups can be flexible when it comes to her principles – if they stand in the way of her love. She holds Mrs. Jennings in contempt, but gladly agrees to be her guest in London, because that's where Willoughby is. All Teacup Maidens place love highest in their personal rankings of importance. If you feel contempt for people in your life who lack your finer sensibilities, it may be time to measure their good qualities, qualities that perhaps you lack. Once Marianne fully realizes how much Elinor has sacrificed for her, Marianne atones by treating her with the utmost sensitivity and respect. When Marianne returns home after her illness, she determines to "enter onto a course of serious study". The Maiden of Teacups does not do things by half – there are no grays in her world. She is capable of great love and enormous sensitivity towards others, though she finds it difficult to relinquish her self-absorption. She is unable to be a dilettante. She gives all or nothing.

Just as Marianne is able to feel the strongest raptures of joy, she is plunged into the deepest of despondencies when she comes down: "Misery such as mine has no pride. I care not who knows I am wretched…I must feel – I must be wretched". She has even been known to undergo bouts of hysteria. Do you, as a Maiden of Teacups, have a tendency to feel utterly euphoric…and then dramatically wallow in your misery? Contrast this fondness for reveling in emotional depths with the Lady of Teacups, Jane Bennett, who determines to do everything in her power to put aside her love for Bingley when all seems lost. This Maiden of Teacups is like a musician who plays for love, not money. Were she performing today, she might be playing for tips at a saloon, because she is disinclined to refit her talents for the vagaries of the market. Art and feeling are all; mundane money is beneath her. Perhaps you are feeling frustrated at the lack of public acclaim for your art – though you have yet to present it in a manner where anyone could actually observe it. Then again, you may not care. As Marianne asks in *Sense and Sensibility*, "What have wealth or grandeur to do with happiness?".

What Would Jane Do?

"Common sense, common care, common prudence, were all sunk in Mrs. Dashwood's romantic delicacy."

Jane Austen, *Sense and Sensibility*

Jane's Advice: Sensitivity without sense is as useless as sense without sensitivity, and far more preposterous. It is difficult to laugh at sense, but sensitivity without the balance of good judgment provides a veritable font for derision. Sensibility is an essential portion in the configuration of a lady, but discretion in application and public displays is necessary, as well.

Knight of Teacups
John Willoughby (Sense and Sensibility)

Card Description
A dashingly-attired young man sits astride a beautiful and spirited horse. In one hand, Willoughby holds the reins loosely, in the

other, he carries a tendril of blondish-brown hair that he stares at lovingly. The man is in his early twenties, attractive and dashingly dressed. The outdoor scene is autumnal and set in a forest. The trees are green with shades of red and brown, and the grasses are thick and lush. The sky is gray and threatens rain.

Storyline

Marianne Dashwood is primed to fall in love, but only with a hero similar to the protagonists in the romantic novels she reads. When she falls and hurts herself outdoors, the appearance of John Willoughby seems both quixotic and destined: he literally sweeps her off the ground into his arms. What could be more fated? How could he be a more romantic hero, especially with "the influence of youth, beauty, and elegance" added to his persona.

Willoughby and Marianne do seem to be a perfect couple:

"They speedily discovered that their enjoyment of dancing and music was mutual, and that it arose from a general conformity of judgment in all that related to either. Encouraged by this to a further examination of his opinions, she [Marianne] proceeded to question him [Willoughby] on the subject of books; her favourite authors were brought forward and dwelt upon with so rapturous a delight, that any young man of five and twenty must have been insensible indeed, not to become an immediate convert to the excellence of such works, however disregarded before. Their taste was strikingly alike."

Willoughby visits the Dashwoods daily, and each meeting has Marianne feeling more, not less, on that account. There is every reason to believe Willoughby has fallen in love with her. He gives Marianne a horse (which, in Jane Austen's time, would only be an appropriate gift for a fiancée or spouse), asks for a lock of her hair, and invites her to his home without a chaperone. When he has urgent business that causes him to leave for London, Marianne is saddened by the loss of his presence, but san-

guine in the belief that they will soon be together again, in a more permanent union.

However, when she arrives in London, Marianne's letters to Willoughby go unanswered. When they meet at a gathering, he openly snubs her, and then sends her a cold, dry letter announcing his engagement. He is to marry the wealthy heiress, Sophia Grey.

It turns out that mercenary behavior is not Willoughby's most egregious sin. Marianne's sister Elinor discovers that Willoughby, as always mastered by his passions, has impregnated a young woman, Eliza Williams, leaving her to fend for herself and their illegitimate child.

Later in the novel, Willoughby learns that Marianne is seriously ill, and, without giving a thought to respectable behavior (or his wife), he dashes to the estate where Marianne and Elinor are staying. As Marianne lies in bed upstairs, Willoughby dramatically reveals his heart to Elinor. He claims that he only married Sophia Grey in order to preserve a lifestyle he believed was necessary for his happiness, more necessary than the great love he felt (and continues to feel) for the impecunious Marianne. Believing she is near death, he feels compelled to divulge the truth, and begs Elinor to let Marianne know she had not deluded herself – he had always shared her feelings. He leaves, a heart-broken man who knows he had found – and lost – his one true love.

Card Interpretation

As the Knight of Teacups, you are very pleasing to others, often obtaining loyalty through your winning ways that you have yet to earn. Even sensible Elinor is moved by Willoughby's articulated love for Marianne, despite her awareness of his despicable behavior. You or someone in your life has a flair for the dramatic, and is an insightful, feeling individual with whom others feel comfortable sharing.

It may be that your feelings run very deep, and you are capable of giving your partner all the romance he or she could desire. You can be quite sentimental, as Willoughby is when he asks Marianne for a lock of her hair. As the Knight of Teacups, you are also quite expressive, with a real gift for articulating your feelings.

Traditionally seen as a complete romantic, the Knight of Teacups is oft-compared to Sir Galahad, a knight on a quest of great feeling and spirituality. Willoughby evinces his sensitivity in every exchange with Marianne. He shares every rapture, every appreciation of beauty and art, and is completely attuned to her every feeling. Because emotions are so fluid, however, he is able to transfer his feelings of love for Marianne to self-love, in terms of living a life of extravagance. Willoughby doesn't know how to stifle his self-indulgence – he impregnates Eliza Williams because he is swept away by his desires, and not constrained by responsibility. If you receive this card in a reading, you may attract romantic interest and develop soul-deep relationships with ease. You may also, however, find it more difficult to sustain a committed relationship. You could possess little emotional discipline or place too high a priority on satisfying your own feelings. You may be guilty of duplicity, primarily because you don't think before you act.

It is possible that you might even feel no compunction in toying with someone else's emotions. Willoughby discloses the following to Elinor:

"Thinking only of my own amusement, giving way to feelings which I had always been too much in the habit of indulging, I endeavoured, by every means in my power, to make myself pleasing to her, without any design of returning her affection."

Sometimes "the hunter gets captured by the game." You might find yourself enmeshed, getting involved with someone you didn't intend to take to heart, only to discover that your feelings are stronger and more complicated than you initially planned.

Note that the cold letter Willoughby writes to Marianne is dictated by his fiancée. This shows how hard it is for a Knight of Teacups to be detached and rational, particularly in terms of communication. If you receive this card in a reading, it may be alerting you not to make promises you don't wish to keep, and to show some discernment in your oral and written correspondence.

What Would Jane Do

"Her thoughts were silently fixed on the irreparable injury which too early an independence and its consequent habits of idleness, dissipation, and luxury, had made in the mind, the character, the happiness, of a man who, to every advantage of person and talents, united a disposition naturally open and honest, and a feeling, affectionate temper."

Jane Austen, *Sense and Sensibility*

Jane's Advice: It is all very well to be feeling, but controlling your emotions, not allowing them to control you, must be your credo. Your natural ability to charm and enchant can serve you well – or ill, depending on intermingling equal degrees of rationality and principled behavior. A true romantic hero must possess all these traits if he is to win the ultimate prize.

Lady of Teacups
Jane Bennett (Pride and Prejudice)

Card Description
The most beautiful of the Queens, this card shows Jane Bennett seated at her window. If you look closely, you discern an almost indistinguishable tear in her eye. She is dressed simply, but with taste. Her face is composed and serene. A teacup is placed on the windowsill. We can see a departing rider in the distance from the window.

Storyline
Jane is the most beautiful of the five Bennett daughters, but her looks are not the only thing that is beautiful about her. She is modest and unassuming, has a sweet and gentle disposition, and her emotions run deep, but never overflow into excessive displays. She believes the best of people, until there is no doubt that they are undeserving of her kind thoughts.

When she falls in love with Charles Bingley, the rich and handsome newcomer to Hertfordshire, he seems equally infatuated, yet his sisters and his best friend, Fitzwilliam Darcy, succeed in separating them, wanting Bingley to marry a wealthier woman, someone who is of his own societal status. Darcy is also not convinced that Jane is in love with Bingley because she is restrained in the manner in which she evinces her affection.

When Bingley leaves for London, Jane believes they will still see one another, but her hopes are dashed. She nurses her heartbreak silently, not sharing her pain with others, but suffering greatly nonetheless. When Darcy asks Jane's sister Elizabeth to marry him, he learns that he has been mistaken in not believing in Jane's love for his friend, but since his greater mistake is in thinking Lizzy will accept his proposal, the matter of Jane's affections doesn't register in terms of importance.

However, once Darcy realizes his mistake, he tacitly give his approval for his friend to court Jane. When Bingley returns to Hertfordshire, Jane has no expectations, but her heart is still committed to him. When he asks for her hand in marriage, she accepts with great joy.

Card Interpretation
This court card's elemental makeup is Water of Water, which means that the individual represented is very emotional. Yet the Lady of Teacups has learned to control her emotions, instead of allowing them to control her. If you receive this card in a reading, the individual is very feeling and compassionate, perhaps too much so. Inclined to see the best in everyone, he or she can be hoodwinked by others' kindnesses, real or imagined. He or she has a tendency to be too trusting, and once his or her heart is engaged, it can remain so forever.

Even though the elemental component is watery and could be considered unstable, the

Minor Arcana

position of Lady is one that shows advancement over the less mature Maiden. While both cards indicate a feeling person, the Lady of Cups has mastered her emotions. It does not mean she is any less tender, but she is able to hide her vulnerability more successfully. Also, unlike the Maiden of Cups, the Lady of Cups has the maturity to focus her empathy on others, instead of being emotionally self-absorbed and/or overly sensitive. Sometimes she seems to understand others' feelings better than they do themselves, and she can be quite psychic in the department of interpersonal relationships.

The person this card represents is often one of unusual physical beauty and grace. However, she is usually unaware, even modest, about her extraordinary good looks. When it is noted that Bingley is paying her great attention, Jane observes, "I was very much flattered by his asking me to dance a second time. I did not expect such a compliment".

In fact, this card character can sometimes be oblivious to much that is going on in the mundane world, because she resides in such an emotional realm. Despite her maturity, she is subject to moodiness and can wallow in her own heartache. Her pride does not always allow others to see her pain, but just as she feels great love, her depressions can be deep and long-lasting. Resilience is not her strong suit.

As a parent, she can be too indulgent. Setting boundaries is always a challenge for the Lady of Teacups, because of her overpowering desire to be loved and her strong sensitivity.

What Would Jane Do?

"Jane united with great strength of feeling a composure of temper and a uniform cheerfulness of manner ..."

Jane Austen, *Pride and Prejudice*

Jane's Advice: Inner beauty may be rarer than physical appeal, but that does not always increase its worth to the average person in society. However, wise observers will value a loving heart beyond measure when it is coupled with compassionate discernment and a

controlled manner. The first quality protects one from being a fool, the second saves one from being extremely wearing.

Lord of Teacups
Charles Bingley (Pride and Prejudice)

Card Description

Charles Bingley, a good-looking, genial man in his early thirties sits at a table, his glass hoisted in the air in a toast. He seems filled with good will towards all. A miniature of the Lady of Teacups is on the table nearby. The table is set for a fine repast. We see his face slightly raised, as if he is listening to someone else, but he is the only person in the picture.

Storyline

Despite being *the* eligible bachelor in Hertfordshire, Charles Bingley is humble and unassuming. Perhaps he is able to maintain his modesty because his closest friend, Fitzwilliam Darcy, is several rungs higher than he on the social ladder. Bingley's general affability and open nature makes him a general favorite in the neighborhood, whereas Darcy's more reserved nature elicits distaste. When Bingley meets the lovely Jane Bennett, he is attracted both by her beauty and her sweet and gentle nature.

The attraction is mutual, but when his sisters and Darcy convince him to return to London, he allows them to convince him that Jane's feelings for him aren't as strong as his. However, he does not forget her and continues to pine for her. When Darcy gives him tacit permission to court her again, he quickly returns to Hertfordshire and Jane.

Card Interpretation

The Lord of Teacups is a pleasant and warm individual who comes across as caring and compassionate. When he asks how you are faring, he genuinely wants to know. He is a positive individual who loves his family and friends, and possibly allows them too much personal influence, as Bingley does in his relationship with Jane Bennett.

He invites confidences with his non-judgmental, empathic manner; like his Lady of Teacups, he tends to see the best in people and can be overly trusting. He is simply less vulnerable, because his place in life is so secure. He would make an ideal therapist or coach, encouraging others to find the good in themselves.

He is always well-liked, but he does not inspire awe or fear, like his friend, Darcy, the Lord of Quills. He tends to be somewhat of a dilettante. He is good at many things, but he does not have the focus or energy to excel at any of them. He has learned to trust his intuition, but in some cases, internal insecurities can make him vulnerable to others' criticism. While the Lord of Teacups has many good qualities, his overwhelming desire to please and keep his environment a harmonious one can stop him from doing what is right in favor of what is easiest, as Bingley does by allowing his family and friend from diverting him from pursuing the woman who loves him. A true and open "giver", he does not always discern whom is worthy of his generosity. Unlike the Lord of Quills, he suffers fools with too much equanimity.

In a reading, this card urges you to be loving and compassionate – and to trust your heart, as opposed to the advice of others.

What Would Jane Do?
"Mr. Bingley had soon made himself acquainted with all the principal people in the room; he was lively and unreserved, danced every dance, was angry that the ball closed so early, and talked of giving one himself at Netherfield. Such amiable qualities must speak for themselves."

Jane Austen, *Pride and Prejudice*

Jane's Advice: An amiable personality is one who is welcome everywhere, and if that person is well-off, so much the better. He will be avidly sought after. He might not make the best general, but society does not demand an iron will and determination. In fact, it often decries such characteristics. If you wish to make yourself well-loved, be open and affa-

ble. If principles matter more to you, join the Navy.

Ace of Quills
Persuasion

Card Description
A sharp silver letter opener is in the center of this card. The things we see clearly are its silvery gleam and its sharpness. It sits on an envelope addressed to Anne Elliot.

Card Interpretation
The Aces are the elementals in the tarot, and so don't represent a part of a story, per se, but are instead the essence of the suit. Logic and rationality are at the heart of the novel *Persuasion*. We meet Anne Elliot after she has refused the suit of naval captain Frederick Wentworth, an impecunious young man whose position, spirit, and brilliance held the

promise of potential success. Anne loves him, but bows to the wisdom of her godmother, Lady Russell, who reasonably believes her goddaughter can do better and persuades her that she will hold him back if they wed. Rational Anne bends to the will of Lady Russell's maternal influence; the bold Frederick Wentworth leaves with great resentment towards them both.

As Anne grows older, she doesn't regret attending to Lady Russell, as she feels their relationship required respect and that prudence should always accompany the prospect of marriage. However, her love for Captain Wentworth never dissipates. When he returns to her circle seven years later, she is looked upon as an on-the-shelf spinster, whereas he has become quite prosperous and a highly sought-after bachelor.

Captain Wentworth seems not to see Anne at all, and she must watch as various relatives put themselves forth to catch his eye. However, when one of them, the rash Louisa Musgrove, nearly jumps to her death on a lark, capable Anne handles the situation with calm and efficient rationality while everyone else, including Captain Wentworth, is immobilized with shock and horror.

This action re-awakens Wentworth's understanding of the woman he had once loved, allowing him to see her for her true worth. Over time, he realizes how much he still loves and admires Anne, and he once again proposes. This time she accepts.

When they discuss the broken engagement of their youth, Anne rationally analyzes the situation thus:

"I have been thinking over the past, and trying impartially to judge of the right and wrong, I mean with regard to myself; and I must believe that I was right, much as I suffered from it, that I was perfectly right in being guided by the friend whom you will love better than you do now. To me, she was in the place of a parent. Do not mistake me, however. I am not saying that she did not err in her advice … But … I was right in submitting to her, and that if I had done otherwise, I should have suffered more in continuing the

engagement than I did even in giving it up, because I should have suffered in my conscience. I have now, as far as such a sentiment is allowable in human nature, nothing to reproach myself with; and if I mistake not, a strong sense of duty is no bad part of a woman's portion."

Meanwhile, Captain Wentworth has a regret of his own. Two years after they parted, he had earned enough money to support a wife. He internally debated renewing his suit, but "was too proud" to do so. Had he been less hot-tempered, and more sensible, they would have had additional years of happiness.

The Ace of Quills represents the pure element of air. The image itself reminds us of the aphorism, "The pen is mightier than the sword," in that logic and reason can triumph over violence and might. Qualities associated with the Quill and its element, air, include intellect, communication, reasoning, verbalization, detachment, articulation, decisions, strategies, judgments, and analytical and psychological approaches.

When this card appears in a reading, you might have an exciting new brainstorm. It's possibly as brilliant as you think it is, but in order for any idea to manifest in the world, it will need to undergo rational scrutiny and be assessed and analyzed.

This card can also invite you to bring clarity to a situation. You can make a list of pros and cons, or do some other form of statistical analysis. The Ace of Quills urges you to penetrate an issue sharply and deeply.

In addition, this card reminds you to think with your head, as well as your heart. Ignoring your desires is self-defeating, but allowing wishful thinking to blur the nature of reality is simply idiotic. The danger this card can represent is thinking without bringing emotion into the equation. Humans are a delicate balance of both qualities, and ignoring one for the other is a mistake, no matter which one is eschewed. Words that come only from the mind can be vicious and cut to the bone, but words from the heart can move mountains, because they combine verbal and emotional intelligence.

The Ace of Quills can also represent a "Eureka!" moment, an instant of blinding insight and clarity.

What Would Jane Do?

"Till that day, till the leisure for reflection which followed it, he had not understood the perfect excellence of the mind with which Louisa's could so ill bear a comparison, or the perfect unrivalled hold it possessed over his own. There, he had learnt to distinguish between the steadiness of principle and the obstinacy of self-will, between the darings of heedlessness and the resolution of a collected mind."

Jane Austen, *Persuasion*

Jane's Advice: Perfect excellence is, indeed, a rarefied quality, one that often remains more in the ethers than the material world. However, in the coolest regions of the mind, wisdom and rationality can intermingle and create a vision of perfection. It is not a perfection that can last in the continued earthly interchanges that demand the washing and needlework get done, but one breath drawn in that heavenly clarity can provide a lifetime of happiness.

Two of Quills
Emma

Card Description

Jane Fairfax is seated on a chair. She holds a pen in each hand and stares straight ahead. On her right stands Mrs. Elton, who is clearly trying to convince her to do something. On Jane's left is Frank Churchill, kneeling eloquently by her side. He looks at her pleadingly.

Storyline

When Jane Fairfax returns to Highbury, it seems her fate is sealed. As the friend of a well-off classmate with whom she has lived with as a sister, she is well-educated, but now that her friend has wed, she must make her home briefly with her spinster aunt and elderly grandmother. Since they are not well-off, she will have to gain respectable employment, probably as a governess, though it is not something she wishes to do.

Unknown to everyone, she is secretly engaged to Frank Churchill, who is the ward of a wealthy couple. His adopted mother is unlikely to approve the match, so no one knows of their relationship. However, when Frank visits his real father in Highbury and begins to flirt shamelessly with the wealthy Emma Woodhouse, Jane begins to question his fealty.

To make matters worse, the well-meaning, but presumptuous Mrs. Elton has found her a position as a governess and is urging her to take it and be grateful, despite Jane's not having asked the officious woman to find her employment.

Jane is in a quandary. Should she trust Frank Churchill and remain engaged to him or should she prudently accept the unpleasant, but possibly necessary, position Mrs. Elton has obtained for her?

Card Interpretation

When this card appears in a reading, you may be of two minds about something. Like Jane Fairfax, you could be torn between trusting your heart or following the dictates of logic, and are feeling blocked and immobilized. You might even feel as if you are teetering on a precipice and a hearty gust of wind could push you over the edge. The balance you are struggling to maintain is a challenge, and though you might seem calm to the outside world, internally you are feeling chaotic and unsure.

There is sometimes a sense of calm in this card, because the individual seems to have made a choice, but it's more of an interim accommodation than a final decision. There can also be a degree of denial in this card, which is sometimes a willful desire not to want to see something unpleasant, but occasionally stems from an intuitive understanding that what appears on the surface can be deceiving.

Unfortunately, additional tension is created when the individual doesn't feel comfortable trusting intuitive guidance, but prefers to deal solely with facts. Jane Fairfax wants to trust her fiancé, but is afraid to do so.

This card can also denote being torn between two sides, or two people who wish you to go in different directions, as Jane is being pulled to one side by Frank Churchill and to another by Mrs. Elton.

Astrologically, the Two of Quills is attributed to Moon in Libra. An emotional planet in a detached air sign makes for a natural battle between thought and feeling. Libra strives for equilibrium, but the Moon fluctuates. It can do nothing else. Only temporary balance can be achieved with Moon in Libra.

Sometimes the best response in such cases is to do nothing, because fate might take a hand. In *Emma*, Frank Churchill's adopted mother dies, leaving him free to become openly engaged to Miss Fairfax. This allows Jane to

ultimately reject Mrs. Elton's proffered employment placement without fearing that she is giving up a possible financial lifeline.

What Would Jane Do?

"When Jane first heard of it, she was quite decided against accepting the offer ...Sure enough, yesterday evening it was all settled that Jane should go."

Jane Austen, *Emma*

Jane's Advice: When you feel you are unable to make a decision that you know both logically and emotionally to be correct, inaction is preferable to action. Decisions based on logic must be lived by someone with a heart, whereas a decision made quickly and emotionally is bound to be repented at leisure. Sooner or later, circumstance will demand that a choice be made, but conditions will inform that decision, so it will be more wisely made.

Three of Quills
Pride and Prejudice

Card Description
Alone in a garden, the beautiful Jane Bennett reads a letter from Caroline Bingley, three tears streaming down her face. Red roses – with thorns – grow nearby.

Storyline
When Jane Bennett first meets Charles Bingley, he seems to be very attracted to her. Her sister Lizzy is apprehensive that Jane's preference for him will be too obvious, but, upon observation, she is reassured that Jane's decorum and sense of what is appropriate will shield her from making a fool of herself.

The relationship between Jane and Bingley seems to progress, but his sisters and his friend, Fitzwilliam Darcy, don't want them to marry. Bingley's affable and trusting nature allows him to be spirited to London and away from the woman he has begun to love.

Jane feels the loss but is unsure where he stands, since he has given her no reason to believe his interest has abated. Since nothing is definitively stated, she goes to London expecting Bingley's family to at least acknowledge her socially, but they snub her – and Bingley never finds out that Jane has even come to town. Jane is also unaware of the particulars, and her trip puts the final nail in the coffin of her hopes for them to have a future together.

Jane never expresses her heartbreak, but feels it deeply. When Bingley finally returns, she tries to show no emotion; she is "anxious that no difference should be perceived in her at all". She refuses to hope that he might want to court her again and feels it would be "weak" to continue to care for him, yet she can not help but find his ways appealing.

Soon enough, her spoken objections come to a halt. And when he asks her to marry him, her answer is a joyous, "Yes".

Card Interpretation
This is not a card people are generally happy to see come up in a reading. It speaks of sorrow, a heart in pain. But since this is a card of Quills, which is aligned to the element of air, we need to recognize the important influence our thoughts have on our feelings.

Like Jane, you might be in a situation where it seems that someone you care about does not return your sentiments. You can fall into a spiral of self-loathing, questioning your behavior or appeal, or you can rationally assess the situation and recognize your worth is not measured by another's affection (or lack thereof).

This awareness does not take away from your sorrow at not having the relationship you want, but it does allow you to continue to be open to the future possibility of happiness. Even though Jane rationalizes that she can no longer afford to care what Bingley thinks of her, she isn't foolish enough to refuse his proposal on the basis of past pain and injury. Someone who allowed herself to wallow in bitter emotions might have done so, but Jane wisely does not invest in such acrimony.

Saturn in Libra is the astrological assignment for the Three of Quills and it speaks to the importance of disciplined (Saturn) balance (Libra). No matter how constraining the circumstance, immersing yourself indefinitely in sorrow and despair will not prove effective or helpful. Three is an odd number, making balance a challenge, but harmony is only attained through rigorous rationality. As humans, we possess an abundance of feelings; this card reminds us to balance them with recognition of the facts. Jane's trip to London strips away any fantasies that Bingley intends to take their relationship to the next level, which allows her to mourn it and find closure. Sometimes love, like the red rose Jane holds in the Three of Quills, has thorns, but that doesn't diminish its potent beauty. Although Bingley ultimately returns to her, Jane would have survived it if he had not – not because her love for him is weak, but because of her quiet strength.

Sometimes this card isn't as dramatic as losing a love. It can indicate a departure or division from the known, which can cause tension and dejection. And, as in the case of Jane and Bingley, this card does not always indicate a permanent breach.

Alternately, it can indicate that the feared worst-case scenario does not come to pass, or is not as dismal as originally believed. In its most perverted form, it can suggest someone over-dramatizing a situation, making mountains out of molehills. Unlike Jane, you could wring your hands and see yourself as a tragic heroine. While this might be satisfying in the short-term, its potential for enduring gratification is limited at best.

What Would Jane Do?

"She does not know, no one can know, how much I suffer from what she says."

Jane Austen, *Pride and Prejudice*

Jane's Advice: Would that those who claim to suffer in silence actually do so. The fact that we know that this is their self-belief indicates the falsity of the claim. There is no life without setbacks and disappointments, but it is within

our power to determine how contented we are with the lives that we are given.

This is not to say that we should welcome sorrow, simply that it is as much a part of life as joy, and it would be hard to recognize one without the other.

Four of Quills
Sense and Sensibility

Card Description

Marianne Dashwood sits up in bed. She is pale, a sign of convalescence. The room is dark, lit by a lantern atop a small pile of books that sits beside her bedstead. The room is rather bare, almost monastic in its lack of furbelows and furnishings

Storyline

Emotionally passionate Marianne Dashwood has loved – and lost. She gave her young heart to John Willoughby, but he has cast her and her heart off to become engaged to an heiress. Marianne had been sure of his love and constancy and grieved publicly and privately. She shows listlessness and apathy, the hallmarks of true depression, as she makes her way through her last days in London before going home.

But before arriving home, she spends time in Somerset and takes a walk about wet grounds. She doesn't change into dry clothes, and develops a cold. Her condition slowly becomes serious, and her sister Elinor fears for Marianne's life.

Card Interpretation

In the Three of Quills, Jane Bennett deals with her heartbreak by remaining positive and philosophical. In the Four, Marianne does not share that restraint, but instead wallows in her emotions to the point where she literally makes herself sick. Note that, in the Jane Austen Tarot, Marianne is the Maiden of Teacups, Jane, the Queen.

We get some clues as to the difference between the two approaches when we examine the astrological association for this card: Jupiter in Libra. Where Saturn contracts,

Jupiter expands – and Libra is ruled by Venus, the Goddess of Love. As opposed to Saturnian restraint, we have Jupiterian abundance. Normally, we think of abundance as a good thing, but when our emotions are so abundant as to wash away our rationality, we endanger ourselves and those around us.

When you receive the Four of Quills in a reading, like Marianne, you may be feeling rather listless and apathetic. Something or someone has drained you dry, and you are not at your emotional or intellectual peak. Rest and respite are called for in serious quantities.

You may blame yourself for feeling so weak. Fault is immaterial compared to the need to take care of yourself. You may not realize the level of your debilitation, but this card is a warning flag that, if you don't take a break, one will be forced upon you.

When Marianne takes ill, she is sure that her reason for living is gone. She sees no point in living without love. Yet soon enough, she comes to love Colonel Brandon with every passionate fiber of her being. No matter how difficult things have been, this is not time to give up hope, With rest comes strength and stability, and changes for the better will inevitably occur if you allow yourself the respite you need.

It may be time to re-order the thinking in your particular universe. Marianne's sickness ultimately changes her from a romantic girl who holds stability and practicality in contempt to someone who cherishes the safety and security Colonel Brandon represents. If your thoughts have been chaotic, it may be time to create a new mental structure for yourself.

What Would Jane Do?

"Marianne had now been brought by degrees, so much into the habit of going out every day, that it was become a matter of indifference to her, whether she went or not: and she prepared quietly and mechanically for every evening's engagement, though without expecting the smallest amusement from any, and very often without knowing, till the last moment, where it was to take her."

Jane Austen, *Sense and Sensibility*

Jane's Advice: One of the chief charms of youth is its idealism. However, one of the chief charms of youth is that it is a period of short duration. Maturity calls for sense, as well as sensibility. Being carried away by passion can result in crises far more serious than the fortunate Marianne's. If your emotions are causing you more pain than pleasure, it may be time to reconsider your choices. Peace and serenity aid in making good decisions; chaos and torment invariably cause more of the same.

Five of Quills
Emma

Card Description

The scene, from Jane Austen's *Emma*, is of an outdoor garden party. The grounds are green and lush, with many flowering trees, showing the English countryside at its best and most unspoiled. The central figures are charmingly grouped in a circle: Emma, a beautiful young woman in her 20's, holds a delicate knife in one hand and is speaking. Her expression is one of condescension and wicked delight; Miss Bates is all dowdy clothes and large spectacles, and she is on the verge of confused tears; Frank Churchill, a dashing and amused young man is enjoying the scene, and Jane Fairfax, Emma's equal in beauty, is composed, elegant, and serene. Leaning against a tree, looking disapprovingly on the revelers is Mr. Knightley, a handsome and distinguished man in his late thirties.

Storyline

Emma, who is somewhat captivated by the flirtatious Frank Churchill, is basking in being the acknowledged center of her society. In the past, she has often been irritated by the kind-hearted, but annoyingly voluble Miss Bates. Emma chooses this moment to say something witty, but cutting to the older woman, partially to impress Churchill, who is known to employ wicked ripostes of his own. When Miss Bates self-deprecatingly says that she can easily say three dull things, Emma replies that the difficulty lies in Miss Bates' limit of saying only three.

Once she understands the sentiment, Miss Bates is too good-natured to blame Emma for her cruel comment. Instead, Miss Bates spirals into a painful and embarrassed oration detailing her own flaws. Later, Mr. Knightley reproves Emma for her vicious comment. He is particularly outraged that Emma, whose lot in life is clearly superior to the less fortunate Miss Bates, would be so gratuitously unkind, pointing out that "Her situation should secure your compassion."

Emma recognizes the truth in his observation. She is as painfully wounded by this true mirror of her own behavior (and losing the estimable Mr. Knightley's respect) as Miss Bates is hurt by Emma's cruel comment.

Card Interpretation

Mental cruelty can occur even in settings as beautiful and innocuous as the English countryside. The reason for this cruelty can be impulsiveness, an inner belief in one's personal superiority, a desire to "show off," or even a sense of inferiority masquerading as confidence – there are many internecine wounds that can lead to cutting comments.

Emma's witticism is lethal precisely because of its accuracy. Truth is always the most damaging and powerful sword. When this card appears in a reading, it is time to question mental cruelty in your own life – and where you stand within its circle. Have you been humiliated by someone's verbal assault? If so, it might be useful to determine the roots of that malice, but ultimately, there's never a good reason for verbal malevolence. A straightforward oral rejection of such attacks is the most appropriate response (as opposed to Miss Bates' trajectory into self-blame). You also might want to contemplate if the comment was particularly injurious because it was so unexpected. It could be time to re-evaluate your relationship with the person who wounded you. At the same time, if the words contain truths that cut to the bone, you might wish to evaluate your flaws accordingly.

If, however, it is you who have been guilty of mental cruelty to another, it is time for you to examine your own motivations. Are you merely honoring wit over kindness, or is there something deeper percolating in your subconscious? Knowing what is at the core of errant words can assist you in not repeating behavioral improprieties. Emma ultimately makes reparations to Miss Bates with both tangible charitable offerings and socially gracious gestures. She is rewarded for her acts of atonement by Mr. Knightley. If you come to determine that recompense is called for, also determine the appropriate method in providing it.

Crowley calls this card the Lord of Defeat, and suggests that the intellect has been enfeebled by sentiment. While that sounds like a description of the unfortunate Miss Bates, it could also apply to Emma, whose interest in Frank Churchill's approbation influences her to say something she later regrets. Is your intellect becoming enfeebled by sentiment?

On a less negative note, you could find yourself with a newfound awareness of personal dynamics, coupled with an unwillingness to repeat old verbal patterns, either of abuse or self-abnegation.

If this is a card that evokes family dynamics for you, there could be a toxicity not seen in the squabbling of the Five of Candlesticks. You may benefit from finding refuge with a healthier family of choice rather than remain enmeshed in the mental cruelty of your family of origin.

What Would Jane Do?

"She had often been remiss, her conscience told her so; remiss, perhaps, more in thought than fact; scornful, ungracious. But it should be so no more."

Jane Austen, *Emma*

Jane's advice: A position of power is a position pregnant with responsibilities. *Noblesse oblige* may be considered a form of arrogance today, but the term is quite literal. True nobility is found in service. If you have been the victim of a verbal barrage, considering the source should provide all necessary solace – unless there is an element of truth contained in said barrage; in which case, any personal improvement you make is a reflection of your worth, and a scourge to the source of reproof. Conversely, gloating is not merely unattractive, but begs inevitable retribution. While the likelihood of consistent success is severely curtailed by both petty and salient annoyances, grace and respect for others in thought and action are always worthwhile ideals for which to strive.

Six of Quills
Persuasion

Card Description

Handsome and dashing Frederick Wentworth wears the uniform of a new naval ensign as he steps on to his first ship, "The Asp". The ship looks rather old and decrepit, especially in comparison to the more up-to-date and seaworthy vessels in the harbor. Wentworth looks behind him to the town beyond the harbor. The weather is rather grey and misty, as if it has recently rained. The waters are choppy, but in the distance, they seem to smooth, becalmed.

Storyline

When Anne Elliot breaks her engagement to Frederick Wentworth, he is determined to make his fortune in the British Navy. He is filled with anger and resentment at what he perceives to be Anne's lack of faith in him and his ambition.

Despite privations and challenging odds, Captain Wentworth succeeds brilliantly and returns to Anne's social sphere. Now he is the sought-after bachelor and she the pitiable spinster – or so it seems. He has arrived at last.

Yet though he thinks he no longer loves Anne, he realizes he does – but only after he feels he has given another young woman, Louisa Musgrove, good reason to think his heart belongs to her. More complications develop, but when the book ends, Anne Elliot and Captain Wentworth are reunited.

Card Interpretation

The Six of Quills is a card of transition. Change is necessary in order to succeed, in whatever terms that matter to you. Like Frederick Wentworth, you might need to travel to realize your potential, but since this is a card of the intellect, it may be that you simply need to broaden your intellectual horizon. Astrologically speaking, this card corresponds to Mercury in Aquarius, which speaks of sudden, occasionally abrupt, change.

When Anne Elliot breaks her engagement to Frederick Wentworth, his response is rational, despite his heartbreak. He knows it is time for him to "move on", despite the fact that it is painful and difficult. It may be that your current situation is difficult, but you are fearful of the uncertainty of leaving the known. You may need to make some painful changes, secure only in the fact that, while your voyage may be choppy, you are going to a better place. Having said that, be aware that you may, like Captain Wentworth, meet a few obstacles before achieving your ultimate destination. You could get sidetracked, as he does with Louisa Musgrove. Your rational intellect should be your compass. When there is a crisis, Captain Wentworth realizes with certainty that Anne Elliot's smart and capable nature is the one that he truly loves and respects.

This card can also presage a literal voyage or journey of some kind. While you may look upon it as simply a vacation, the Six of Quills suggests that it may give you a new mental perspective as a bonus. When you receive the Six of Quills in a reading, depending on its position in the spread, movement is accentuated, both literally and intellectually. The good news is that it indicates that this movement will lead you to improved circumstances.

What Would Jane Do?

"But he was confident that he should soon be rich: full of life and ardour, he knew that he should soon have a ship, and soon be on a station that would lead to everything he wanted. He had always been lucky; he knew he knew he should be so still."

Jane Austen, *Persuasion*

Jane's Advice: If your current conditions are unpleasant, know that you have the intelligence and skills to improve your lot in life. Courage and wit will take you far, and it is a fact that fortune favors the brave. Remaining in a situation that brings you little pleasure is self-defeating and disrespectful of your abilities.

Have confidence in yourself and go forth into your future.

Seven of Quills
Mansfield Park

Card Description

Mrs. Norris, an elderly woman with a pretty, but mean, lined face, puts some fruits into her apron, as if to steal them. Her face is averted, as if she is looking behind her to insure that no one is seeing her petty larceny.

Storyline

Mrs. Norris is one of the most malignant characters in the Jane Austen canon. We learn most about Mrs. Norris through her words, though her actions are also questionable, though covert. She will express charitable thoughts, but her behavior shows that her first priority is getting her own needs and desires met.

When Sir Thomas Bertram leaves her in charge of the young people's welfare at Mansfield Park, her skewed values, which are rooted in prestige and money, cause her to make many poor decisions. She indulges the already-spoiled Bertram sisters, Maria and Julia, but offers gentle Fanny only contempt and frequent demands. She welcomes the Crawfords into the family circle, and ignores how Henry Crawford emotionally manipulates Maria and Julia. Mrs. Norris encourages Mr. Rushworth's suit towards Maria, seeing only his wealth and not that he is a buffoon and Maria does not love him. In fact, Mrs. Norris plans a family trip to his home, Sotherton, where she makes off with donated goodies from their larder.

When the family decides to put on a risqué play, Mrs. Norris sees nothing wrong with it, and even allows them to alter Sir Thomas's rooms to build a theatre. She unsuccessfully pressures Fanny to participate in the play, reminding her, as always, of how much she owes the Bertrams.

Mrs. Norris is very active and wishes to be perceived as the initiator, the spark that makes everything run. When Sir Thomas comes home, he puts a stop to the playacting, and her main disappointment is that she has not been the one to announce his arrival (even though she anticipates his displeasure in the dramatic goings-ons and tries to hide her part in them). When Sir Thomas says something to her about it, Mrs. Norris "was ashamed to confess having never seen any of the impropriety which was so glaring to Sir Thomas, and would not have admitted that her influence was insufficient". Yet she isn't so ashamed that she doesn't pilfer some of the green baize that had been used for the stage curtain for her own abode.

Mrs. Norris hopes she makes amends for her error in judgment about the play when Maria marries Mr. Rushworth, since she has been the one to promote the match. However, when Maria runs away with Henry Crawford, her judgment comes into question yet again. When Henry deserts Maria, Mrs. Norris, who has always made a pet of her, tries to get the family to receive her. This final want of propriety ends with Mrs. Norris's leaving the area to "devote herself to her unfortunate Maria, and in an establishment being formed for them in another country, remote and private, where, shut up together with little society, on one side no affection, on the other no judgment, it may be reasonably supposed that their tempers became their mutual punishment".

Card Interpretation

The Seven of Quills has a rather malign reputation. The Rider-Waite-Smith version of the card shows a man making off with some swords, looking like he's definitely getting away with something, probably robbery. The keyword for this card in the Thoth deck is "futility". Yet Waite calls this "a good card" and even writes of it, "a country life after a competence has been secured", which fits Mrs. Norris' situation if you replace competence with incompetence. Quills are associated with the element of air, which rules thoughts and communication. Sometimes this card, like Mrs. Norris, represents someone whose mode of communication is devious, or at least, not completely straightforward. When this card appears in a reading, you may not be telling – or hearing – the whole truth of a situation. Many of Mrs. Norris' difficulties occur because of her prejudices and partialities. The Seven of Quills indicates that it may be time to examine motivations – your own and/or someone else's.

Astrologically, this card is connected to the Moon in Aquarius. The watery, emotional Moon is not comfortable in the more detached, airy realm of Aquarius. The Moon reflects our basic needs and desires and, in Aquarius, attempts to rationalize or intellectualize them. But needs and desires are often decidedly non-rational, and the attempt to determine their rightness on a logical level forces the individual to resort to intellectual chicanery and pettifoggery. When this card comes up in a reading, you may want to see if you are trying to stretch logic to support an emotional inclination.

Mrs. Norris is always trying to prove how important and helpful she is to Sir Thomas. She goes out of her way to be frugal on even the smallest items and offers these savings to prove her worth. While this is quite annoying, it speaks to her own sense of emptiness and loss – her husband has left her relatively impecunious and, since she worships money, this lack demeans her in her eyes. Is discontent causing you to feel envious or hyper-critical of others? In what areas are you feeling empty or lacking, and what mental tricks do you employ to comfort yourself? If they aren't successful, perhaps you need to re-examine your value system.

This card can also speak to evasions, successful or bootless. If you feel as though you are hiding something, as Mrs. Norris does with a costume in *Mansfield Park*, how is this concealment harming you? Perhaps bringing things into the open will improve your situation.

Sometimes expressions of flattery or other pleasantries cause you to make poor choices in your friends or acquaintances. We can see this in Mrs. Norris' choice of the willful, ego-centric Maria Bertram over the gentle and principled Fanny Price. Select your intimates with discernment.

Lastly, this card can reflect intellectual theft, as when Mrs. Norris claims to come up with a good date for a dance, although it had been decided beforehand. Someone may be pumping you for ideas and then claiming them as his or her own – or conversely, you might be misappropriating others' innovations.

What Would Jane Do?

"Mrs. Norris, having fidgeted about, and obtained a few pheasants' eggs and a cream cheese from the housekeeper, and made abundance of civil speeches to Mrs. Rushworth, was ready to lead the way... "What else have you been spunging?" said Maria..."

Jane Austen, *Mansfield Park*

Jane's Advice: When the henhouse is robbed, the loss is easy to distinguish. The lack of eggs in the larder makes the theft very obvious. But there are more subtle machinations that are harder to discern, yet condition just as much distress. Someone who copies your mannerisms and serves them up as her own has stolen every bit as much from you as someone who takes your purse. Listen carefully to what others say and observe even more carefully what they do before you trust them with the secrets of your heart – or your pet ideas.

Eight of Quills
Mansfield Park

Card Description

Edmund Bertram stands with his eyes closed, but faced towards the beautiful Mary Crawford, who plays a harp "as elegant as herself". Both are seated in a living room, "placed near a window, cut down to the ground, and opening on a little lawn, surrounded by shrubs in the rich foliage of summer". Bertram's hands are behind his back. An unlit candle sits on a table next to him.

Storyline

Gentle and sensitive Edmund Bertram is very attracted to newcomer Mary Crawford. Her sophistication concerns him, but her looks, wit, and harp playing attract him as compellingly as ever the Sirens lured their prey. He convinces himself that though she has been misguided by living a cosmopolitan lifestyle, her good heart and inner wisdom have saved her from corruption.

Mary is attracted to him, too – but she has no interest in being a clergyman's wife. She uses her wiles to first convince him to act in a play he disapproves of and then she tries to dissuade him from his chosen career path. He submits to her on the first matter, but he is firm about taking his ordination.

During this odd courtship, Edmund uses his cousin Fanny as his confidante. While Fanny conceals her romantic feelings for her cousin, she tries to support him in his choice. However, her vision of Mary is not blinded by infatuation and clearly sees Mary's flaws and unsuitability. Though Fanny gently tries to draw his attention to evidence of Mary's moral gaffes, Edmund refuses to see them.

However, when Mary's brother Henry runs off with Maria Rushworth, Edmund's married sister, he is appalled. When Mary treats their elopement as a minor social inconvenience, he is repulsed. And when she suggests that the death of his brother Tom would be a blessing for Edmund, as it would make him the sole heir to Mansfield Park, it is the death knell for any future they might have together. Edmund can no longer blind himself to Mary's true nature.

He breaks things off with her, finally and completely. After a time, he comes to love Fanny romantically as well as platonically, recognizing her as his ideal mate.

Card Interpretation

When the Eight of Quills appears in a reading, you may, like Edmund, be momentarily blinded by love or some other delusionary influence. The expression "Denial is not just a river in Egypt" could be this card's slogan. The Nile, incidentally, is a large body of water, and water is the element that symbolizes love and feelings, feelings that can overrun and drown the intellectual perspicacity of even a thoughtful person like Edmund.

The astrological association for this card is Jupiter in Gemini. Jupiter embodies the property of expansion and Gemini is the highly active intellect. Thoughts can amplify at an alarming rate – like weeds blooming until they overtake flowers. First, you observe to yourself, "This person is nice". Once you are romantically attached, you begin to believe your beloved is at the level of an Albert Schweitzer or Mother Teresa. The result of this teeming mental energy becomes obvious to any outsider: perspective can be lacking when this card appears in a reading.

Crowley calls this card the Lord of Interference and this mental dissension can cause personal and professional chaos in your life, as Edmund's passion for Mary convinces him to act in a play that is at odds with his moral convictions and spurs him to reconsider his chosen vocation.

While you may be filled with conviction, your thoughts are unclear at this time and your rational self is muddled. You may be acting based on incomplete or inaccurate information. Ironically, the facts may be right in front of you, but you are selecting only the data that you wish to receive. You may be ignoring clear evidence that disproves your hypotheses, as Edmund does with Mary. At one point, she states, "Selfishness must always be forgiven", and though her tone is merry, her actions are, indeed, selfish. Yet Edmund continues to see her as selfless.

You may even be casting a blind eye on your own code of ethics, as Edmund does when he obtains a horse for Fanny for the purpose of exercise, but then allows Mary to use it to Fanny's detriment. Mary's superior gifts as a horsewoman make him forget that the purpose of the horse was to improve Fanny's health, not serve as a romantic offering.

This card can signify that you feel or think that you are compelled to do things that you don't wish to do. Edmund extends a break from Mansfield Park to avoid Miss Crawford and her many charms, but as soon as he sees her again, he falls back into infatuation. It is only too easy to fall back into old patterns of denial.

Alternately, this card suggests that you may have been blind and fettered by wrongful thought, but light has just begun to dawn. You are beginning to see that you are not as ensnared as you initially thought. The good news that accompanies this card is that self-imposed blindness, while a handicap, can be cured. You need only take off your blindfold.

What Would Jane Do?

"He is blinded, and nothing will open his eyes; nothing can, after having had truths before him so long in vain."

Jane Austen, *Mansfield Park*

Jane's Advice: While love induces an enviable state of bliss, it is also akin to a form of madness. Rationality and discernment go out the window at the appearance of "fine eyes" or a fine figure. Love may be the nectar of the gods, but when humans imbibe of the divine drink, they often do not have the head to handle it. Be sure you sober up before making any lifelong commitments – they are often decided upon in haste and repented at leisure.

Nine of Quills
Northanger Abbey

Card Description

Catherine Morland lies upright in bed. Her room is simply decorated and there's a large, unopened hamper at the foot of the bed that clearly has a lock. There is also a small desk with a pen holder that contains nine pens. A candle burns by Catherine's bed, casting undecipherable shadows about the room.

Storyline

Catherine Morland could not be more thrilled to be invited to the home of her friend, Eleanor, by her father, General Tilney. Not only does the man she worships, Henry Tilney, live there part of the time, their abode is an abbey. As a fan of gothic novels, Catherine can't imagine anything more romantic. The potential for secret passageways and nooks filled with mystery abounds. On the ride to Northanger Abbey, Henry regales her with the exciting and dramatic possibilities that await her, and asks, facetiously:

"And are you prepared to encounter all the horrors that a building such as 'what one reads about' may produce? – Have you a stout heart? – Nerves fit for sliding panels and tapestry?".

Catherine asserts that she will not be afraid, yet when she spies an "immense heavy chest" in her room, she explores its contents with a rapid heartbeat and trembling hands... only to discover that it holds... a white cotton bedspread.

But this mundane discovery does not calm her imagination that evening. As Henry presaged in his mesmerizing talk on the ride to the abbey, it's a dark and stormy night and she discovers an ebony cabinet she hadn't noticed in the daylight. With increasing terror, she searches it, finally uncovering a sheaf of papers. Unfortunately, in her excitement, Catherine extinguishes her candle and is alone in the dark, having no knowledge of the contents of the mysterious manuscript. She creeps into bed, tossing and turning with fear and curiosity, and that is the image that we see on the Nine of Quills card.

In the morning light, she discovers the mystifying nature of her discovery is but an inventory of linens.

These occurrences do not cure Catherine of her flights of over-imagination. Soon thereafter, she begins to – wrongly – suspect the General of having killed his wife.

Card Interpretation

Anxiety is an emotion with which we are all familiar, and if we are creative individuals with active imaginations, our anxiety is all the more powerful and intricate. Catherine's love of gothic novels has made her overly sensitive to the potential for horror in everyday objects, and Jane Austen has a bit of fun at her heroine's expense in narrating these embarrassing incidents. Before we laugh too loudly at Catherine's silly behavior, it may behoove us to remember our own sleepless nights when we've contemplated potential disasters that never actually took place or tossed and turned over personal embarrassments that we now see as inconsequential in the grand scheme of things, if we remember them at all.

Mars, the red planet of action, in Gemini, the mercurial sign of the intellect, is the astrological attribution for the Nine of Quills, and we can see Catherine's mind working overtime to

her own detriment – as it often does with our own feverish thoughts. In *Northanger Abbey*, Catherine has nothing to fear from the furniture, but she is correct to instinctively mistrust General Tilney. While she incorrectly imagines he has killed his wife, she is right to intuitively fear the General, though not for any supernatural reasons. When he discovers that she isn't an heiress as he had wrongly believed, the General rudely banishes Catherine from Northanger Abbey with the intent of obliterating her from his family circle.

If you are intuiting that someone is not to be trusted, don't dismiss your suspicions because you have no concrete evidence. You don't have to remove yourself from this person's sphere or make groundless accusations – in fact, that is not advised – but don't place yourself in a position of vulnerability with this person either.

My grandfather used to say that 99 percent of the things we worry about never come true. If that's the case, the wisest use of our mental energies is to focus on innovative ways to handle the one percent of the challenges that do occur in the real world, instead of allowing our imaginations to run wild and engage us too deeply in the spectral domain.

What Would Jane Do?

"She shuddered, tossed about in her bed, and envied every quiet sleeper. The storm still raged, and various were the noises, more terrific even than the wind, which struck at intervals on her startled ear... Hollow murmurs seemed to creep along the gallery..."
Jane Austen, *Northanger Abbey*

Jane's Advice: There is more to fear in the trials and tribulations of society than in the goriest gothic novel. Being judged on social standing and properties, rather than one's innate gifts and abilities, is more likely to result in physical, mental, and emotional suffering than any visit to a threatening precipice, or anything hidden in a cave or closet. The things we most fear often never come to pass, yet our instinctive repulsions need to be honored, for what our soul shrinks at in novels may take more pernicious – and mundane – form in real life. An active and experienced mind will ultimately be able to discriminate between real and imaginary foes.

Ten of Quills
Pride and Prejudice

Card Description
Elizabeth Bennett sits at a desk, holding a letter with taut hands. We see the words "Lydia..." "elopement..." "Wickham..." and "ruined..." Elizabeth's face is pinched and she is holding back tears. Darcy is walking out the door, followed by Elizabeth's glance.

Storyline
When Fitzwilliam Darcy dismisses Elizabeth Bennett as not being pretty enough to dance with, she is affronted and amused. As their acquaintanceship deepens, he falls under her spell, but she doesn't notice his attraction to her, in part because she has no interest in him. She is therefore surprised when he proposes. She turns him down for a number of reasons, and expects never to see him again. However, when she is assured he is not going to be at his home, Pemberley, a national showplace, she agrees to visit. However, Darcy has unexpectedly returned to Pemberley and she encounters him.

Lizzy is impressed not only with the beauty and grace of his home, but Darcy's engaging and affable manner. He treats both her and her family with great respect, and even his servants speak well of him. Suddenly, she begins to see Darcy in a new, more positive light, and begins to value his earlier proposal, even though her rejection left no room for a reprise of those sentiments.

When Darcy calls on her, Lizzy has just received a letter that informs her that Wickham, a man she once fancied but whom

Darcy reviles, has eloped with Lydia, her youngest sister. This means societal ruin not only for Lydia, but her sisters' reputations as well. Lizzy informs Darcy of the news, and realizes that any potential relationship she might enjoy with him, a man she is beginning to admire, will never come to fruition.

Card Interpretation

When this card appears in a reading, you may feel, like Elizabeth, that you have reached a point of no return. Circumstances may seem hopeless, or you might feel overpowered and defeated. Often this card is seen as a message that a situation or relationship has come to an end, a complete standstill, no matter how much you might want to revive it or pretend it's not defunct.

On the other hand, this card heralds that the accompanying problems and stresses of trying to fan the flames of a dead fire have come to an end. And every ending is a beginning unto itself. This card's astrological attribution is Sun in Gemini, and the sun comes up every day. Gemini is the sign of the twins; when one is in its fall, the other is at its rise. No sooner does one dream die than another takes its place.

When Jane and Bingley become engaged, the Bennett family is "pronounced to be the luckiest family in the world, though only a few weeks before, when Lydia had first run away, they had been generally proved to be marked out for misfortune". Had Lydia not run off with Wickham, Darcy could not have intervened, saved the day, and won Lizzy's heart completely.

To use a garden analogy, this card indicates that the plant has withered on the vine. It either makes way for new and better flowers to bloom or, if it's a perennial, revives the next year. But for the present, you can neither see it nor smell it, so it's as good as dead to you. Lizzy's amorphous hopes for a possible union with Darcy are realized, but only after some emotional uncertainty on her part. In fact, her relationship with Darcy flowers beyond her wildest imaginings, but that doesn't alter the fact that Lydia's virtue can never be retrieved.

When this card appears in a reading, the time has come to accept and mourn a loss or an ending. It may well be that the loss eventually makes for greater gain, but that does not provide much comfort in the immediate future. Occasionally this card appears when the ending has already come and been accepted, and indicates that the new day beckoning in the distance is close at hand.

What Would Jane Do?

"Every thing must sink under such a proof of family weakness, such an assurance of the deepest disgrace ...never had she so honestly felt that she could have loved him, as now, when all love must be vain."

Jane Austen, *Pride and Prejudice*

Jane's Advice: The price of reckless abandon, especially for a woman who is not from a wealthy family, can be steep. Yet even more dangerous is the belief that a serious setback, no matter how precipitous or wounding, forces us to despair indefinitely. It is impossible to ignore pressing pain, but accepting what is (or what will never be) is essential to one's serenity and peace of mind, as well as one's future happiness. Weep and languish if you must, but not indefinitely, else you remain in a rôle that no longer suits you and repels those around you.

Maiden of Quills
Emma Woodhouse (Emma)

Card Description

Emma Woodhouse, a graceful young woman is drawing a likeness of her friend, Harriet, who is a less attractive, less wealthy, less elegant and younger woman. The art is polished but shows a far prettier, idealized model.

Storyline

Emma Woodhouse is described by Jane Austen as:

"handsome, clever, and rich, with a comfortable home and happy disposition, seemed to unite some of the best blessings of existence;

and had lived nearly twenty-one years in the world with very little to distress or vex her."

In fact, the novel begins with a self-congratulatory Emma gloating about her success at matchmaking. She is convinced that had she not formed the brilliant idea of placing her former governess and an elderly single man, Mr. Weston, in close proximity, the match would not have been made. While Emma asserts that she plans to remain single for the rest of her life, she wants to unite others in matrimonial bliss.

When she meets Harriet Smith, she also welcomes the role of being an advisor to the younger woman. When Harriet confides that she has an admirer, Robert Martin, Emma assures her that she can and should do better. Emma then "matches" her new friend with the local clergyman, Mr. Elton, and encourages Harriet to fall in love with him. Unfortunately, Emma mistakes Mr. Elton's attentions as being intended for Harriet, when he, in fact, is interested in Emma. She both offended and humiliated by his eventual proposal.

Though it seems she has learned her lesson, Emma next considers Frank Churchill as a potential mate for her friend. However, the confidence Emma has instilled in Harriet backfires when Harriet chooses the finest man in the neighborhood, Mr. Knightley, a man Emma belatedly realizes she wants for herself. Despite Emma's superior understanding of others' and their motivations, she makes a lot of mistakes in her assessments. Frank Churchill is secretly engaged to Jane Fairfax, yet Emma indiscreetly encourages Frank to gossip about and speak badly of her. Emma is afraid to allow Mr. Knightley to speak to her about something serious because she fears it will be an avowal of his love for Harriet, when, in fact, Emma herself is the woman he loves. Her numerous analytical mistakes allow her to realize she has much to learn about human nature, and, by the end of the book, she is less arrogant about her superior abilities at manipulating other people's lives.

Card Interpretation

Intelligence without experience can lead to prideful mistakes. The Maiden of Quills in a reading represents someone who is very bright and quick, but not necessarily wise. In other words, her deductions can be accurate to the extent that she has complete information – but unfortunately, she isn't always able to obtain all the facts. Like Emma, this card suggests someone who thinks she knows what's best for others, but doesn't even know what is best for herself. When this card appears in the reading, you might want to make sure you know all the facts before taking action.

Sometimes this card suggests someone who uses her intelligence in order to manipulate events; Emma knows exactly how to draw Harriet's attention away from Robert Martin and on to Mr. Elton. Sometimes, it's simply someone who loves to argue and debate, as reflected by Emma's badinage with Mr. Knightley.

The Maiden of Quills is a clever debater and loves to win her point, yet she sometimes gets hoisted on her own petard, as Emma repeatedly does in the novel.

One must remember that the Maiden makes youthful mistakes. This doesn't mean that this card only applies to young people, but, in a reading, can suggest that you need maturation on a particular issue or approach, even if you are a senior citizen. Experience is a great teacher, but sometimes specific experience must be acquired when dealing with an isolated situation.

When the qualities of air are prominent, there can be a lack of true empathy. Note how disbelieving Emma is when Knightley must assure her repeatedly that Harriet Smith has chosen to marry Robert Martin. Despite Harriet's repeated displays of amorous interest in any man who shows her attention, Emma can not understand such emotional flexibility, because she lacks that trait.

Both the Maiden and Knight of Quills are mentally quick – at least as quick as their Lady and Lord counterparts. The difference is that their cleverness is often diffuse or excessive. Emma notes to Frank Churchill (the Knight of Quills) there is "a likeness in our character" and it is true. In fact, in tandem their wit flows long and occasionally with a tad too much venom. When Frank hides his engagement to Jane with snide comments about her to Emma, she is too much of a lady to match his level, but she participates in equal part on speculations as to Jane's influence over a married man. Combined, these two have a preponderance of "air". Astrologically, the Maiden of Quills is Earth of Air, whereas the Knight of Quill is Air of Air. Frank Churchill's excessive air makes him far more of a manipulator than Emma, who is honest at the core. However, when she and Frank get together, their focus on cleverness to the exclusion of compassion sometimes leads to toxic results, as shown in the Five of Quills.

What Would Jane Do?

"Emma is spoiled by being the cleverest of her family."

Jane Austen, *Emma*

Jane's Advice: A bright young lady with the benefits of wealth and education needs the edifying hand of discipline in order to acquire wisdom. Without restraint, intelligence has no check, but veers into the nooks and crannies of the labyrinth of life. Only equally intelligent and firm guidance can protect that quicksilver from diffusing or exploding.

Knight of Quills
Frank Churchill (Emma)

Card Description

This rider, Frank Churchill, is dashing indeed. He is elegantly coiffed and his attire is perfect, even a bit affected. He is riding on a river road with his eyes straight ahead.

Storyline

Frank Churchill is quite the eligible man of mystery when he enters Highbury society. The son of the genial Mr. Weston, he has been adopted by his wealthy but difficult aunt and uncle, and is the beneficiary of their largesse, as well as servant to their whims.

When Mr. Weston weds Emma Woodhouse's governess, the dearest wish of both their hearts is that Frank and Emma fall in love, and they hope that when Frank visits them at Highbury, that will transpire. What they don't know is that Frank is already secretly engaged to Jane Fairfax; through much of the novel this information is concealed.

Despite his engagement, Frank is very convivial and charming to Emma. He appeals to Emma with his wit, and also his clever gossip and innuendoes about Jane Fairfax, a woman Emma grudgingly acknowledges as her superior in accomplishment and grace.

Frank's intelligence and dash is in great evidence when he comes across some gypsies harassing Emma's friend Harriet, and comes to her rescue, as pictured in the card. This event convinces Emma that Harriet and Frank are meant for one another, and Emma decides that her own feelings for Frank, though warm, are decidedly platonic. When they attend a picnic, they egg one another on in witty exchanges until Emma says something quite cutting to an old family friend, which she later regrets. When Harriet confides that her love interest is not Frank Churchill, Emma is surprised. She receives a further blow to her intellectual pride when she learns of Frank's secret engagement, and is grateful that her heart was not affected. She does resent his callous lack of concern for her feelings – he has no way of knowing that his allurements didn't make her fall in love with him, after all.

However, Frank's way of expressing his love for Jane and his reasons for his concealment are so clever and engaging that even the upright and moral Mr. Knightley can't hold a grudge against him, once he realizes that Emma doesn't love Frank, but himself.

Card Interpretation

The Knight of Quills astrological attribution is Air of Air. This elemental confluence bestows speed, wit, intelligence, and a decided self-interest unleavened by emotional vulnerability. This doesn't mean that the card is an indicator that the person in question can not or does not love, simply that he is deliberate and calculating, even when he's in love. Frank Churchill loves Jane Fairfax and doesn't care that she's penniless, but he enjoys flirting with Emma to make Jane jealous. While Jane is uncomfortable with hiding the truth of their relationship, he takes a wicked pleasure in it. When the Knight of Quills insists on his own wretchedness at being so deceitful, his sister in air, Emma Woodhouse, remarks:

"Not quite so miserable as to be insensible to mirth. I am sure it was a source of high entertainment to you, to feel that you were taking us all in. – Perhaps I am the readier to suspect, because, to tell you the truth, I think it might have been some amusement to myself in the same situation. I think there is a little likeness between us."

Yet Emma is far more sincere than Frank Churchill, despite their kindred spirits.

This card in a reading indicates quickness, both of movement and intellect. Because of the native intelligence of the individual, the

Knight of Quills rarely puts a wrong foot out, but when he does, he risks losing everything, as Frank does when he torments Jane Fairfax into considering a governess position. Yet the Knight of Quills is a master with words, and can generally seduce anyone into doing his bidding.

You don't want to get into a debate with the Knight of Quills. He not only has incredible intellectual firepower, he has no scruples about using it, and will not hesitate to use cutting, cruel words. In argument, the air quality of detachment can turn into cold, reserved viciousness or callous imprudence. If you are the Knight of Quills, remember that words can never really be taken back and the wounds inflicted by piercing remarks never completely heal.

This card's answer to any question is, "Take action!". Move quickly and surely, with all your wits about you. The Knight of Quills occasionally loses a battle, but is almost always ultimately successful in the long-term, unless he outsmarts himself. His sure-footedness ensures survival.

What Would Jane Do?
"The young man's spirits now rose to a pitch almost unpleasant."
   Jane Austen, *Emma*

Jane's Advice: High spirits and youth are as natural a match as romance and ladies of a certain age. Yet heedless, undirected spirits can precipitate heartache as much as overly romantic recklessness can ruin an entire family. Cleverness untempered with kindness is memorable only for the pain it causes in others. When intelligence is subservient to compassion and wisdom, the journey may be less diverting, but it will also prove to be more harmonious.

Lady of Quills
Anne Elliot (Persuasion)

Card Description
The oldest of the Queens/Ladies, Anne Elliot is a dark and attractive woman in her late twenties. She sits in a chair avidly reading Adam Smith's *Theory of Moral Sentiments*, but despite her avidity, her posture is perfectly straight. She is in an elegant room that has seen better days.

Storyline
Anne Elliot is a loving woman of strong values. Despite her family's worship of appearances over values, Anne ensures that the household runs smoothly while her older sister treats her unkindly and assumes the airs of the lady of the house. In her youth, Anne was convinced to break her engagement with the man she loved, Frederick Wentworth. When he enters the Navy, her romantic opportunities wither after she turns down a marriage proposal from a wealthy man she does not love.

Seven years pass. Anne remains in love with Frederick, who has returned from a successful stint in the Navy and is now considered an eligible bachelor whom even her sister contemplates as a possible suitor. However, Frederick's focus seems to be on other, younger women in their social circle, and Anne must watch their flirtations, feeling old and on-the-shelf. At one point, she plays piano for the others to dance, as if she were no longer of an age to engage in such merriment. When one of the young women, Louisa, impulsively tries to leap into Wentworth's arms from a stone wall, she falls and loses consciousness. While everyone else is immobilized with fear, Anne capably mobilizes help for the young woman, reminding Captain Wentworth of her many good qualities and that he is, in fact, in love with her. However, he believes she is to marry her cousin, William Elliot. Anne does not want to marry him, but when she discovers that he is disingenuous and grasping, her determination is renewed. When Frederick overhears Anne saying that she believes women remain more loyal in love than men do, he writes her a note renewing his request for the honor of her hand in marriage. Anne is only too delighted to accept.

Card Interpretation
The Lady of Quills combines a perfect balance of mind and heart, which is echoed through the elemental assignment of water of air. Intelligent and rational, she is also a woman of feeling and sensitivity, but she never allows her emotions to drown her discernment. We see this combination in Anne Elliot again and again. She sees her family for what they are, yet cares about them despite their vagaries. While everyone else is quick to welcome William Elliot back into the bosom of their family, she wonders how a man who had been so dissolute has become such an exemplar of appropriate and gentle behavior, even as she refuses to judge him unfairly. And her love for Captain Wentworth, begun in the bloom of youth, lasts forever and for good reason, showing what a wise judge Anne truly is.

When you receive this card in a reading, you, too, may be a wise judge, rational and logical, yet you're still a feeling, loving person. Like

Anne, you may allow people to take advantage of your kindness, yet you are always aware of their egocentricities and petty subterfuges.

You may also be called upon, like Anne, to make hard decisions, ones based on your intellect even when your heart decries the choice. Even though Anne wishes she had married Frederick Wentworth when he asked, she honored the counsel of the woman who had served as her mother and closest advisor. Even though her advice was incorrect, Anne believes she was right to listen to her – even after she agrees to marry Captain Wentworth a second time and has suffered for many years because she did listen to her friend. Doing the right thing is sometimes more important than initial pleasure or satisfaction.

In the past, this card has had the reputation of signifying a bitter, spiteful woman, because what is perceived as strength and toughness in men is often seen as stridency. Some think women should act with gentleness even in a crisis. Also known as the widow card, this Lady of Quills is often a woman who has suffered, like Anne Elliot has suffered over her lost love, Frederick Wentworth. Suffering rarely ennobles anyone, but it does, of necessity, teach one how to survive in this challenging world.

When this card comes up in a reading, you might indeed be the sadder-but-wiser woman who has learned to say the word, "No", as Anne does to her cousin's proposal. Don't allow anyone to pressure you into doing something against your own self-interest.

Some might consider the individual represented by the Lady of Quills cold or calculating. She is neither: Anne, for all her virtue and morality, is as open to love as any Maiden of Teacups. When she begins to think that Frederick may still have some feelings for her, Austen writes of Anne, "She hoped to be wise and reasonable in time; but alas! Alas! She must confess to herself that she was not wise yet". However, a Lady of Quills can retain her sense of logic in almost any situation; when she is reading an old letter of her cousin's that shows him to be callous and disingenuous,

she reminds herself that "seeing the letter was a violation of the laws of honour, that no one ought to be judged or to be known by such testimonies, that no private correspondence could bear the eye of others". Few Maidens of Teacups (or most anyone, for that matter) would inject such fairness or rationality at such an emotionally tempestuous time.

But that is one of the great strengths of the Lady of Quills. Just as Anne is cool-headed during Louisa's accident, she can be sensible when others lose their heads. Those of us with less clarity find it comforting to project coldness on others rather than own our muddled emotionalism.

Because she is so rational, the Queen of Swords doesn't always trust the truth of her heart. Lady Russell is able to convince Anne to break her engagement to Captain Wentworth, despite her faith in the rightness of their love – and his ability to eventually make his way in the world and provide for her. She is right on both counts, but she and Captain Wentworth suffer for many years and almost don't reunite because she doesn't have enough confidence in her emotional accuracy. If you know something in your heart, stop trying to attack that wisdom with logic and rationalizations. The heart possesses its own understanding and it can't be quantified with facts.

Other positive qualities of the Lady of Quills are ones that Anne Elliot possesses: competency and capability, intelligence, incisive readership and scholarship, and a general air of quiet accomplishment. While others are self-congratulatory or self-promotional about their gifts, the Lady of Quills tends to be modest about them, even self-critical about her few mistakes. Even when she recognizes her own gifts, she does so, as she does her suffering, in silence. As always, balance is the key – even a thoughtful Lady of Quills should indulge in some baths of self-love and nurturance once in a while.

What Would Jane Do?

"Every emendation of Anne's had been on the side of honesty against importance. She wanted more vigorous measures, a more complete reformation, a quicker release from debt, a much higher tone of indifference for everything but justice and equity."

Jane Austen, *Persuasion*

Jane's Advice: Discernment without emotion is unbearable; pictures of perfection make me sick and wicked. Yet emotion that receives no check is a river in which one drowns – and, alas! not quietly and in a dignified manner. This is a time to look rationally, even harshly, at the particulars of a situation. There is no cruelty in this. In order to love wisely, one must actually be wise.

Lord of Quills
Fitzwilliam Darcy (Pride and Prejudice)

Card Description

Fitzwilliam Darcy, a tall, dark, handsome, and perfectly attired gentleman is seated at an ele-gant desk, writing a letter with an old-fashioned pen. It is clear he has already written quite a bit of the letter, and is posed with the pen in a thoughtful position, clearly thinking about what he's going to write next and how he's going to phrase it. The room around him is a library filled with books and paintings of various ancestors who look much like him.

Storyline

Our first glimpse of Fitzwilliam Darcy is that of a haughty gentleman who should be taken down a peg. Unlike his affable friend, Charles Bingley (Lord of Teacups), who finds great pleasure at a country dance, Darcy has only contempt for all he surveys. He sees Elizabeth Bennett (Lady of Candlesticks) and refuses to dance with her, since she is only "tolerable" in the looks department. Lizzy overhears him and is both amused and affronted.

But fate continues to bring the two together, and Darcy finds himself enchanted by Lizzy's lack of pretensions, her wit, her intelligence, and even her "fine eyes". It doesn't hurt that, unlike most women, she is obviously uninterested in him as a suitor. As he becomes more and more engaged by her charms, he congratulates himself that his superior social status protects him from becoming romantically attached to her. He notes that Lizzy seems to have some interest in a man he despises, Wickham, and he expresses his contempt for him to her. This makes Wickham all the more attractive to Lizzy, and Wickham is only too happy to spin her a tale of the cruel treatment he has received at Darcy's hands, reinforcing Lizzy's dislike.

Soon thereafter Darcy takes Charles Bingley to London to keep him from getting "snared" by Lizzy's beautiful sister, Jane. But when Lizzy visits her friend Charlotte, Darcy enters her society again, as his aunt is Charlotte's husband's patroness. When Lizzy discovers that Darcy has been the one that has kept Bingley away – on purpose – from her beloved sister, he sinks even lower in her estimation.

However, Darcy understands his own attractions better than he does Lizzy's. He is a wealthy gentleman with an impressive landed estate. He can not imagine that Lizzy would not welcome a marriage proposal, since all the advantages of money and society would be on her side. However, when he proposes, she rejects him – and when he asks why, she has a stockpile of reasons. In addition to insulting her with his proposal, wherein he makes it clear that he loves her despite his awareness of her inferiority, Darcy has also treated Wickham unfairly and interfered in her sister's love life.

Darcy is stunned and leaves, but later sends her a letter clarifying his position. It seems Wickham's tale was untrue, and he was the actual villain of the piece. Not only that, Darcy only took Bingley away because he didn't think Jane cared for him. At first, Lizzy doesn't wish to believe his words, but soon their truth begins to settle into her understanding.

When she goes touring England with her aunt and uncle, they want to go to Pemberley, Darcy's estate. Lizzy refuses until she learns Darcy will not be there, but fate lends yet another hand because a change of plan ensures that he is. Instead of treating Lizzy and her family in his usual superior manner, Darcy goes out of his way to ingratiate himself with them. Lizzy is surprised and impressed with this new kindness and begins to consider him in a more positive light.

However, when Lizzy discovers her sister Lydia (Maiden of Candlesticks) has eloped – with Wickham! – she tells Darcy, knowing he will be appalled and she will never see him again. But Darcy's strong sense of responsibility, along with his love for Elizabeth, causes him to subvert his pride. He deals directly with Wickham, bribing – and forcing – him to wed Lydia, who indiscreetly informs Lizzy that Darcy was involved in the affair. When Lizzy and Darcy meet again, she expresses her gratitude. At that time, he renews his proposal of marriage, a proposal she joyously accepts.

Card Interpretation

Intelligence, circumspection, and prudence are all qualities of Mr. Darcy – and the Lord of

Quills. When you receive this card in a reading, it suggests someone whose intellect is occasionally exceeded only by his pride, but that does not take one IQ point away from the person being described. Super-intelligent people do run the risk of believing that, because they are so often correct, they are always correct. They can also dismiss feelings and intuition at their peril – all the most successful C.E.O.'s talk about the importance of trusting one's gut, yet the Lord of Quills isn't as connected to that portion of the anatomy as he is his brain.

Like Darcy, you might feel you know what is best for others simply on the basis of your superior acuity. While you could be correct on one level, you might want to factor emotions into the equation – they are a necessary part of any successful calibration. Darcy learns this by the end of *Pride and Prejudice* when he finds he must earn Lizzy's love (not to mention how he bollixes up Bingley's affaire de coeur).

The Lord of Quills does not suffer fools gladly – or at all. However, don't let his appearance of calm rationality fool you. Elementally, this card is the Fiery Part of Air, so never discount the aspect of heat when this card appears in a reading. Despite his veneer of reason, the Lord of Quills is never cold or passionless. Darcy is a perfect case in point.

Like this card, it could be that your standards are very high. Some may perceive you (or the Lord of Quills) as being arrogant, but your intellectual equals will appreciate your clever wit and elevated conversation, and no one could deny that you hold yourself to a higher standard than anyone else.

It may be that you act as a mentor or guide for your family and friends, as Darcy does with his sister and his friend Bingley. You have an excellent command of facts, but be sure you don't twist them to suit your preferences – and don't forget to enter the human factor of emotion into your calculations.

And when you're socializing, you might want to remember that not everyone has your advantages. Politeness and thoughtfulness are qualities that every good ruler inculcates when dealing with the public.

What Would Jane Do?

"Mr. Darcy soon drew the attention of the room by his fine, tall person, handsome features, noble mien . . . he was looked at with great admiration for about half the evening, till his manners gave a disgust which turned the tide of his popularity; for he was discovered to be proud, to be above his company, and above being pleased..."

Jane Austen, *Pride and Prejudice*

Jane's Advice: The gift of intellect is a blessing, indeed; however, it can become a curse if used as a weapon instead of a device for superior communication. While the public square is filled with fools and simpletons, why grow querulous on the subject? One can derive amusement from them, and even, occasionally, learn from them.

Ace of Coins
Sense and Sensibility

Card Description

A gleaming, old-fashioned gold coin sits at the center of this card. The profile imprinted on the coin is that of Elinor Dashwood, the Queen of Coins in the Jane Austen Tarot.

Card Interpretation

The Aces are the elementals in the tarot, and so don't represent a part of a story, per se, but are instead, the essence of the suit. Even the title of *Sense and Sensibility* offers us insight into the theme of the book, which emphasizes the importance of pragmatism and common sense, as opposed to the fine sentiments of "sensibility," which would correspond in modern terminology to sensitivity.

The novel begins with the death of Elinor and Marianne's father. On his deathbed, he asks his son to take care of them financially. His son agrees, but then his wife persuades him to do less and less for them than he initially planned.

The two main characters exemplify the divide between sense and sensibility. Practical, consistent Elinor Dashwood represents sense; her younger sister, Marianne, embodies all that is sensitive and feeling. Both women fall in love, but their approach to that exalted state is quite different. Elinor is careful, and tries not to show her feelings until she is sure they are returned. When she discovers that the man she reasonably believes loves her is already engaged to another, her heart breaks, yet she never allows anyone, even her beloved sister, to see her pain. She even keeps the information a secret because that is what her loved one's alleged fiancée wants!

When a mysterious stranger appears out of nowhere and literally sweeps Marianne off her feet, she falls in love completely. Willoughby is everything she could want: romantic, smart, sensitive. She behaves without restraint, in a way that would be considered improper for her time.

When Willoughby goes to London, Marianne follows him, convinced that he will be delighted to see her. When he snubs her, she causes a scene in public. She discovers he is engaged and can not hide her heartbreak, but displays it again and again in the public eye. There is no check on her feelings, and she wanders in the rain, courting illness. She is only too successful in that pursuit; she almost dies.

Elinor eventually lands the man she loves, with her dignity and good sense intact. Marianne weds the man she disdained at the beginning of the novel as being too old and prosaic. And she learns to love him with every fiber of her being, which leads us to believe that Jane Austen recommends the qualities of perseverance, stability, and good sense.

When the Ace of Coins appears in a reading, it suggests some new, material gift or undertaking. You might find yourself inspired to start an income-producing project, or an addition to your home, human or concrete. You might wish to start to budget, or in some other tangible way, impact your financial situation. Alternately, you might want to begin a diet or exercise program – the suit of Coins speaks to all things physical, and that includes the body. The expression of this card is pragmatic, sensible. While you might have elaborate visions, the Ace of Coins demands a step-by-step process, where you must address the first level before attempting to ascend to the next. The elemental assignment of this card is Earth, in all its physical glory, but it's a seed, not the finished product.

What Would Jane Do?
"He meditated within himself to increase the fortunes of his sisters by the present of a thousand pounds a-piece."
Jane Austen, *Sense and Sensibility*

Jane's Advice: People's thoughts can change in the blink of an eye – or with an insinuating comment from a parsimonious wife. Wishing is not possessing, and verbal offers are not money in the hand. If there's something you want, expectation alone will not provide it.

Move steadily and surely – and even then, you may not reach your desired goal. But you will be at least one step closer to it.

Two of Coins
Sense and Sensibility

Card Description
The scene is of a large room with couples dancing. We see John Willoughby (Knight of Cups) engaged in conversation with an unattractive young woman who is dressed in extremely fancy ball dress. Large diamond earrings dangle in her hair and she wears an ornate diamond on her furbelowed gown. Marianne (Maiden of Cups) watches the pair, her face pained. Willoughby looks back longingly at Marianne, but resolutely continues to speak with the woman who does not attract him, except with her riches.

Storyline

When Marianne Dashwood meets John Willoughby, she is immediately infatuated with him, and the romantic feelings seem more than returned. She is convinced by his actions that they will marry. When he goes to London, she is disconsolate until she can go there, too. She is sure he will be delighted to see her and their relationship will graduate to the next level: marriage.

However, Willoughby ignores her letters, which confuses but does not frighten her. She is sure there must be a very good reason for his silence. Yet when she meets with him at a social gathering, he snubs her and seems to be involved with another woman. Marianne, heartbroken, makes a scene, allowing the entire party to know of her vulnerability and heartache.

Shortly thereafter, she receives a coldly-worded letter from Willoughby telling her of his forthcoming marriage. He has included the letters she wrote to him, along with the lock of her hair that he had begged her for just a short time before.

Her despair turns into physical sickness. Willoughby's choice of a wealthy woman over Marianne is ultimately a bitter one. When he learns Marianne is ill, he rides to her and confides to Elinor, Marianne's sister, that he made a terrible mistake in choosing another woman simply for material reasons.

Card Interpretation

When the Two of Coins appears in a reading, physical reality is shifting in some tangible way, as it does in *Sense and Sensibility*; Marianne's belief that she is going to be marrying Willoughby disintegrates before her eyes. Like her, you might be struggling to maintain your balance, but when your world shifts, it's hard to stay grounded.

You might be trying to do too many things at one time. Willoughby wanted to keep Marianne on a back burner and his new bride-to-be happy as well. It wasn't possible for him to have them both. You may be in a similar position, where you have to prioritize. Willoughby chooses financial security over

love, and coins are about practicality, so you may wish to err on the side of pragmatism. On the other hand, Willoughby ultimately regrets his avaricious choice – yet he manages to enjoy his life, just the same.

Astrologically, this card is attributed to Jupiter in Capricorn. The desire for material success (Capricorn) is expanded (Jupiter). Money under a mattress does not have the same return as funds placed in a bank – this card urges mobility and movement over maintaining the status quo. But this card, sadly, doesn't make that movement easy – for every action, there is a reaction, as Willoughby learns when he rejects Marianne for his heiress.

As with so many things in the tarot, the way to approach the situation is balance. Don't take on too much, but don't take on too little, either. Recognize the need to stretch yourself, but don't stretch so much that you lose your shape or balance. This is not a time of great difficulty, but it may be stressful trying to maintain equilibrium. Go with the flow, recognizing that this, too, shall pass.

What Would Jane Do?

"He could not then avoid it, but her touch seemed painful to him, and he held her hand only for a moment. During all this time he was evidently struggling for composure."

Jane Austen, *Sense and Sensibility*

Jane's Advice: Our common sense does not always walk hand-in-hand with our hearts. We are often torn between our desires and our needs. Sometimes we make decisions we regret, and not only when we follow our hearts. We can momentarily be so swayed by pragmatic considerations that we agree to things we later regret. Sometimes we must even withdraw our word, and that causes its own brand of shame and heartache. Life turns us in some strange directions, but that does not mean we can remain static – because that is no life at all.

Three of Coins

Emma

Card Description

In a refined English garden, Emma is drawing Harriet Smith in an idealized pose. Behind Emma is Mr. Elton, who is clearly making suggestions. The image on Emma's page is far prettier than the real Ms. Smith – Emma is creating a better woman, not only in her physical features, but also her attire, hairstyle, and posture.

Storyline

Emma has great intentions for self-improvement and plans to do many edifying things with her new friend Harriet Smith, but in the face of her deferential admiration, Emma soon focuses on improving Harriet.

In an attempt to focus on her artistic studies, Emma uses Harriet as her model. This action serves as a metaphor, as Emma is, like Pygmalion, shaping Harriet to share her

vision of the world. Harriet is infatuated with Robert Martin, and he with her, but Emma does not think he is good enough for her friend because of his social status. When Martin proposes, Emma warns Harriet that their social interaction will have to end if she marries someone so beneath Emma's sphere. Harriet, completely under Emma's thrall, rejects the man she loves.

Emma has selected the local curate, Mr. Elton, as an appropriate mate for Harriet and advocates with both parties to build their attraction for one another. Emma attributes Mr. Elton's attentions to her friend as romantic interest, and in large part due to Emma's teasing and cajoling, the impressionable Harriet develops a tendre for him. Unfortunately, Mr. Elton's attentions are a result of his desire to court Emma. When he tries to propose to her, she is mortified and immediately rejects him. Uppermost in Emma's mind is guilt that she has put her friend in a vulnerable position, though that guilt shares space with shame at her own blindness.

Emma then chooses Frank Churchill as a potential mate for Harriet, but she has learned her lesson and is less overt in her encouragement of the match. Emma constantly delineates the qualities of a "superior" man to her young mentee. Poor Emma is horrified when her student learns too well. Harriet has given her heart not to Frank Churchill, but George Knightley, whom Emma now realizes she herself loves.

Once Mr. Knightley proposes to Emma, she is both relieved and freshly embarrassed. She now sees the error of her ways. She has tried to mold Harriet in her image, but Emma's big mistake had been to be so flattered by Harriet's deference that she failed to see her friend – and herself – as they really were. One hopes that Emma has learned from her mistakes and will focus on her own self-improvement instead of attempting to manipulate the lives of others.

Card Interpretation

The Three of Coins is a card about apprenticeship and learning something concrete. The image depicts one young woman sketching another. The artist's technique is not accomplished, yet she literally attempts to make her reach exceed her grasp by making the model more beautiful than she, in fact, is. If you wish to learn your craft, you must focus on what is real and true, instead of imagining you are more gifted than you are or attempting to run before you can walk, artistically speaking.

Emma begins the book at one stage of life – overly confident in her own abilities to "make a match". She tries very hard to achieve her aims, yet her growth truly begins when she sees herself and her own limits more clearly. Sometimes we need to persevere in order to make concrete changes in ourselves, and that means making mistakes and learning from them. But without perseverance, there is no possibility of growth.

The Three of Coins is also a card about planning. Emma uses numerous stratagems in order to achieve her goals. When her plans don't come to fruition, it is because she is missing an important piece of the puzzle. Don't allow yourself to be blinded by flattery or wishful thinking, as Emma is with Harriet. Mars in Capricorn is the astrological attribution for the Three of Coins. We can easily read this as solid physical effort consistently applied in order to achieve goals, a kind-of persistent charging ahead. As a mountain goat will keep climbing in order to reach the top of the mountain, so you must persistently charge ahead if you want to reach the pinnacle of your chosen craft or profession.

However, while you charge, be sure you are going in the right direction. Mars in Capricorn's persistence can translate into stubbornly repeating the same mistakes, and ending up on the wrong mountaintop entirely, as Emma does when she must deal with Mr. Elton's unexpected proposal and then again when she must face Harriet's expression of love for Mr. Knightley.

At one point, Emma is totally disgusted with herself and feels like a complete fool. Do not be disheartened and give up when you find yourself in error. Making mistakes is a necessary part of learning one's craft. Focusing on what you learn and learning from your missteps is what will progress you on your path, not berating yourself for your blunders.

What Would Jane Do?

"You do not know it I dare say, but two or three years ago I had a great passion for taking likenesses, and attempted several of my friends, and was thought to have a tolerable eye in general. But from one cause or another, I gave it up in disgust."

Jane Austen, *Emma*

Jane's Advice: While consistent application without talent will never beget great art, persistence in vain is not a criminal act. To possess aptitude without concordant steady commitment, however, is an offense against divine providence. Develop regular and faithful habits and they will serve you and your purpose better than any self-gratifying or self-abnegating commentary.

Four of Coins
Sense and Sensibility

Card Description
Mr. and Mrs. John Dashwood are in the same room in Norland where his father died. There are several pound notes on the table that were originally on Mr. Dashwood's side, but only one remains. The rest are being pulled by Mrs. Dashwood to her side of the table. Elinor, Marianne, and their mother re-appear here, but in a large painting that is slowly fading.

Storyline
John Dashwood promises his dying father that he will provide for his widow and daughters, but his wife, Fanny, convinces him to do far less for them than he originally intends. Instead, when they move into the Dashwood home they have inherited, they allow his father's new family to continue living there on sufferance. However, Fanny's rapacious insensitivity as she wrests all the power due to the new head of a household, along with her pointed expectations that her sister-in-law Elinor is not good enough to marry Edward Ferrars (Fanny's brother), convinces Mrs. Dashwood and her children to move elsewhere.

When they move, Fanny even begrudges them their nice china and silverware!

Later on, John Dashwood is quick to take advantage of his family's wealthy relation, Mrs. Jennings – as well as to imply that it's really her duty to do be generous financially to *his* sisters. He even goes so far as to suggest to Elinor that she and her sister deserve to be beneficiaries of Mrs. Jennings' will. Everyone should be generous, except himself. He encourages Elinor to set her cap for Colonel Brandon, since he's financially well-off. While he does not have the generosity of a brother, he acts as if he has the proprietary rights of one. He has the audacity to complain to her about his expenses, though he is wealthy and she has nothing.

While John and Fanny are stingy with his stepmother and her children, they have a din-

ner for the well-off Middletons. They only give in the hope of a good return for their money. At the party, John is so intent on capturing Colonel Brandon for Elinor that he lauds her by criticizing Marianne's looks in comparison to hers.

When John suggests they to invite his sisters to stay with them, Fanny invites Lucy and Anne Steele instead, hoping to keep Edward away from Elinor. She is horrified to discover Edward has secretly been engaged to Lucy – and when she does, kicks her out of her home. When Colonel Brandon offers Edward a position, John wants all the details, yet conceals them from his wife, as it will upset her to know that her brother isn't completely penniless, despite the fact that the money is not coming out of her pocket.

Card Interpretation
There is often a sense of scarcity and a corollary need for stability and security embedded

in the Four of Coins. John and Fanny Dashwood are relatively prosperous, yet are so envious of others that they feed one another's selfish, least evolved instincts. John's original plan is to honor his promise to his dying father and be generous to his second family, but Fanny does not find it difficult to convince him to begrudge them their due and become self-congratulatory about the pittance he finally offers them. When this card appears in a reading, you might realistically need to budget or cut back on something tangible, but you also might feel more needy than you actually are. Your need for stability might be based more on fear that has no basis in reality, or past financial hardship that no longer exists.

Fanny is particularly covetous and cheeseparing towards the less fortunate Dashwood women. There is a sense that relationships are not based on emotions, but advantage or convenience. Fanny is like her mother, who uses her money as a tool to manipulate her children's lives. Her mother says little, which is another form of withholding behavior that this card can represent – a self-contained attitude that suggests that an even exchange of ideas puts one at a disadvantage.

When one is so fixed on tangibles such as money, it is easy to misconstrue others' feelings, as John Dashwood does when he tears Marianne down to Colonel Brandon, the man who loves her. For her part, Fanny is ungenerous and slighting to her sisters-on-law, and thinks she is punishing them by not socializing more with them. They are smart enough to be grateful to be removed from her company, if not to receive her slights.

Receiving this card in a reading is a reminder to ask yourself – am I feeling on solid ground or am I being irrationally insecure? What am I holding on to? And is it more valuable to me than my relationships with others?

Conversely, you may want to "tighten up" your pursestrings. You may need to start budgeting your finances in a more solid, stable way; like John and Fanny Dashwood, you might have children to consider, or other responsibilities.

What Would Jane Do?
"Having now said enough to make his poverty clear, and to do away the necessity of buying a pair of ear-rings for each of his sisters, in his next visit at Gray's his thoughts took a cheerfuller turn…"

Jane Austen, *Sense and Sensibility*

Jane's Advice: One might think that those with wealth would be the most freely generous, but this is not often the case. They would say that the only reason they are able to maintain their wealth is through avid protection of their finances. The recitations of their many pecuniary responsibilities could almost inspire a poor person to offer what few funds she had to alleviate their suffering. However, a smart woman, no matter how tightly constrained, should find a way to avoid such charitable opportunities.

Five of Coins
Persuasion

Card Description
Mrs. Smith sits on a threadbare sofa in a dark and cold room. She wears a shawl, but one can see she is shivering. She is too thin, the sign of someone who doesn't get enough food. Her feet are soaking in a small tub of water and there is a cane by her side. Yet she is trying to live in a manner that fits within her means and still remain a gentlewoman, and that is apparent from all that surrounds her. A miniature of herself ten years before, when she was in the bloom of youth and quite wealthy, sits upon her desk.

Storyline
Unlike the rest of her family, Anne Elliot does not bestow her affections based on an individual's wealth or societal position. When the Elliots go to Bath, they go to great lengths to be recognized by the Dowager Viscountess Dalrymple and her household. When Anne joins her family in Bath, she finds the Dalrymples poor company – they are neither gracious nor particularly intelligent.

Anne learns her former school friend is also in Bath and visits her. The former healthy and wealthy Miss Hamilton is now the widow Mrs. Smith, a sickly and poor woman who has come to Bath for the healing waters. While her marriage had been a happy one, neither she nor her husband had been very thrifty. Now she is both alone and in financial straits.

Despite her problems, Mrs. Smith is relatively bright and cheerful. Anne is impressed with her friend's "elasticity of mind, that disposition to be comforted, that power of turning readily from evil to good, and of finding employment which carried her out of herself, which was from nature alone. It was the choicest gift of Heaven; and Anne viewed her friend as one of those instances in which, by a merciful appointment, it seems designed to counterbalance almost every other want".

Anne does not advertise that she has renewed her relationship with her old schoolmate, but when the Dalrymples invite the Elliots for an evening when Anne has prior plans to visit Mrs. Smith, she is happy to beg off of the engagement. Her family, predictably, is horrified that she is neglecting wealthy relatives to spend time with the impoverished Mrs. Smith. They harangue Anne about refusing to break her plans. Even Anne's cousin and potential suitor, Mr. Elliot, who admires her loyalty and kindness towards her friend, doesn't understand why Anne doesn't value the social standing of the Dalrymples.

Card Interpretation

When the Five of Coins appears in a reading, it suggests an unstable period of real and tangible concerns. Like Mrs. Smith, you could have physical and/or financial problems. You may be unnecessarily worried about these matters, but the likelihood is that you have good reason to be concerned. Astrologically speaking, Mercury in Taurus is attributed to this card. Mentally quick Mercury is not happy encased in the slow, sodden earth of Taurus, and so the unrest is both mental and elemental. There is still uncertainty, which causes stress, but also the hope that there is a way out of the difficult condition.

Another comfort is that you are not alone. The image on the Five of Coins in the Rider-Waite-Smith deck shows a man and woman standing outside a chapel in the snow, one injured. In the Jane Austen version, Mrs. Smith has a candlestick, a symbol of divine fire. Like the characters depicted in these images, you have a source of spiritual assistance to which you can turn.

Just as Mrs. Smith is alienated from most of polite society, Anne's evolved state is alien to her status-seeking family. And just as they look down on Mrs. Smith, we know that the Dalrymples disdain the Elliots. No doubt a Duke would scorn the Dalrymples. Even if you are feeling isolated or unfortunate, someone else might perceive you as being a child of fortune. Putting things in perspective might help you to feel more blessed than injured.

In the Continental System, this card is seen as bad for money, but good for love. Like Mrs. Smith, you might have (or have had) a loving partner who thought more of present pleasures than future problems. This card reminds you that, while love is a blessing, it's hard to appreciate anyone or anything when your stomach is growling or you are worried about being evicted from your home. If your finances and health are fine, this card suggests you may be in spiritual poverty. Seek the sacred, but spend and budget wisely at this time.

What Would Jane Do?

"She was a widow and poor . . . She had had difficulties of every sort to contend with, and in addition to these distresses had been afflicted with a severe rheumatic fever, which, finally settling in her legs, had made her for the present a cripple."

Jane Austen, *Persuasion*

Jane's Advice: Privilege and wealth are not fixed, but "elasticity of mind, that disposition to be comforted, that power of turning readily from evil to good, and of finding employment which carries you out of yourself is a... gift from Heaven", and it is a permanent one. Resilience and foresight allow you to recover from hardships better than a gift of money, because inner qualities last. The latter does not.

However, if someone wants to offer you financial assistance, so much the better. If and when you have the power to give, you will do so with equal generosity.

Six of Coins
Persuasion

Card Description

Two women are seated in a small, impoverished living room. One is Mrs. Hamilton Smith, the poor woman depicted in the Five of Coins. An afghan covers her legs and she looks particularly fragile. The other is Anne Elliot, who looks out of place in her elegant clothes. Mrs. Hamilton Smith holds out a box of papers to Anne.

Storyline

As mentioned in the previous card description, despite her family's disapproval, Anne Elliot continues to visit an old school friend, Mrs. Smith, a sickly, poor widow. It seems to everyone that Anne is in the position of a Lady Bountiful, condescending to be kind to a woman who is not her equal in money or social status.

Mrs. Smith does want something from her friend. When she hears rumors that Anne is going to marry her cousin and heir to Kellynch, Mr. Elliot, Mrs. Smith asks in a veiled way if Anne will be a true friend to her and influence her husband-to-be to help her in a financial matter. When Anne assures her that she has no intentions of marrying Mr. Elliot, Mrs. Smith gives Anne something very valuable – the letter we see in the Six of Coins. The letter verifies that Mr. Elliot has been all that is corrupt, profligate, and disdainful of his legacy. Now that he has spent all of his money, he places new importance on his title and inheritance. He plans to marry Anne in order to ensure that he will actually inherit, though; he worries that Anne's father will remarry and have a son, taking his place as heir. The letter shows Mr. Elliot's true colors, and had Anne considered him a potential mate, she would have done so no longer after reading it.

Even though Anne had never been in danger of marrying him, the information is still valuable to her and allows her to deal with Mr. Elliot with intelligence and a complete lack of self-doubt.

Ironically, Mr. Elliot had rejected Mrs. Smith's many letters requesting his assistance, assistance he owed to her in her husband's name, if nothing else. He little imagined that Mrs. Smith would one day have the power to harm his cause.

Card Interpretation

We often benefit most when we intend to be a benefactor or benefactress to others. Acting out of gratitude for former kindnesses, Anne Elliot distinguishes Mrs. Smith with her company and her kindness, never asking or expecting a return. Mrs. Smith more than repays her with important information about a man who has the potential to cause great trouble for Anne and her family. When you receive the Six of Coins in a reading, you may be in what seems like a position of power or a position of supplication, just as the two women who sit on the sofa in the card. Whether you are the giver or the receiver, remember that both acts can be ones of generosity and reciprocity.

You might be like Anne, the person who seems to be the Lady Bountiful, yet she derives pleasure from Mrs. Smith's company, as well as useful information about Mr. Elliot. You receive something from everyone whom you assist, in one form or another.

Mrs. Smith hopes to gain from her relationship with Anne when she believes Anne will marry a man who can help her financially (and who owes much to her without Anne's intercession). Instead, Captain Wentworth, Anne's eventual husband, is the one to come to her rescue. The key is that Mrs. Smith articulates what she needs and assistance is found, even though it is not in the form she expects. If you are in need of help, let the universe know that you are ready to receive it by asking for aid from an appropriate party. While that individual might not be the eventual donor, you have put things into motion. Your request for sustenance is now in the Universe, ready to be fulfilled.

When someone comes to you for help, if it is in your power to assist without harming yourself, only good can come of your willingness to give generously. Life takes mysterious twists and turns and you never know when you will be in Anne's position – or Mrs. Smith's. On the other hand, if you are not equipped to provide support, or feel that you are being drained by a particular individual, neither of you is helped by your emptying your own resources.

Astrologically, the Moon in Taurus is attributed to the Six of Coins. The Moon, the planet that represents our deepest needs, is comfortable in hospitable, stable, earthy Taurus. Our tangible needs will be met and possibly exceeded when we receive this card. Whether we are the donor or the donee is almost immaterial, because each receives something necessary and sustaining.

What Would Jane Do?
"Anne was shewn some letters of his on the occasion, answers to urgent applications from Mrs. Smith, which all breathed the same stern resolution of not engaging in a fruitless trouble, and, under a cold civility, the same hard-hearted indifference to any of the evils it might bring on her."
Jane Austen, *Persuasion*

Jane's Advice: The Bible says it is better to give than to receive, but both actions are blessings. Generosity is repaid, though often not by the recipient. However, the virtue of giving and the good feelings it engenders is sufficient repayment for most people. The others receive their reward by the notice of others who observe their generosity, precisely because viewers are the intended recipients of the act.

Seven of Coins
Emma

Card Description
Robert Martin, a strapping, sweating man is working hard in the field, planting seeds in the earth. Harriet Smith looks on admiringly in the distance. Robert Martin looks back at her with hope and interest.

Storyline
Harriet Smith makes a conquest when she visits the Martin sisters. Their brother, Robert, a hard-working gentleman farmer, falls in love with her, and she with him. But her new friend Emma Woodhouse advises her that Robert Martin is beneath her. If Harriet marries him, she and Emma will no longer be able to be friends, because they will move in different social circles. Harriet is quite impressionable and values Emma's opinion so much she turns down Robert Martin's well-written proposal of marriage.

Robert Martin continues to work hard and he continues to love Harriet, despite her refusal of his offer. Whenever he or his family sees Harriet, they are polite, but they are aware and grieved that she has rejected him. Harriet falls for two different young men, but neither of them reciprocates her feelings. When Robert asks her for her hand in marriage again, this time she is happy to accept him.

Card Interpretation
When you receive the Seven of Coins in a reading, you have a goal that is just out of reach, as Harriet Smith is for Robert Martin in the image. There is an inevitable wait for the results you desire, but if you continue to apply yourself wholeheartedly, you will

receive unexpected bounty, as well as the reward you anticipate. Robert Martin doesn't give up on Harriet, but he doesn't allow his feelings for her to interfere with his work. He remains a complete and productive individual, worthy of Mr. Knightley's praise. If you find yourself attracted to someone who doesn't seem to return your feelings, immerse yourself in being effective and productive. As Voltaire writes, "Let us cultivate our garden". Eventually, you will either be successful enough to ensnare the one you desire or you will no longer care, because you have so many other flowers in your garden to give you pleasure.

Saturn in Taurus is the astrological attribution for this card. Despite Crowley giving this card the keyword of "Failure", the message of this astrological combination is that discipline, slow and steady, wins the race. Saturn rewards perseverance and commitment, and no one is steadier and more persevering than

Taurus. You may feel that you have worked hard and received no bounty from your efforts, but this card suggests that if you keep applying yourself to your labors, like Robert Martin, you will eventually win your prize.

Robert Martin is a gentleman farmer. This card evokes working with the earth, and understanding the nature of cycles even if you can't always predict timing accurately. Understand that everything has its season. Much as we might wish for fall in summer, we must labor under the hot sun of August before we feel the breezes of September.

Before Robert Martin first proposes to Harriet, he seeks advice from Mr. Knightley. If things aren't moving as swiftly or in the direction you would like, a mentor or someone wise in the area in which you are laboring might be able to help speed up the process.

But of all things this card preaches, patience is its greatest message. If you give up on something you really want, you will berate yourself for a much longer period than the one you are spending wishing for something to come to fruition. Understand that what is meant to happen will happen when the time is ripe, and your continued application is the only element that will move the desired situation closer.

What Would Jane Do?

"I never hear better sense from any one than Robert Martin. He always speaks to the purpose; open, straightforward, and very well judging. He told me every thing; his circumstances and plans, and what they all proposed doing in the event of his marriage. He is an excellent young man, both as son and brother."

Jane Austen, *Emma*

Jane's Advice: Planning for success can be a bothersome process, but the rewards of planning are great. Anticipation can add to the ultimate reward, but, if too great, can overwhelm the experience out of all proportion to the actuality. A garden can provide pleasure and sustenance, but no matter how many times you water an aster, it won't grow until

July at the earliest. Determine to be pleased by whatever flower is in season, and sow the seeds you wish to grow year round.

Eight of Coins
Persuasion

Card Description

This card shows Anne Elliot doing all the things she is a master of: taking care of a child, making accounts of the possessions in her home/estate, Kellynch, playing the piano, reading, directing Captain Wentworth to carry Louisa after she falls.

Storyline

Though Sir Walter Elliot is the ostensible head of his household, we quickly realize that his middle daughter, Anne, is the one who gets things done, though she gets neither the support nor the respect warranted by her stewardship. She recognizes when the family finances necessitate budgetary restrictions, organizes their move, monitors her sister Mary's children (better than Mary does), and, when the spirited Louisa has an accident, cool-headed Anne is the one who organizes her rescue while the others around her are immobilized by fear.

Anne is not merely composed and organized. She is smart, sensitive, and well-read, as well as sensible and feeling. She is also an accomplished pianist and a lay counselor – at Uppercross, everyone makes her their confidante. When Captain Frederick Wentworth returns to Anne's social sphere, he is looking for a wife, and seems to ignore his former fiancée's charms for the youthful, spirited Louisa. Yet he can't help but notice Anne's rationality and her capable ways – and when he sees how ably she handles the crisis with Louisa, he realizes his admiration is equal only to his love for her.

Card Interpretation

Because this card often has a workmanlike theme and Austen never writes about work, I was initially at a loss to find an appropriate card within her oeuvre. But the accomplished Anne Elliot embodies the qualities of the traditional Eight of Coins: intelligence successfully utilized on the practical level, mastery, skillful organization, capability, and productivity. You can see these qualities reflected in the card, and, when this card comes up in a reading, it suggests that you own these qualities as well.

It may be that you have achieved a level of mastery in one particular field, or that you possess proficiency in a variety of areas. Whichever it is, your native intelligence combines with perseverance in order to thoroughly excel in whatever you put your mind to. The astrological assignment for the Eight of Coins is Sun in Virgo, which suggests a precise, yet grounded approach being an essential part of who you are. Virgo is an earth sign, the domain of the practical and tangible, but it is ruled by smart and speedy Mercury. This card offers the best of both worlds – pragmatism and intelligence.

Another possibility is that you are the unseen hand that effects many valuable projects and possibilities to succeed, but do not get credit for it. In *Persuasion*, virtue (and Captain Wentworth) is its own reward, but if you feel your work is neither acknowledged nor appreciated, you might want to think of ways to alter that. It might mean you have to change your situation, or find other ways to receive fulfillment from your efforts.

Another message this card might have for you is that you are ready to move on to a higher plane of existence. You may have gone as far as you can in one area, and need to seek greener pastures. For Anne, becoming a wife is that greener pasture, but for you it could be a raise in pay or position, another job, or another avenue of expression. This card is particularly relevant to creating anything tangible, such as art, music, writing (Mercury rules communication), or craftsmanship.

Adversely placed, this card could have other, less pleasant meanings. You might be drained by the constant demands upon your time, as Anne is early in the novel. The Eight of Coins can also be a reminder that, in order to

achieve mastery, you must apply yourself to the task. Talent alone accomplishes nothing. On the other hand, skill without values or base materialism can be counterproductive. Not everything that is created should be. Strive always to do the very best, most informed, work that you can. When in doubt, choose "honesty against importance ... more vigorous measures, a more complete reformation, a quicker release from debt, a much higher tone of indifference for everything but justice and equity".

What Would Jane Do?
"If Anne will stay, [there is] no one so proper, so capable as Anne."

Jane Austen, *Persuasion*

Jane's Advice: We all know industrious souls who achieve much, but have not the discernment to achieve well. Their creations are the ones we try to fob off on those of whom we are least fond. Alternately, there are those whose ideas are brilliant, but come to naught. Potential without application is pure vapour. When labor and intellect align, however, the results seem divinely inspired.

Nine of Coins
Emma

Card Description
Mr. Woodhouse sits on a roomy stone bench in the midst of a beautifully manicured and blooming garden. He is draped in a blanket around his feet, which are propped up on a footstool, and he wears a scarf securely about his neck. He looks expansive and comfortable in his little outdoor kingdom. In the immediate background is his large and elegant estate.

Storyline
While all others hail governess Miss Taylor's marriage to Mr. Weston as a significantly positive life-changing event, Mr. Woodhouse feels nothing but pity for her. She must leave the happy home at Hartfield he and his daughter Emma have provided for her. He can't imagine any person more delightful than his daughter, nor any home as safe and comfortable.

Safety and comfort are the watchwords that Mr. Weston lives by. He constantly frets over his diet, as well as any guests who come to visit, because health is a paramount concern for him. He is convinced that his doctor is the finest in the country and urges everyone to avail themselves of his services.

When his daughter Isabella, a valetudinarian like her father, comes to visit, he points out that no one who is away from his beloved Hartfield can really look very healthy, and they spend their time together playing dueling doctors, each being sure that theirs is the best.

While Mr. Woodhouse occasionally must visit others outside of his home, he does so rarely, which allows Emma to venture into a social life unhindered by her father's observations or opinions. Devoted as he is to his daughter,

he has no clue as to her romantic interactions. When Mr. Knightley proposes to Emma, he knows that he must leave his own home to move into Hartfield if they are to wed, because Mr. Woodhouse is so averse to any change in his home-life. The idea of his daughter marrying anyone and leaving home is repellent to him. Though he cares for Mr. Knightley as a son, Mr. Woodhouse only approves of the marriage when he feels that, since there have been robberies in the neighborhood, it will add to the safety of all if Mr. Knightley comes to live at Hartfield.

Card Interpretation
Serenity, health, and home are the priorities of the Nine of Coins. When this card appears in a reading, your priorities are not about excitement, but about settling down in some way. This card can sometimes signify pregnancy, with all the nesting instincts that come with that state. Like Mr. Woodhouse, you might be

disinclined to socialize except on your own terms, preferably in your own home. You could be very health-conscious, and expect others to follow your dietary approach – or at least listen sympathetically to your daily listing of health concerns and their remediation. You probably also dislike change, and do all you can to avoid it.

Venus in Virgo is the astrological attribution for this card. Venus stresses pleasure and comfort and, in the sign of Virgo, makes those desires particular and a bit fussy. Virgo is an earth sign, but an earth sign ruled by Mercury, and needs things to be "just so" on the physical plane. You may take great joy in your physical surroundings, and, like Mr. Woodhouse, spare no expense to beautify them. You may be very particular in how you experience those surroundings as well, taking care to avoid any unpleasant weather or other "disturbances in your field".

With this card, there is an enjoyment of solitude, although, like Mr. Woodhouse, you are happy enough to socialize on your own terms. Also like Mr. Woodhouse, you derive great pleasure from the company of your family and think it superior to any other social situation. You might be blind to the faults of those you love – Mr. Woodhouse sees Emma as the soul of perfection – and you will do anything you can in order to ensure their happiness, if they are attentive to your needs.

The Nine of Coins is a card of material well being. Creature comforts are necessities and there is a great serenity in this card. While the scene can be a bit stultifying, it is very safe and comfortable. One drawback to this card is that one can become isolated or oblivious to the outside world, as Mr. Woodhouse often seems to be. As he says in *Emma*, "The sooner every party breaks up, the better". This is antithetical to the Nine of Teacups motto, which would be: "The later every party breaks up, the better".

Another negative possibility is that one can become selfish and overlook others' needs in order to maintain the pleasant status quo this card represents. Much as Mr. Woodhouse does when he tries to stop Emma from marrying the man she loves in order to keep his circumstances pleasant and stable, you could be fighting a change that holds the potential for the betterment of all concerned.

What Would Jane Do?
"Mr. Woodhouse taken from Hartfield! – No, he felt that it ought not to be attempted."
Jane Austen, *Emma*

Jane's Advice: There are few issues more fascinating to an individual than the state of one's comfort and health, but these same issues are considerably less scintillating to others. Everyone can agree that home is the repository for comfort and pleasure, except teen-agers who are hungry for excitement and the unknown. Age convinces most of us that excitement and the unknown are overrated in comparison to a nicely roasted meal and the restfulness and repose of sleeping on your own bed.

Ten of Coins
Mansfield Park

Card Description
This card depicts a scene that shows old values triumphant, including Sir Thomas Bertram, the patriarch, in front of Mansfield Park, but the people are on the ground (earth). Fanny Price and Edmund Bertram stand in front, holding hands, united, and Lady Bertram stands next to her husband.

Storyline
When gentle Fanny Price comes to live with her wealthy relatives at Mansfield Park, she is afraid of all of them, but particularly, her uncle Sir Thomas terrifies her. To her female cousins, she is an object of disdain (when she is considered at all), and her eldest male cousin, Tom, disregards her. Her languid aunt uses her as a servant. The only family member who treats her well is her cousin Edmund, and she quickly comes to worship him. As she matures, that adoration turns into romantic love.

Despite her fears, Fanny flourishes in the solidity and order of Mansfield Park. However, when Sir Thomas and Tom travel to Antigua and two sophisticated Londoners join the neighborhood, that consistent structure deconstructs. Soon Edmund, who is supposed to become a clergyman, finds himself enchanted by the beautiful and vivacious Mary Crawford, while her brother Henry charms Fanny's cousins Maria and Julia into competing for his affections.

Only Fanny is immune to the allure of the Crawfords. She sees Mary Crawford as being completely undeserving of her beloved cousin Edmund, and recognizes Henry's careless flirtatious manner as the heartless and egotistical behavior it is. When everyone (except a most unwilling Fanny) tamper with Sir Thomas's den in order to create a stage for risqué theatricals, it seems as if the established order of Mansfield Park has been transformed into a den of iniquity.

Sir Thomas arrives in time to stop the play and he immediately tries to undo the damage that has been wrought upon his household. But his lack of involvement with his family has its costs; they have been corrupted without his solid values. Julia is a foolish girl, and Maria marries a fool for his wealth and status. Sir Thomas, fooled by Henry Crawford's seeming respectability, encourages his suit for Fanny's hand; he never expects the morally dissolute Henry to elope with the married Maria when Fanny turns him down.

But in the end, Fanny, whose values have been molded by the best aspects of Mansfield Park, returns to it, and ends up marrying the sadder-but-wiser Edmund, who finally sees Mary Crawford for what she is. Stability and tradition will be cemented into the family structure once again.

Card Interpretation

In some ways, Fanny's journey through Mansfield Park reflects the card pattern of the Ace through Ten of Coins – she has moved from financial incapacity to solidity and stability, with some stumbles along the way. The Ten of Coins is a card of structure and symme-

try, and indicates an established and concrete order. It is an augury of financial security and prosperity.

While this card represents the best of family traditions, it can also signify some of the worst. Wealth and status might take priority over love and ethics. There might be an abuse of power, a form of family blackmail, as when Sir Thomas sends Fanny home to punish her for not accepting Henry Crawford's proposal of marriage. This card sometimes comes up when you need to reject some or all of what your family of origin represents. It can even indicate a rejection of a community or organization that you have been a part of in the past.

Alternately, you might be the one who is overvaluing the material to the detriment of other elements in your life. Sir Thomas's association with Antigua involves the enslavement of others, the embodiment of unethical behavior in order to benefit financially.

On a more mundane level, you could be finding the order of your life fulfilling – or, conversely, re-organizing, standardizing, or streamlining your habits or life patterns to form a more satisfying whole.

The Ten of Coins is the last Minor Arcana card, and, as such, is the sum total of them all. In that sense, it has accumulated all the best and worst qualities and found a way to put them together in solid form. In many artistic renditions of this card, one sees a pattern of the Kabbalistic Tree of Life, which shows the structure of our evolutionary earth journey.

This card, an illustration taken from the end of the novel, indicates that you have successfully completed one level on your journey. Astrologically speaking, this card's attribute is Mercury in Virgo. While Mercury can be flighty, in its "home" assignment of earthy and meticulous Virgo, it is grounded, precise, and very content. Perhaps it's time to consider what you wish to master or achieve next, instead of remaining in such a comfortable, but static condition.

What Would Jane Do?

"With so much true merit and true love, and no want of fortune and friends, the happiness of the married cousins must appear as secure as earthly happiness can be."

Jane Austen, *Mansfield Park*

Jane's advice: There is no substitute for love and merit, but life's path often requires prosperity as well for a truly happy ending. However, when you achieve a secure berth, love often makes it way into the vicinity as well. There are no guarantees and we never know where our paths may ultimately wander, but wholesome values (and some money in the bank) will stand you in good stead wherever you end up.

Maiden of Coins
Charlotte Lucas, Pride and Prejudice

Card Description

Charlotte Lucas is sitting at her kitchen table writing out a dinner menu. She has a no-nonsense look about her and her clothes are rather plain, as is her brown hair and brown eyes. The kitchen window overlooks a blooming country garden with vegetables, as well as some flowers. The Maiden of Coins can not see outside the kitchen window from where she is sitting. Everything looks very comfortable and cozy, including her seat.

Storyline

Elizabeth's dearest friend, Charlotte Lucas, is sensible and intelligent. She is also a not-particularly-attractive young woman who wants to get married. The discussions the friends have are emblematic of their priorities. Elizabeth is glad that Jane's romantic interest in Bingley is veiled by her cheery composure; Charlotte opines that Jane could lose Bingley by not displaying more overt signs of affection. In another conversation, Elizabeth sneers at Darcy's interest; Charlotte suggests that any attention by a man of Darcy's status should be valued.

When Lizzy's cousin, the fatuous Mr. Collins, asks her to marry him, she refuses despite family pressure. She doesn't care that he is to inherit her family home and ignores the financial benefits that she would accrue by wedding him.

Her friend Charlotte kindly spends time with him, and, in less than a week, the news arrives: Mr. Collins and Charlotte are engaged. Lizzy, who values her friend's intelligence and common sense, can't believe she would attach herself to such a buffoon. But Charlotte acknowledges that she understands Mr. Collins' character, and will be perfectly satisfied to have a comfortable home, as she is not a romantic. Charlotte feels that Mr. Collins will be the only man ever to ask for her hand, and what he offers is her best possible future. Charlotte's intelligence and sense are good prognosticators. When Lizzy visits the newlyweds, she observes that Charlotte has arranged her nest for the utmost comfort and the ability to avoid Mr. Collins' company for most of the day. Charlotte "doesn't hear" his more idiotic comments and seems very happy.

And when the more romantic Lizzy finds herself happily engaged to Mr. Darcy, her dear – and pregnant – friend Charlotte comes to wish her well.

Card Interpretation

Elementally speaking, the Maiden of Coins is Earth of Earth. That's quite a preponderance of earth. Pragmatism and the lure of the tangible can overpower the more refined inclinations of spirit (Candlesticks), emotions, (Teacups), and the intellect (Quills). When this card appears in a reading, you (or the individual the card represents) may be, like Charlotte Lucas, willing to sacrifice any of the aforementioned elements for practical or mundane reasons. Your physical and/or financial concerns take precedence over everything at this time. Sometimes this is necessary, but if it is a consistent behavior, your may be missing out on some valuable, if ephemeral, things in life. This card speaks of what may well be a biological need for nesting and nurturing. Charlotte Lucas may deserve better than Mr. Collins, but she is convinced that he is her only and/or best chance to make a home and have a family. You may currently be less discerning or demanding than usual for similar reasons. Settling for "a bird in the hand" may well be worth the proverbial two in a bush, but Charlotte Lucas lived during a very different time for women. Be sure that you can make your home as comfortable and personally satisfying to you as Charlotte Lucas does when choosing a partner of any kind.

The Maiden of Coins needs stability and can be a conformist. This is not the card of a rebel or a free-thinker, but someone who values placidity and a secure place in her social environs, as Charlotte does. If, like Charlotte, you have an interfering individual like Lady Catherine de Bourgh in your life, you may not want to challenge her head-on, but simply accede to her in public and do as you wish in private. Like Charlotte, you are straightforward and dislike dissimulation, but prefer it to dissension.

When this card comes up for you in a reading, it can speak to a need for a more stable environment, which sometimes demands a

change from the status quo, if your present situation is not physically comfortable or satisfying. It may be necessary for you to examine your current circumstances and see if they accord with your priorities. This is a time to take care of your needs, even if your friends and acquaintances neither approve nor understand. You must be the arbiter of your values and lifestyle.

What Would Jane Do?

"Without thinking highly either of men or of matrimony, marriage had always been her object; it was the only honourable provision for well-educated young women of small fortune, and however uncertain of giving happiness, must be their pleasantest preservative from want."

Jane Austen, *Pride and Prejudice*

Jane's Advice: While wit and sagacity are laudable, they are not edible. In times of want, one soon recognizes the importance of financial security, but women of good sense must always be cognizant of its significance. Sadly, there are too many men and women who wish never to consider such mundane matters; you often hear from them when they have need of funds.

Knight of Coins
Edward Ferrars (Sense and Sensibility)

Card Description
Unlike the other Knights in the Jane Austen Tarot, Edward Ferrars is not on horseback, though we see a horse tethered to a tree in the background. Edward is walking down a dirt path leading to a cottage during the in-between time when it is neither fall nor winter. The leaves on the trees are dying, and one gets a sense that it is a cold, windy and desolate time in this young man's life. On his finger, he wears a ring that he touches as he walks. He is young, but seems unusually mature and sober.

Storyline
In the first flush of youth, Edward Ferrars engages himself to Lucy Steele. He is drawn to her physical beauty and vivacity, qualities that lessen in importance as he grows in age and discernment and realizes that she is shallow, cunning, and ignorant. Years later, he meets Elinor Dashwood, who is not only attractive, but has depth and values that resonate with his own, and he slowly wins her heart with his modest and steady sincerity. However, he honors his prior engagement (though his integrity does not demand that he acknowledge his engagement to his mother, whom he knows will not approve of the match to Ms. Steele).

When Lucy informs his family of their engagement, Edward's mother disinherits him. Edward does not know how he will be able to afford marriage, but determines to make his way somehow. Lucy cleverly and secretly wins the heart of Edward's brother, who is now the family heir, and elopes with

him. Edward is at last free to marry Elinor, a woman to whom he is far more suited.

Card Interpretation
Unlike the romantic Knight of Teacups or the dashing Knight of Candlesticks, the steady Knight of Coins, as embodied by Edward Ferrars, seems rather dull at first glance. We are not alone in thinking so; Marianne, Elinor's dreamier sister, finds Edward's methodology abhorrent:
"He was confused, seemed scarcely sensible of pleasure in seeing them, looked neither rapturous nor gay, said little but what was forced from him by questions, and distinguished Elinor by no mark of affection. Marianne...began almost to feel a dislike of Edward..."

This card signifies an individual who keeps his thoughts and feelings tucked away, and is neither eloquent nor voluble. At the time of Marianne's assessment, he is engaged to another woman. But even if he were not, he'd be unlikely to shower Elinor with beautiful word bouquets. The person this card represents in a reading says what he means and means what he says. He just doesn't say all that much! But what he does say is sincere.

One thing in Edward's favor is that he knows who he is and has no delusions of grandeur. He embraces his prosaic nature ("Thank Heaven! I cannot be forced into genius and eloquence", he exclaims at one point) and acknowledges that he is not particularly lively. His self-description:
"I am so foolishly shy, that I often seem negligent, when I am only kept back by my natural awkwardness. I have frequently thought that I must have been intended by nature to be fond of low company".

is disarming in its openness and humility – at least to those who love him, as Elinor does. If you receive the Knight of Coins in a reading, recognize this card as one who is not at all flashy and is rather shy – but also genuine and self-effacing.

The Knight of Coins can be too much so,

doubting his self-worth to his detriment. This insecurity almost causes Edward Ferrars to create a future with a coarse wife who is distinctly his inferior intellectually, financially, and in class, because he meets and commits to Lucy Steele before he is completely formed.

Another quality of the Knight of Coins is that he is eminently practical. He describes a house as "fine" because "it unites beauty with utility". He could easily consider a top-of-the-line vacuum cleaner a "fine" birthday gift for his wife, and wonder why she is less than enthusiastic about her present. But he is also quite observant and often notices the emotional interplay of others, as Edward notes Marianne's feelings for and allusions to Willoughby, even when she thinks she is being subtle.

Sometimes this card can indicate a period of inertia. Until the Knight of Pentacles knows which direction he wants to go, he tends to stay still. Sometimes he can stay so still that his dreams pass him by completely. He does not have an innate drive or lust for life, and sometimes allows others to focus his direction, as Edward Ferrars does in terms of his career. This is not a Knight who acts impulsively, but sometimes he doesn't act at all, which can be frustrating for him and his loved ones.

This Knight can move quickly, once he has definitely decided upon a course of action. As soon as he receives a letter from Lucy notifying him that she has eloped with his brother, he immediately rushes to Elinor to ask her hand in marriage. Love helps him to overcome his usual self-doubt. This time he has no reason to regret his choice, because it is not made in haste, ignorance, nor youth.

What Would Jane Do?
"I have more pleasure in a snug farm-house than a watch-tower."

Jane Austen, *Sense and Sensibility*

Jane's advice: Fables remain current because they contain eternal truths. The tortoise triumphs over the hare because slow and steady really does win the race – in the long run.

This is not a time to rush to judgment, but to move patiently and stealthily. Choose both wisely and well the first time, because instinct does not always serve its master.

Lady of Coins
Elinor Dashwood (Sense and Sensibility)

Card Description
Elinor Dashwood sits on a chair looking out the window, sketching a scene of the lovely gardens outside. She is dressed sensibly and tastefully, though her clothes are neither fancy nor elaborate, and her surroundings are cozy and comfortable, though not lavish. The room is well-lit and inviting, and a basket of needlepoint sits at her feet; she has clearly put it aside to focus on her sketch in the late morning light. There are few books on the shelves, but the ones that are there are classical and wholesome histories.

Storyline

Two loving sisters could scarcely be more different than Elinor and Marianne Dashwood. Elinor, the eldest, is the epitome of decorum and practicality. Austen describes her thus:

"Elinor... possessed a strength of understanding, and coolness of judgment, which qualified her, though only nineteen, to be the counsellor of her mother, and enabled her frequently to counteract, to the advantage of them all, that eagerness of mind in Mrs. Dashwood which must generally have led to imprudence. She had an excellent heart; – her disposition was affectionate, and her feelings were strong; but she knew how to govern them: it was a knowledge which her mother had yet to learn; and which one of her sisters had resolved never to be taught."

That other sister is Marianne, who is the Maiden of Teacups in the Jane Austen Tarot. Elinor falls in love with the not-very-dashing Edward Ferrars, and his behavior toward her has given her good reason to believe that her affections are returned. Yet she is completely discreet and airs neither her belief in that returned love nor her own feelings, even as her mother and Marianne advertise both, to Elinor's distress. She is considerably more upset when she learns that Edward is secretly engaged to Lucy Steele, a scheming young woman who accosts Elinor with this information as a method of warning her off of her fiancé. Yet even in the face of this galling adversity, Elinor manages to keep outwardly calm and circumspect, saying nothing of her own feelings and hiding her inner emotional turmoil.

In the meantime, Marianne's emotional volatility has caused her to fall quickly into a romance with the dashing John Willoughby. Her behavior is the counterpoint to Elinor's: rash where Elinor's is cautious; open where Elinor's is discreet. Even Marianne's immediate immersion into love and passion reflects its opposite in Elinor's measured and slow-to-blossom affections. When Willoughby leaves for London, the sisters' mother is convinced that he and Marianne are secretly engaged because Marianne has visited his private quarters and given him a lock of her hair. Elinor, deliberate in her method of drawing conclusions, is not so sure, yet hopes this is true, since Marianne's behavior would be extremely imprudent if given without a firm offer of marriage.

When Elinor and Marianne are invited to visit London, Marianne is willing to tolerate Mrs. Jennings' vulgar hospitality in order to get a chance to see Willoughby. Elinor, loath to meet the engaged Edward Ferrars, is less enthusiastic, but agrees to go for Marianne's sake. Elinor suspects Willoughby of no longer having a serious interest in Marianne when he doesn't come to call despite several letters from her. But the trusting Marianne is unconvinced even when he publicly snubs her. It takes a cold, dismissive letter from Willoughby announcing his engagement to another woman to make her realize that he has played her false. Unlike Elinor, who suffers in silence, Marianne's distress is both dramatic and overt.

Elinor spends her time comforting her sister, stoically concealing her own broken heart. Because Lucy Steele tells Elinor of her engagement to Edward Ferrars "in confidence," Elinor feels honor-bound to maintain that confidentiality.

Finally, Edward's mother learns of his engagement to Lucy and disinherits him. She had disfavored a match with Elinor but would have preferred her to the impoverished, socially inferior Lucy.

Elinor, freed from her vow of silence, can finally share the information with her sister, who feels profoundly guilty at her own emotional excesses, and admires Elinor more than ever when she realizes how much Elinor has suffered in silence. Soon thereafter, Elinor and Marianne attempt to return home, and Marianne becomes seriously ill. Elinor nurses her back to health, and is soon rewarded for all her sacrifices – Edward returns to her with the news that Lucy has married his brother, and asks for her hand. Both recognize that he is unable to support a wife until he reconciles with his mother, which he does, and the two marry soon thereafter.

Card Interpretation

The Lady of Coins can sometimes be seen as unfeeling, because she is in such external control of her emotions. When this card appears in a reading, you may be feeling emotional tumult on the inside, but not allowing yourself the luxury of indulging in a public acknowledgment of your real sentiments. However, you might also be perceiving things as being more negative than they actually are. Even when you are supremely happy, you don't over-enthuse, but maintain an outer serenity.

Elinor recognizes Willoughby for what he is long before Marianne does, because she notes his behaviors with an impartial eye, despite her genuine liking for the man and her hopes that he will be worthy of her sister. You, too, as the Lady of Coins, are likely an astute judge of character, because you observe an individual's actions, and are not misled or seduced by false words. Denial and delusion hold no appeal for you.

The Lady of Coins does not demand dramatic displays of affection, but likes to see palpable symbols of love. In *Sense and Sensibility*, Elinor is pleased when she thinks Edward wears her hair in his ring, and is dismayed when she discovers it is not hers, but Lucy Steele's.

The Lady of Coins is a hard worker and caretaker. When Elinor nurses Marianne, or handles family concerns, she does so with diligence and no expectation – or receipt – of gratitude.

While no mercenary, she recognizes the importance of money. Elinor cares not for grandeur, which she recognizes "has but little to do with happiness". She values art and nature; when fantasizing about great wealth, Elinor suggests she would use it to obtain "every print of merit". She is practical and will not marry someone unable to support her. We no longer live in a time when a woman must depend on a man's earning capacity, but this card suggests an individual who is a pragmatist when it comes to finances.

The Lady of Coins represents someone who is no conformist, but is also not someone who

makes waves. She keeps her opinions to herself – but she keeps them.

What Would Jane Do

"My doctrine has never aimed at the subjection of understanding. All I have ever attempted to influence has been the behavior... When have I advised you to adopt their sentiments or conform to their judgment in serious matters?"

Jane Austen, *Sense and Sensibility*

Jane's Advice: Be sure to keep your own counsel and your individual values. You need not, however, advertise them to the entire county. Prudence and patience, combined with practicality, are not merely their own reward, but help one to attain one's just deserts. The sound of a rattle signifies nothing, but the dulcet tones of measured harmony fall gently on every ear.

Lord of Coins

Colonel Brandon (Sense and Sensibility)

Card Description

Colonel Brandon, a flannel vest underneath his brown waistcoat, is seated and looks out the window. Outside is a beautiful, lush-but-manicured garden – the grounds are extensive. The room in which he overlooks his estate is old-fashioned and well-appointed, but not ostentatious, with leather chairs and leather-bound books shelved on the walls. The floor is covered by an oriental rug. His face is impassive, but his hand covers his heart, indicating that he is capable of deep, if undisplayed, emotion. His "throne" is a roomy leather chair, one that is both comfortable and solid.

Storyline

Our first impression of Colonel Brandon is that of a solid, stolid individual, hardly the stuff of what heroes are made. Marianne Dashwood, the young woman he falls in love with in an unprecipitate manner atypical of a Lord of Coins, certainly doesn't see him in a heroic, or even romantic, light.

"He was silent and grave. His appearance however was not unpleasing, in spite of his being in the opinion of Marianne… an absolute old bachelor, for he was on the wrong side of five and thirty; but though his face was not handsome, his countenance was sensible, and his address was particularly gentlemanlike".

Still, when she plays on the pianoforte, he is the only one who says nothing, but actually pays "her only the compliment of attention; and she felt a respect for him on the occasion." Although it is obvious to others that Colonel Brandon is interested in Marianne, she describes him as "infirm" and says, quite seriously, that while he isn't quite ready for the graveyard, his altered age of thirty-five has "nothing to do with matrimony". He even wears a flannel waistcoat, which she perceives as a sign of "aches, cramps, rheumatisms, and every species of ailment that can afflict the old and the feeble", instead of the sober and practical action emblematic of Colonel Brandon's personality.

Elinor, Marianne's sister, esteems Colonel Brandon for his gentlemanly traits, noting that he is also well-traveled and well-read. She even berates Marianne for her dismissive attitude towards him, recognizing that Marianne doesn't value him because of the mundane nature of his qualities, negating him because he isn't a sensitive, artistic type.

This casual contempt does not deter Colonel Brandon from continuing to visit and spend time with Marianne; his affections grow regardless of her disregard. He invites their circle to visit his brother-in-law's estate, and includes Willoughby, the dashing man who appears to have attached himself to Marianne. However, Colonel Brandon must cancel the arrangement at the last minute – he has received a letter that mandates his immediate removal to London. He doesn't discuss the nature of his business, but it involves his ward, whom Willoughby has impregnated, which gives him additional concern for Marianne's emotional and personal safety.

When the Dashwood sisters come to London, primarily so that Marianne can see Willoughby again, Colonel Brandon asks Elinor if rumors that Marianne is engaged are true, yet does not divulge his ward's situation. It is only when Willoughby's engagement to another woman is public knowledge that Brandon shares what Willoughby truly is and has done, and he tells the story only to ease Marianne's broken heart, not to curry favor by destroying his competition. When Marianne falls ill, Brandon rides to her rescue, though not so dramatically as Willoughby has earlier in the novel: he merely travels to her home to bring her mother to her. Marianne heals emotionally as well as physically, and begins to recognize the sterling qualities of the infirm, over-the-hill Colonel Brandon. When the novel ends, their marriage promises the greatest of happiness for both parties.

Card Interpretation

Colonel Brandon is steadfast in his love for Marianne, even when it seems unlikely that his feelings will ever be returned. He is ultimately rewarded for his devotion. When you receive this card in a reading, it indicates that you are utterly loyal once you bestow your affections, and dogged in your pursuit of them. The expression, "Slow and steady wins the race" is apropos when it comes to your mode of behavior. You may not shower someone with streams of pleasant words and dramatic gestures, but you can always be relied on, in both good times and bad.

Brandon withholds the story of his ward's pregnancy until there can be no question that his sharing the information is in Marianne's best interest, and not his own. As a Lord of Coins, your integrity is of the highest caliber and you know how to maintain confidences. You are both discreet and an individual of few words, but you mean every one that you say.

The Lord of Coins is someone whose wealth is often for what they are best known. Even so, "security" and "comfort" are what matter most to Colonel Brandon and there is nothing extravagant or flashy about him. You might be very well-off, or simply "comfortable," but money is neither your bane nor your master. Even if you don't wear a flannel waistcoat, you are sensible about your finances, your health, and your lifestyle. You may not receive the acclaim you deserve when someone first meets you, but your sterling qualities are eventually discerned by all who get to know you. Just as Colonel Brandon listened silently to Marianne's playing but appreciated it with the greatest sensitivity of anyone in attendance, still waters run deep in your case. Quietly, you observe everything, even things that are neither concrete nor obvious.

What Would Jane Do?

"Colonel Brandon was now as happy, as all those who best loved him, believed he deserved to be…"

Jane Austen, *Sense and Sensibility*

Jane's Advice: Patience is a virtue that often earns its own reward, especially when companied with the coin of the realm. Steady behavior, applied steadily, can provide you with the material gifts you seek. But the last thing you need is the advice of an impoverished spinster – your own sagacity can not be questioned, as your heart's desire has been achieved, again and again.

Reading with the
Jane Austen Tarot

Tarot of Jane Austen

How to Use the Cards

There are many ways to use the Jane Austen Tarot. Beginners will find that pulling a daily card is a painless way to learn the cards. While mastering the tarot takes time, journaling about one card image and what it might mean on a symbolic and literal level is valuable. In the morning, shuffle and select one card and describe it in your journal. Keep it in mind during the day as you observe occurrences and qualities/behaviors that relate to that image. That night, note those connections in your journal. Once a week, re-read your notes – you might see issues and concerns presaged by your daily readings.

More experienced readers often use layouts (also called spreads) to examine an issue more fully. Familiarity with the cards, and comparing and contrasting them with other cards in a layout allows you to interpret them with detail and specificity.

Receiving a majority of Major Arcana cards in a spread may reflect that you (or the person you are reading for, sometimes referred to as the querent) are experiencing some life-changing and life-challenging lessons. A predomination of a particular suit can also indicate an emphasis on that suit's domain. If your spread contains a number of Candlesticks, energy, passion, enthusiasm, and movement are highlighted. Teacups reflect emotions, love, relationships, as well as the psychic realm: dreams and the properties of the sixth sense. Several Quills in a reading might suggest a detached, intellectual approach is called for, or that the thinking mode is currently predominating in your life. Coins refer to all that is tangible, including your physical senses and surroundings, health, and work. An overview of a spread can help you to decipher the general message or trend of the reading, with individual cards giving you more specific answers.

While social mores have changed since Jane Austen's books were written, her understanding of the human condition transcends time; her timeless wisdom makes her a perfect choice for the High Priestess card. Additionally, Austen's emphasis on truly appropriate social deportment is based on an internal wellspring of probity and grace. This, in conjunction with Austen's modernity in valuing the individual human spirit, allows us to create relevant spreads based on her novels, since the inherent values contained within them assist us now in successfully structuring our own lives with harmonious and principled symmetry.

Many people think of Austen as the original and greatest writer of the romance novel. While it is true that love and marriage are primary plot points, the importance of money and even right livelihood are central to her work as well. Since these are often the primary subjects on querents' minds, the following spreads, all based on Austen's writings, providing a template for answering these universal concerns. However, you are free to alter them or design your own spreads, customizing them to specific issues and questions you (or a querent) may have.

Love and Friendship Spread

The following spread is based on the characters and their qualities in *Pride and Prejudice*. It is a good layout to use when you have a specific new romantic prospect in mind.

Card 1 – What is most intriguing (Darcy-esque) to me about him/her?

Card 2 – What is hidden or concealed (Wickham-esque) in his/her character?

Card 3 – In what ways are we most pleasing to and harmonious with (Bingley-esque) one another?

Card 4 – What is foolish or buffoon-like (Collins-esque) about him/her?

Card 5 – Is a long-term relationship (like the Bennetts') with this person wise or foolish?

Alternately, if you are wondering what you should be looking for in a partner, you can redo the questions, keeping the nature of the characters in mind.

Card 1 – What would I find most intriguing (Darcy-esque) in a partner?

Card 2 – What must I be careful to observe (Wickham-esque) in his/her character, to know if he/she is sincere?

Card 3 – What qualities should we share in order for harmony to reign (Bingley and Jane-esque)?

Card 4 – What obvious flaw can I learn to adjust to or live with (the Collinses)?

Card 5 – What qualities or goals must we share for our relationship to last for the long-term (like the Bennetts')?

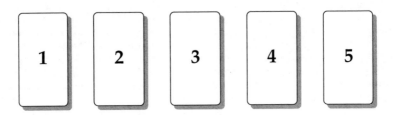

Reading with the Jane Austen Tarot

The Power of Persuasion Spread

If you and your partner are having a disagreement, this layout, based on *Persuasion*, may help you to achieve some clarity on the issue:

Card 1 – My thoughts on the issue

Card 2 – My partner's thoughts on the issue

Card 3 – Influences on my opinion (background, advice of family and friends, current situation in life)

Card 4 – Influences on his/her opinion (background, advice of family and friends, current situation in life)

Card 5 – What can keep us apart on this issue?

Card 6 – What will bring us together on this issue?

Be sure to look at the way each pair works together (or conflicts), as it will shed additional light on the best way to come to a win-win agreement for you both.

In the tarot, the suit of Coins represents the material world and worldly success. *Sense and Sensibility* forms the basis for many of the Coins cards in the Jane Austen Tarot, so it was natural to draw upon the characters and situations from that book for this spread. Each card position is based on one of the Coins cards in the Jane Austen Tarot.

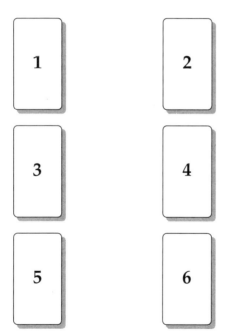

Sense and Sensibility Prosperity Spread

Card 1 – How can I begin to create prosperity in my life? (based on the Ace of Coins)

Card 2 – What must I balance in order to create prosperity in my life? (based on the Two of Coins)

Card 3 – Where do I need to cut back or be careful to budget in order to create prosperity in my life? (based on the Four of Coins)

Card 4 – What youthful mistake(s) do I need to avoid or rectify in order to create prosperity in my life? (based on the Knights of Teacups and Coins)

Card 5 – What inner resource(s) can I draw on to create prosperity in my life? (based on the Lady of Coins)

Card 6 – What outer resource(s) can I draw on to create prosperity in my life? (based on the Lord of Coins)

Card 7 – What romantic delusions do I have about the world that I need to cast off in order to create prosperity in my life? (based on the Maiden of Teacups, Four of Swords)

Card 8 – What life-changing event has taught me lessons I can use to transform my life and make it more prosperous? And what were those lessons? (based on Death)

I used this reading for an artist who is notorious for undercharging for her work and has issues surrounding prosperity and being paid what she is worth. Her cards were as follows:
Card 1: Ten of Teacups
Card 2: The High Priestess
Card 3: Justice
Card 4: Five of Quills
Card 5: Six of Candlesticks
Card 6: Lady of Coins
Card 7: Eight of Coins
Card 8: The Wheel

One thing the querent can do in order to begin to create prosperity in her life is to utilize her families, both her family of origin and her chosen family (her husband, her close friends). Instead of being the one to nurture them and

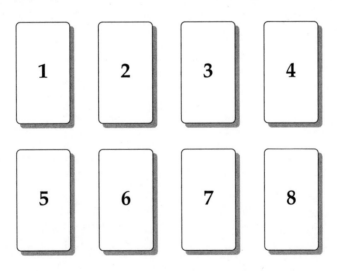

ensure their worlds are comfortable and filled with rainbows (Ten of Teacups), the querent needs to ask others to help her create a foundation in which she can create her beloved art. Because she is so used to sensing her family's needs, she expects it to be reciprocal. They would be willing to help her, but she needs to let them know specifically what she wants and needs.

The querent intuits what she needs, but she tends to be silent about it. She could take a lesson from Jane Austen (the High Priestess), whose only family duty was handling breakfast, giving her time to write. The querent needs to act on what she knows at her deepest core, which is that her art deserves a wider audience. She needs to balance her need for introversion (the part of creating that she loves) with the necessary interactions with people in order to promote her art. Some of this she can pass on to family members; Jane Austen's father and brother handled many of her publishing negotiations and transactions.

In order for her to create prosperity in her life, the querent is going to have to re-think her views on fairness and equity (Justice) when it comes to the marketplace. The querent prices her work as she would like other artists to price theirs – but, of course, they don't. She is so concerned about being fair to others that she is unfair to one person: herself. She also needs to recognize that some of her more time-intensive work is not going to be as lucrative as mass-producing some of her other items. She will have to learn to balance her own desires as an artist with what people want to buy.

As a child, the querent endured negativity and cutting remarks (Five of Quills) from her mother, and this impacted her self-esteem. In addition, she later became part of a culture that thrived on self-deprecation. Humility is a survival technique that no longer serves her, particularly as an artist.

One inner resource the querent forgets is that she really likes to compete and win (Six of Candlesticks). She is happy to expend whatever effort is necessary in order to triumph. This inner resource can be channeled for success in her field.

In the Lady of Coins, the querent has the gift of creating art itself – it's depicted in the very image! Her talent is enough to bring her success. In addition, there may be a practical, sensible woman of her acquaintance who could help her with the mundane aspects of marketing her work.

The delusion the querent must rid herself of is that of having to do everything herself. Like Anne Elliot, she is able to do many things so capably that she takes on many responsibilities (Eight of Coins). However, the business (Coins) aspect is something the querent dislikes, and she either has to steel herself to do it or get some help from friends and family. There is even a middle ground, where she does some of it, but gets assistance from others. The querent needs to find a healthy balance that works for her and those around her.

In the past, the querent has transformed on numerous occasions, as the wheel of life has turned. She has changed partners, homes, cultures, and careers (The Wheel). She has recently come to another passage in her life, and can take what she has learned in adapting to those changes to triumph in a new phase – that of the successful artist.

The preponderance of Major Arcana cards lets us know that a major life change is knocking at the querent's door – and the absence of Teacups indicates that this isn't about the querent's feelings. The changes she needs to make are in the way she thinks and physically acts – and that will move her in the spiritual direction she so desires.

The Bildungsroman Spread

The term Bildungsroman refers to a specific literary genre, the novel of education/ formation within the context of a defined social order. The principal subject is the moral, psychological, and intellectual development of a usually youthful main character. Jane Austen's novels are all Bildungsromans. This spread utilizes the vessel of story, as well as the ingredients for self-actualization.

1. Protagonist – the person for whom the reading is conducted

2. Theme – the theme or current life-lesson of the protagonist

3. Right Partner – qualities/characteristics of the "ideal" partner for the protagonist

4. Work Ethic/Fulfillment – the kind of work that will fulfill the protagonist

5. Healthy Connection to/Understanding of Roots – Approach to making peace with the past

6. Spiritual Fulfillment – What the protagonist needs to attain spiritual satisfaction

Those of you who study the esoteric tarot recognize that these four levels of "formation," interestingly enough, correspond to the Kabbalistic four worlds: Right partnership/Yetzirah; Work ethic/fulfillment, Briah; Value of Roots, Assiyah; and Spiritual Fulfillment, Atziluth.

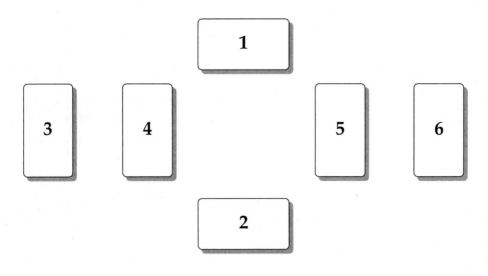

The Künstlerroman Spread

A variation for artists on the previous spread is the Künstlerroman Spread.
A Künstlerroman is similar to the Bildungsroman, but speaks to the artist's path of formation.
I recently used this spread for a writer who was planning a major revision of a novel. Her cards were as follows:

Card 1: The Maiden of Candlesticks
Card 2: The Lord of Teacups
Card 3: Nine of Coins
Card 4: Six of Quills
Card 5: Queen of Coins
Card 6: The Lovers

The Maiden of Candlesticks represents the querent/author. We conducted the reading during summer (the season of Candlesticks), a period in which she had spent more time seeking pleasure than working seriously on her novel. In part, this is because she measures spiritual fulfillment in terms of her loved ones (Lord of Teacups) and her sons were home from college. Even though the querent/author loves the editing process, she had begun to see her work as a burden. The Maiden of Candlesticks will do anything to avoid something she sees as dull drudgery.

We talked about ways to re-stoke the fire of creativity and rekindle her spiritual intentions based on other cards in the reading. Also, with the appearance of two Coin cards in the reading, one of which was the Lady (as opposed to the Maiden), we determined that practicality and physical effort needed to be priorities in order for the querent to complete her manuscript as desired. This would help in the desired transition from Maiden to Lady. Finally, the querent needed to be a bit more selfish, like the Maiden of Candlesticks. Her children are nearly adults, and she no longer has to subsume her needs in order to take care of her family.

The "right partner" or form she needed was the Nine of Coins, the card of home and hearth-loving. Because the writer follows a shamanic practice, we discussed her doing her morning meditation outside, with a notebook for her to jot down any book-related ideas. If feasible, she could even do some writing outside. This would feed her spirit and re-light her creative fire. Interestingly, this card looks like autumn, the season we were about to enter. The obvious meaning of this card was for the querent to stay home more, and put in the physical time to re-write her novel.

The Six of Quills showed the positive and negative aspects of the querent's work ethic/motivation. On one hand, it depicted her mental travels, as her imagination is an important part of her vision as a novelist. The card itself reminded her of a favorite childhood novel, *Treasure Island*. It also illustrated the concept that completing the novel would assist her financially, moving her into "smoother waters."

The negative aspect of this card spoke to her frequent fantasies about travel, fantasies that seem much more enticing than the reality of sitting at her computer pounding out words. We tried to focus on the pleasures of imaginary mental trips, as well as their resulting funds leading to actual physical vacations to interesting lands.

It was easy to see the connection between the form and the integration of roots into her art, as the Lady of Coins is able to manifest the daily application the Nine of Coins demands. This card also represented the querent's mother, who taught her through her expert needlework how to create things of beauty, as well as modeling a willingness to rip apart and redo any physical imperfections. In addition, her mother's love of solitude allowed her to be disciplined and productive, something the querent admired.

The only Major Arcana card fell in the position of Spiritual Fulfillment. The Lovers speaks to discernment and choice. When Darcy picks Lizzy over Caroline, he is choosing a challenge, a woman who must be earned, not an easily-won conquest. The querent needs to accept that, in order to write the book she wants, she has to take the worthwhile, but more challenging path.

The Bildungsroman and Künstlerroman spreads are innately suited to utilizing card connections (see below) to supplement interpretations.

Card Connections

When a reader uses a tarot spread, s/he tries to tell the "story" of it to the querent. What are the querent's characteristics, particularly the ones that impact the current situation? One determines the plot, which is advanced via the Minor Arcana, and the theme or pattern or life-lesson, which is represented by the Majors. The Court Cards are the dramatis personae, expressing qualities and flaws, even personality quirks. The querent's characteristics not only infuse the situation with his or her essence, they can suggest approaches to make sure the story has a happy – or, at least, a best-case-scenario – ending.

Those readers who use an image-based style can gain additional symbolic insights. Does an animal or other symbol repeat in the reading? What color(s) predominate in the cards? Which way are the characters facing, and do they face one another or look away from each other? What does that tell you about the situation or the individuals' mindsets? All of these observable details add to the complexity of your reading.

Many advanced readers analyze the composition of a spread, tabulating overtly or covertly, the number of Majors, Minors, and Court Cards, as well as noting which suit(s) predominate and if there are multiple numerologically-related cards (for example: even in a 10-card spread, The Lovers and a pair of sixes would emphasize reciprocity, if that is the reader's keyword for the sixes).

Much like a well-designed carpet, these interwoven threads enable the reader to easily recognize patterns, giving the reading resonance and cohesion. The Jane Austen Tarot, composed as it is of characters and scenes from the author's oeuvre, offers additional intricacies in the area of association. Numerous cards are connected by the fact that they share a distinct, discrete world – the novels on which they are based. And, in most cases, Austen has provided specific interactions between each of the characters in the novels (and their card counterparts).

You can separate the cards by the novels on which they are based (available in the synopses section). You might note that 21 cards are based on *Pride and Prejudice*, Austen's most popular novel. If two cards based on that novel appear in a spread, you can enhance the reading by thinking about how those two characters/situations interact with one another and weave that backstory into your reading.

Below you will find three of these possible combination interpretations using the Fool. The card is based on Elizabeth Bennett's "foolhardy" walk to Netherfield, which she takes in order to ascertain that her beloved sister is being cared for properly. Her fate is altered by this "leap of faith."

* The Fool/The Hierophant (based on Mr. Collins' character) – The Hierophant wants the Fool to be more traditional and circumspect; the Fool has no use for the Hierophant's tired platitudes or concern for external appearances

* The Fool/The Lovers (the triangle of Elizabeth, Caroline Bingley, and Mr. Darcy) – The Fool's appeal lies in her atypical, uncalculated behavior and style, and the querent might want to play to that appeal – premeditation is not her friend. For the Fool (querent) to even consider settling down, understanding and appreciation of his/her unique qualities is essential.

* The Fool/The Hermit (Mr. Bennett) – Kindred spirits, these two. They both seek "the road less traveled" and have individual concepts of integrity and what constitutes "good society." The Fool is considerably more interested in human interaction than The Hermit.

Now – how might these play out in a spread? If the querent's "Past" card is The Fool and the Present is The Hermit, we would know that the querent might have taken some risky steps in the past that have led to solitude and reflection. That possible scenario would be suggested by any deck. Add the *Pride and Prejudice* storyline, and we can add some additional insights. The querent might have been too trusting (à la Lizzy's original feelings for Wickham) and now needs to be a bit more vigilant (unlike Mr. Bennett, who rues his decision of allowing Lydia to go to Brighton unchaperoned).

If, however, the querent's "Past" card is The Fool and the "Present" is the Hierophant, in addition to the traditional meanings of someone who used to be more carefree, but is now more interested in tradition or a serious approach to religion or spirituality, we see that the querent must watch out for pomposity or ponderousness.

While I could detail each combination, I would have to write another book to do so. I leave each reader to think about and create his or her own combinations. If you are familiar with Austen's work, this card combining will immediately give you a distinct advantage in learning to read with the Jane Austen Tarot.

Finally, I include a template for you to use when analyzing any tarot spread, in order to more clearly see the card connections and use them to enrich your readings.

Card Connections Checklist

Spread layout:

Suit/Elemental Connections between the cards:
Candlesticks/Fire:
Teacups/Water:
Quills/Air:
Coins/Earth:

Repeating Numbers:

Card Analysis:
Majors:
Minors:
Courts:

Image-based Connections:
Repeating colors:
Repeating Symbols:
Directions:
Mood:

# of Reversals:

Story Connections:

Synopses

These
synopses of Jane
Austen's books are
provided for two reasons.
For those who have not read all
of her novels, they serve as an
overview for putting the cards into
context. For those who have read some
or all of the Austen oeuvre, the capsule
summaries include a list all of the cards
and the books on which they are based,
forming a sort of "cheatsheet" for seeing the
connections between the cards at a glance.

The synopses are woefully inadequate in
terms of conveying the flavor of Austen's
work or even providing a full accounting
of the books. I urge you to read all of
Austen's work if you want to enrich
your understanding and
perspective of these cards – and,
of course, have the great
pleasure of reading the
books themselves.

Emma

The Empress, The Wheel of Fortune, Temperance, The Moon, The Sun, Judgment, The World, Ace of Teacups, Seven of Teacups, Nine of Teacups, Two of Quills, Five of Quills, Maiden of Quills, Knight of Quills, Three of Coins, Seven of Coins, Nine of Coins

Young Emma Woodhouse believes she has nothing to gain from marriage because she is very well-off and the complete mistress of her father's house. She takes pride in having arranged a match between her governess, who had served as a mother figure-cum-dear friend and companion, and Mr. Weston, a sociable widower. Once they marry, Emma's loneliness motivates her to become friendly with the pretty and very romantic Harriet Smith, a young woman of mysterious family origins.

Because Emma sees now herself as a successful matchmaker, she determines next that the local rector, Mr. Elton, would be a fine match for her new friend. Neighbor and family friend George Knightley scoffs at Emma's alleged credit for arranging nuptials, but she ignores his advice and convinces Harriet to reject a proposal from her current suitor, Robert Martin, in favor of the socially superior Elton. Harriet, with a soupçon of regret, obliges and transfers her romantic fantasies to Mr. Elton.

Mr. Knightley thinks Robert Martin is a fine match for Harriet and encouraged him to propose to her. He is dismayed to learn that Emma has higher hopes for her friend, as he is disappointed for Mr. Martin. Mr. Knightley believes Elton will never marry Harriet and says as much to Emma, who is sure she knows better than he does, based on his attentiveness to Harriet. When Emma drew a picture of Harriet, Elton offered to have it framed and writes a clever joke that alludes to a romantic interest.

Emma is confident that she knows best how to read these signs and is under the impression that her matchmaking efforts are paying off when Mr. Elton proposes – to her! She rejects him, but reserves her sympathy for Harriet, whom she has lured into heartache. She tries to atone for her misguided attempts at matchmaking by finding Harriet another lover, though she has learned from her mistake to be less overt about it. While Emma (and the Westons) had initially considered Mrs. Weston's soon-to-be rich young stepson, Frank Churchill, as a romantic prospect for herself, Emma generously transfers him – in her mind and hopes – to Harriet.

Harriet grieves for the loss of Mr. Elton, who quickly rebounds from Emma's rejection by marrying an overbearing but wealthy woman from another town. When Harriet acknowledges soon thereafter that she is attracted to another man, Emma wrongly assumes it is Frank. Since he rescued them both from being importuned by gypsies and is charming and clever, she is sure that romantic Harriet couldn't resist such actions. One thing Emma and Frank have in common is their delight in discussing Jane Fairfax, a young woman whom Emma somewhat resents for being held up as a paragon of accomplishment. Frank suggests Miss Fairfax might have a married admirer, and Emma encourages his naughty gossip. At another gathering, Mr. Elton snubs Harriet by refusing to dance with her and Mr. Knightley, despite opining that Harriet is a rather silly woman, asks her to dance. Emma is proud but not surprised that Mr. Knightley does this – she knows he is a gentleman with a truly chivalrous nature, despite his brusque exterior.

Emma also encourages Harriet to think herself worthy of a man like Frank Churchill – after all, Harriet is far superior to the silly, prideful Mrs. Elton. At a picnic, Frank teases Jane Fairfax about a gift from a mysterious admirer and flirts shamelessly with Emma. She not only basks in his attentions, but behaves rudely to Jane Fairfax's annoyingly loquacious, but kind aunt, Miss Bates. Mr. Knightley reproves Emma for her behavior; she is distraught because she knows she has deserved to lose his good opinion of her.

Mrs. Elton obtains a governess job for Jane Fairfax without her permission. Jane needs to make a living but cringes from the thought of taking on such a position. However, after the picnic, she agrees to do so. Mr. Knightley learns Emma has made gracious gestures to both Miss Bates and Jane Fairfax and is proud of her, even though Miss Fairfax has politely rejected Emma's overtures.

Shortly thereafter, Frank Churchill writes to the Westons with some shocking news: he has secretly been engaged to Jane Fairfax all along, but needed to receive his guardian's blessing before making the engagement public. Emma gets another unpleasant surprise when she humbly begs Harriet's pardon for encouraging a romance between herself and Frank, and it turns out that Harriet's object of desire is Mr. Knightley.

Emma is appalled, but has only herself to blame for Harriet's belief that she is worthy of Mr. Knightley – Emma had supported, even created, that inappropriate self-confidence. As Emma spends a dark night realizing how many mistakes she has made, the biggest one comes to light: she doesn't want Harriet to marry Mr. Knightley for the simple reason that she wants him for herself. Until then, Emma hadn't realized how much she loves him.

When Mr. Knightley comes to visit the next day, Emma fears that he will tell her that he loves Harriet and avoids such a personal discussion. Finally, Emma allows him to speak, and Mr. Knightley confesses his love for her and asks her to marry him. While Emma feels badly that Harriet will suffer, she's not foolish enough to think of giving up her own happiness. Fortunately, after a very short period, Harriet decides it is really Robert Martin whom she loves, after all. More fortunate still, he has been patiently waiting for her to return his love and has asked her again for her hand in marriage.

One thing still stands in the way of Emma and Mr. Knightley's joy. Mr. Woodhouse, Emma's father, hates change and wishes Emma to honor her oft-repeated decision to never marry. Mr. Woodhouse tries to prolong the inevitable, until minor robberies in the neighborhood convince him that it would be a good thing if Mr. Knightley comes to live with them, after all.

Lady Susan

The Devil, Nine of Candlesticks

Lady Susan – a beautiful, manipulative widow reminiscent of Madame de Merteuil in *Les Liaisons Dangereuses* – has deposited her daughter, Frederica, into a boarding school, hoping to forcibly persuade her to marry a rich buffoon, Sir James Martin, who, like many men, has fallen prey to Lady Susan's wiles. When Lady Susan is ousted from a friend's home for sleeping with said friend's husband, she takes refuge at the home of Charles and Catherine Vernon, her brother and sister-in-law.

The estate was once Lady Susan's, but when her husband died, it was entailed to his younger brother. Lady Susan made no secret of her resentment at the time, so Catherine is forewarned about her character, yet Lady Susan's decorous behavior initially inclines her sister-in-law to be charitable. However, this inclination turns to dismay when Lady Susan's daughter runs away from school and Catherine observes that Frederica is terrorized by her mother, who is also busy seducing Reginald de Courcy, Catherine's beloved brother.

Frederica has been forbidden to disclose to her aunt or uncle that her mother is trying to force her to marry against her will. Out of desperation, Frederica writes a note to Reginald asking him to intercede for her with her mother – since Lady Susan never considered the possibility that her timid daughter would have the temerity to consider him as a potential resource. Lady Susan is furious, and allows her true self to briefly emerge. Reginald decides against marrying her when he sees her for what she is. Lady Susan ultimately must marry Sir James Martin herself, in order to salvage what is left of her reputation, and Frederica and Reginald eventually wed.

Mansfield Park

The Magician, The Emperor, The Chariot, Strength, The Hanged One, Two of Candlesticks, Three of Candlesticks, Three of Cups, Four of Cups, Six of Cups, Eight of Cups, Seven of Swords, Eight of Swords

Fanny Price is Austen's most moral – and least sparkling – protagonist. At the age of 10, Fanny is brought to live with her wealthy aunt and uncle, the Bertrams, and their four children at Mansfield Park. She is shy and misses her family, her brother William in particular. Mrs. Bertram is not unkind, but she is self-absorbed and has no time for anyone but herself. Sir Thomas Bertram is distant, stern, and intimidating. The eldest son, Tom, and the daughters of the house, Maria and Julia, feel superior to Fanny and do little to welcome her into their world. The only one who is kind to the scared little girl is the younger son, Edmund Bertram. He ensures she has what she needs to write to William and generally looks out for her welfare.

Fanny develops into a quiet and pretty young woman, one who is obedient and eager to please her adoptive family. She is also in love with her cousin Edmund, who has been so kind to her. Not particularly strong herself, she serves as a helper to her Aunt Bertram. She also frequently does chores and runs errands for her other aunt, Mrs. Norris, a woman who prides herself on her good works, but who really manipulates others to spend their money while she holds on tightly to her own. Edmund has continued to watch out for Fanny over the years, and has even bought her a horse so that she can get exercise.

Sir Thomas leaves with Tom to oversee some business interests in Antigua. Other changes take place in the established order of their lives. The Grants move into the Mansfield Park parsonage, bringing with them Mrs. Grant's nephew and niece, Henry and Mary Crawford. While Maria has a rich but dim beau in James Rushworth, both she and Julia are immediately infatuated with the charming and flirtatious

Henry Crawford and compete for his attentions; Mary has captivated Edmund with equal ease. Soon she and Edward are riding together, Mary appropriating Fanny's special horse with Edmund's permission. All of this is quite painful to Fanny, who suffers in silence.

Mrs. Norris has done everything she can to further a match between Maria and James Rushworth, and plans a family visit to his home, Sotherton. She wants to cement her worth in the eyes of Sir Thomas by arranging a financially beneficial marriage for Maria – but she is quick to use the connection for her own personal advantage as well. The Crawfords are from the city, and, as such, are a bit spoiled and cynical. Henry takes delight in making two sisters compete for his attentions, and Mary determines that she should ensnare Tom, since he is the eldest brother and will inherit Mansfield Park. While she has feelings for Edmund that she can not deny, his insistence on joining the church (with no potential of social or financial growth) makes him completely unacceptable to her. She tries repeatedly to make him change his planned vocation through mockery and persuasion.

When Maria becomes engaged to Mr. Rushworth, she does not stop flirting with Henry. Edmund sacrifices his own place to ensure that Fanny is able to go to Sotherton. Henry and Maria end up in a private tête-a-tête on the grounds, while Fanny is left quite alone and ignored. When they leave, Maria teases her Aunt Norris, who is carrying a pile of gifts, about "sponging" off the Rushworths.

Edmund wants Fanny to share his good opinion of Mary Crawford and hears only what he wants to hear when they discuss her. Tom returns home early from Antigua, accompanied by a friend, Mr. Yates, and they determine to put on a play, *Lover's Vows*. It is a somewhat racy play, and while everyone else is eager to act in it, Edmund and Fanny refuse on moral grounds: they are sure that Sir Thomas would not approve. Mary convinces Edmund to participate, but no one can change Fanny's mind. The play gives Maria and Henry more opportunities for flirtation while they "practice their lines," and Edmund and Mary use their time together similarly, both of them becoming quite infatuated with one another. When Sir Thomas comes home right before the play is to take place, he puts a stop to it immediately.

Sir Thomas is outraged that his own office has been used for the purpose of putting on a play, and worries what other silliness has occurred while he has been away. He hadn't expected his wife to do very much, but Mrs. Norris, whom he expected to keep order and decorum in his absence, has disappointed him.

The glowering presence of Sir Thomas convinces Mr. Yates to make himself scarce, and Henry Crawford soon leaves the area, as well. Realizing that he is not about to make her an offer of marriage, Maria weds Mr. Rushworth, taking Julia with her on her honeymoon. With no other young women of her age available, Mary makes overtures of friendship to Fanny, and soon begins to really appreciate her. Fanny is fascinated with Mary against her will, but sees her flaws quite clearly. Fanny's clarity on that count is influenced by her undiluted partiality for her beloved cousin Edmund. Mary loves all things worldly, and Fanny prefers the purity of nature, but they find things to appreciate in the other.

When Henry returns, he decides to make Fanny fall in love with him for the sake of fun and ego. She has become even prettier, and he is bored. Fanny barely notices Henry – partially because she is in love with Edmund and partially because her uncle has permitted her to invite her adored brother William to visit Mansfield Park.

Fanny takes great delight in spending time with William, who is equally happy to see her, though his focus is on his budding naval career. Sir Thomas is delighted to see Fanny blossoming, and holds a dance in her and William's honor. Henry manages to give Fanny a necklace through the auspices of his sister, but she'd prefer to wear the simpler one given to her by Edmund. Fanny's obvious disinterest, coupled with her looks and genuine goodness, causes the hunter to get captured by the game: Henry falls in love with her and asks her to marry him. Despite the fact that Fanny is poor and Henry could give her every social and financial oppor-

tunity, she rejects him. She is in love with Edmund, and she neither trusts, loves, nor respects Henry, whom she sees through when she bothers to think about him. It is painful to her on a number of levels when Edmund, Mary, and Sir Thomas all encourage and pressure her to accept Henry's marriage proposal. Fanny's rejection of him makes Henry all the more interested and eager to marry him, but Sir Thomas, who is concerned that Henry will lose interest, exiles Fanny to her birth family in Portsmouth for an extended visit, hoping that a reunion with miserable poverty will bring her to her senses.

While Fanny is disheartened by the disorder and chaos in her home, as well as the unsatisfying relationship she has with her parents, she sees that her sister Susan is eager to become more like her, and they bond, Fanny becoming Susan's mentor. When Henry comes to Portsmouth to renew his proposal, he is so solicitous of her and her circumstances are so depressing, she is tempted to accept. But her love for Edmund makes it impossible for her to do so, and Henry leaves with assurances that he will win her yet.

Tom becomes very ill and must return home from London, with even Lady Bertram exciting herself into concern over his condition. To make matters worse, Henry, who has returned to London, convinces the married Maria to run away with him, making her a social pariah. Mary blames Fanny for this turn of events – if she had accepted him, Henry wouldn't have behaved so badly. Even though Tom steadily improves, the Bertram family realizes how badly they need Fanny and Edmund comes to retrieve her from Portsmouth, along with sister Susan. Adding further excitement, Julia elopes with Mr. Yates – but at least neither of them is married.

Mary's response to Henry and Maria's immoral behavior is more amused than horrified or condemning. This response makes Edmund finally realize Mary is completely inappropriate for him and he ends his relationship with her, though his heart is broken. It mends relatively quickly; he soon realizes that Fanny is the perfect wife for him, and they wed.

Northanger Abbey

Five of Candlesticks, Knight of Candlesticks, Two of Cups, Nine of Swords

Northanger Abbey is Austen's most playful and ultimately most modern work, an affectionate but en pointe satire of the gothic novel. Catherine Morland is almost an anti-heroine; she is not particularly beautiful, rich, smart, or wise. Her family is neither obscenely wealthy nor ridiculously poor, she lives in the small town of Fullerton, and, is generally unremarkable in every way.

When Catherine is invited by her neighbors, the Allens, to accompany them to Bath, she is delighted to do so. She is almost immediately befriended by Isabella Thorpe, a pretty and adulatory young woman whose brother John is at school with Catherine's brother, James. Soon thereafter, Catherine meets Henry Tilney at a dance in the public rooms, and she finds is attracted to him immediately, although his wit is often incomprehensible to her more simple, direct sensibility. Her obvious captivation charms him, too. Bath is a much busier place than Fullerton, and soon John Thorpe and James Morland make their way there. John Thorpe seems quite loutish to Catherine, but as he is Isabella's brother and John's friend, she tries not to see it. James and Catherine are in agreement that Isabella is a wonderful girl – and Isabella seems as delighted with James as he with her.

That night, James asks Isabella to dance and Catherine has promised to dance with John, who has momentarily disappeared. When Henry Tilney asks her to dance, she wishes she could accept, and so is made even more miserable having to listen to John Thorpe's boring, self-absorbed patter. She does have the opportunity to meet Henry's sister, Eleanor.

The next day, Catherine hopes to become better acquainted with Eleanor Tilney, but is swept up almost against her will in plans with John, James, and Isabella. Because Catherine must ride with John Thorpe, she really has an unpleasant time and feels very frustrated. When she next dances with Henry, it is somewhat spoiled by John's insistence that she promised to dance with him. Catherine is soon much happier when she makes plans to go for a walk with Eleanor and Henry the next day.

However, John manipulates Catherine into believing Eleanor and Henry have forgotten their plans so that Catherine will join him, Isabella, and James on a trip to Blaize Castle. She really does want to go to Blaize Castle, but they ultimately don't have time to get to that desired place. Catherine apologizes and her genuine dismay breaks through his initial reserve. They plan to go for a walk the following day and Mr. Thorpe takes it upon himself to cancel the walk so they can go to Clifton together. Both Thorpes and John try to coerce her to break the engagement. This time, Catherine's conciliatory nature takes a back seat to her desire to honor her word (and see her beloved Henry Tilney!). She refuses, despite John's blustering harangues and James and Isabella's entreaties and attempts at evoking guilt.

The walk has the effect of increasing Catherine's admiration of Eleanor and Henry's superior intellect and charm, and Catherine meets their father, General Tilney, a gruff but courtly gentleman who seems delighted with her.

Isabella can't remain angry with Catherine either, because she has exciting news to share – she and James are engaged. Isabella hopes that the Morlands will approve the marriage and is anxious to be assured that they will. James rushes to Fullerton to discuss the marriage with his parents. In his absence, Henry's brother Captain Tilney comes to Bath and Isabella flirts outrageously with him, obviously infatuated. Everyone can see it but Catherine, who thinks Captain Tilney is the only culpable party, despite Henry's disagreement on the issue.

Soon, Catherine has something more exciting to consider. General Tilney has asked her to come and stay at Northanger Abbey, as company for Eleanor. After receiving permission from the Allens, who are returning home to Fullerton, and her parents via letter, she is en route with Henry as her driver. As they share a love of Gothic novels, he regales Catherine with a dramatic tale of what will happen to her at Northanger Abbey. While he is joking, she takes him quite seriously. When she comes across a mysterious box, she is sure it is filled with terrifying contents, but comes to discover they are rather prosaic. More importantly, she becomes convinced that General Tilney has killed his wife, based on certain of his behaviors and actions and a great deal of feverish imagination on Catherine's part. When Henry realizes that Catherine suspects his father of murdering his wife, he is shocked but is careful not to embarrass her too greatly after initially teasing her about her overactive imaginings.

Catherine receives a letter from James telling her that he finally had to break his engagement to Isabella. Isabella's preference for Captain Tilney is too marked, and, despite James' request, she refuses to end her relationship with him. Catherine is greatly grieved by this development, not realizing it is a result of Isabella considering Captain Tilney a superior financial prospect.

Unlike James, however, Captain Tilney is not interested in marriage and lets Isabella know that in no uncertain terms. Isabella is quick to contact Catherine to intercede for her with James, insisting that he had simply been irrationally jealous. Catherine has become sophisticated; she is not fooled by Isabella's smooth words and finally recognizes her for what she really is.

Even so, Catherine is shocked when General Tilney evicts her from Northanger Abbey with no prior explanation. He has openly encouraged her to form a union with his son, Henry, and she doesn't understand how she has offended him. General Tilney's treatment of her is truly worthy of a Gothic villain – he doesn't even ascertain whether she has the money to get home by herself. Eleanor, a true friend who is shocked and embarassed by her father's cruelty, gives her the funds to travel home.

When Catherine returns to Fullerton, her mother finds it odd that she has been sent home so unceremoniously, but doesn't ask many questions. Soon Henry Tilney comes to visit. He proposes marriage – but they will have to wait, because their marrying is against his father's wishes and he will not sanction it. General Tilney had mistakenly believed that Catherine was wealthy (the Thorpes were under the impression that this was so, explaining Isabella's initial avid interest in James), but when, by coincidence, he meets up with John Thorpe, he is told that the family is, in fact, impoverished. Consequently, General Tilney no longer wants them to marry.

Fortunately, Eleanor soon marries her childhood sweetheart, who has unexpectedly come into a title and a fortune. This unexpected bounty gives her enough influence on her father so that she is able to convince him to approve Henry's marriage to Catherine, and all ends happily.

Persuasion

The Tower, The Star, Ten of Candlesticks, King of Candlesticks, Six of Quills, Queen of Quills, Five of Coins, Six of Coins, Eight of Coins

Anne Elliot is a smart, sensitive, and sensible young woman whose family has none of these qualities. Her mother is deceased, and her father, Sir Walter, is a self-absorbed snob who has so wasted the family fortune that he must now rent the family seat, Kellynch Hall. Anne's elder sister Elizabeth is an arrogant and overbearing spinster who dwells on her own consequence and belittles Anne's, and her younger sister, Mary, is a whining hypochondriac. Mary is the only married sibling, and her spouse, Charles Musgrove, originally sought to marry Anne.

But Anne had turned him down. More than seven years before the story begins, Anne had been briefly engaged to Frederick Wentworth, and her heart has never wavered in its faithfulness to him. She broke off the engagement due to the advice of Lady Russell, a woman who had been a second mother to her. Lady Russell wanted her to break the engagement because Frederick was not Anne's social or financial equal; Anne became convinced it would be in Fredericks's best interest if he had no encumbrances. He joined the British navy to make his fortune when Anne broke their engagement, and did so quite angrily and resentfully; Anne is convinced that he will never forgive her.

When *Persuasion* begins, Anne is in her mid-twenties, considered "off the shelf" in terms of being marriageable. It is bad enough that she must content with leaving her family home, but she soon learns that the lessees are Frederick Wentworth's sister and brother-in-law, the Crofts. When Sir Walter and Elizabeth depart for Bath, they take the ingratiating Mrs. Clay for a companion, leaving Anne to visit Mary as a solace, as well as an unpaid nurse and caretaker.

A few weeks after Anne comes to stay with Mary, they visit the Crofts at Kellynch. They learn that Mrs. Croft's brother, Captain Frederick Wentworth, will be visiting them soon. In a stroke of coincidence, Frederick was the captain of Mary's now-deceased brother-in-law's ship, when he was in the Navy. When Frederick comes to visit Mary's Musgrove in-laws, he makes a good impression on the whole family. Charles' sisters, Henrietta and Louisa, are particularly taken with him, and it is evident to all that Frederick is looking for a wife. When Frederick first sees Anne, he comments that she is much-altered and that he wouldn't recognize her, making her feel old and dowdy. Her realization that now he is a far more eligible bachelor than she is a potential bride is painful, indeed.

Anne must watch as Frederick flirts with both Henrietta and Louisa at various social events, though she tries to avoid them. When they travel as a family to Lyme, it seems as if Louisa has captured Captain Wentworth's heart. When Louisa impetuously leaps off of a stone stairway into Frederick's arms, he catches her. She insists upon doing it again! This time she falls to the ground, leaving her unconscious. While all the others lose their heads in fluttering anxiety, Anne calmly organizes Louisa's rescue. After a visit from the doctor and an agonizing waiting period, Louisa slowly recovers, but must remain for an extended period of time in Lyme before she can be moved. Frederick's anxiety over Louisa's health is palpable. While this concern is due to guilt, rather than love, Anne has no way of knowing that and her heart suffers further anguish.

Anne joins her father and sister (and Mrs. Clay) in Bath; Lady Russell is there, as well. Anne's family is actively consumed in joining its "rightful" place in Bath society. They don't understand why she would spend time with Mrs. Smith, a former schoolmate, who is now an invalid and lives on the poor side of town. When Anne honors an engagement with her friend over a visit with the Dalrymples, her family is outraged. Meanwhile, Lady Russell confides to Anne her hopes that she (Anne) and her cousin William Elliot, who will inherit Kellynch, will fall in love and marry.

Elizabeth is sure that she would be a more suitable spouse for their cousin, even though he has spurned her once. His reputation had been that of a dissolute and debauched reprobate, but in Bath he seems rehabilitated and, as such, a highly sought after potential mate.

William seems more interested in Anne than Elizabeth, who barely notices the slight. Meanwhile, Bath becomes even more crowded, as the Crofts, with Captain Wentworth following behind, arrive, as do the Musgroves. When they attend a concert, Captain Wentworth observes William Elliot's pursuit of Anne. It is rumored in Bath that William and Anne are engaged, and, seeing William's obvious interest, Frederick is afraid that the rumors are true. On her next visit, Anne apprises her friend Mrs. Smith that she has no intention of marrying William Elliot. Mrs. Smith is then free to disclose that he is not rehabilitated at all – he is spending time there in order to ensure that Mrs. Clay doesn't marry Sir Walter and have children, as then he would no longer be in line to inherit Kellynch Hall. She even has evidence that William Elliot is an immoral and unjust man. Anne, who has remained constant to Frederick despite his evidenced interest in another woman, values the information, but never plans to accept William Elliot, despite Lady Russell's urgings to do so.

When Anne sees Frederick again at the Musgroves', they are surrounded by others. Surprisingly, during her rehabilitation, Louisa has fallen in love with and become engaged to Captain Benwick, a depressive man whose heart had been broken when his fiancée, Fanny, died. Fanny's brother, Captain Harville expresses that his sister would never have forgotten him so quickly. Anne agrees with that assertion, claiming faithfulness for her sex, saying, "We certainly do not forget you as soon as you forget us. It is, perhaps, our fate rather than our merit. We cannot help ourselves". Captain Wentworth overhears her, and gaining hope, writes her a letter asking for her hand in marriage. They end up walking home together, and Anne happily accepts his proposal.

Pride and Prejudice

The Fool, The Hierophant, The Lovers, The Hermit, Justice, Four of Candlesticks, Six of Candlesticks, Seven of Candlesticks, Eight of Candlesticks, Maiden of Candlesticks, Lady of Candlesticks, Five of Teacups, Ten of Teacups, Lady of Teacups, Lord of Teacups, Three of Quills, 10 of Quills, Lord of Quills, Maiden of Coins

At his wife's urgent behest, Mr. Bennett, the father of five unmarried daughters, visits Netherfield in order to make the acquaintance of Charles Bingley, an eligible bachelor. Mr. Bennett considers his three youngest daughters rather foolish, but he loves the eldest, Jane, for her goodness and is particularly partial towards Elizabeth, because of her wit and spark. When Mr. Bennett introduces Bingley to the family at a public dance, Jane and Charles are immediately attracted to one another. Mr. Bingley's friend Mr. Darcy accompanies him to the dance, and is dismissive of Lizzy's looks. He refuses to dance with her, which alternately amuses and annoys her.

When Jane is invited to Netherfield by Bingley's sisters, Mrs. Bennett is overjoyed. Desperate to get her daughters married off, she concocts the scheme of sending Jane on horseback, hoping that the impending rain will compel the Bingleys to invite Jane to spend the evening. Jane falls ill with the 'flu, requiring a stay of several days. Lizzy, concerned for her sister's health, goes to check on her and is also invited to remain and care for Jane. While Darcy initially scorns Lizzy, to his chagrin, propinquity greatly increases his attraction to her.

When the Bennett sisters return, the self-important Mr. Collins comes to call on their family with the intention of "extending the olive branch" of peace. Their families have been estranged. Collins is to inherit the Bennetts' home, Longbourn, since the Bennetts have no male heirs, and Mr. Collins asserts his wish to marry one of their daughters (who are famed for their beauty), keeping the estate in the family. Mrs. Bennett is both relieved and delighted.

Initially Mr. Collins sets his sights on Jane, as she is the eldest and most beautiful, but he easily turns his attentions to Elizabeth when he is informed that Jane is practically engaged. When he proposes, he refuses to believe Lizzy's rejection is sincere, chalking it up to maidenly modesty. Mrs. Bennett does all she can to coerce her daughter into accepting his proposal, but Mr. Bennett supports Lizzy's decision with ironic humor. When Lizzy continues to rebuff Mr. Collins, he turns to her friend Charlotte Lucas, who is delighted to accept him, despite his fatuous self-importance and her superior sense and sensibility.

A new and pleasing soldier, George Wickham, is introduced into the Bennetts' social sphere. He confides in Lizzy that Darcy has cheated him of his financial birthright. Lizzy is quick to sympathize with Wickham and uses this confidence as an additional reason to dislike Darcy, a dislike she is sure is reciprocal.

While Mr. Bingley seems attracted to Jane, he and his family move back to London indefinitely. Jane quietly suffers a broken heart, especially when she visits London and contacts Bingley's sister, with no positive response. Lizzy also goes on a visit to the newlywed Collinses at Charlotte's request; the last person she expects to see again is Mr. Darcy. They meet at the home of Mr. Collins' patroness, Lady Catherine de Bourgh, who is also Darcy's aunt. Lizzy also meets Darcy's cousin, Colonel Fitzwilliam. He inadvertently apprises Lizzy that Darcy has colluded with Bingley's sisters to keep Charles away from a woman (not realizing that Lizzy is that woman's sister). Darcy's interest in Lizzy grows stronger with each meeting, and almost against his will, he declares his love and proposes marriage, certain that she will accept with gratitude. She is relatively poor and he is one of the richest and most eligible bachelors in England, as he reminds her in his proposal. This incenses Elizabeth, who not only rejects him, but enumerates and details his offensive behaviors – his proud manner, his maltreatment of Wickham, and his interference in her sister Jane's love life.

Darcy stalks off in anger, but later writes and delivers to Elizabeth a letter that clarifies his behavior. He tells her that Wickham's tales of his stolen birthright are completely false, even confiding that Wickham almost succeeded in eloping with Darcy's young sister Georgiana. In the letter, he adds that he was unconvinced of Jane's feelings for Bingley because of her all-embracing amiability. Repeated readings of the letter make Elizabeth realize that she has been guilty of unfair prejudice towards him. Upon reflection, lengthy reconsideration of Lizzy's words make Darcy reflect upon his own behaviors with honest self-criticism, igniting a desire to change. Darcy even encourages Charles to renew his attentions to Jane.

When Lydia is invited to Brighton, Mr. Bennett's wife easily persuades him to allow her to go without an appropriate chaperone. When Lizzy travels with her aunt and uncle, she again meets up with Darcy, this time at his family estate. He is markedly gracious to her and her family and they take pleasure in one another's society until Lizzy receives a letter with dire news: feckless Lydia has run away with Wickham – and marriage is not imminent. After Lizzy confides this news to Darcy, she returns home, saddened to realize that her sister's action removes any possible furthering of a relationship with a man whom she now loves.

This disgrace to the family name rouses even the disengaged Mr. Bennett to regret. Mr. Collins sends a letter to the Bennetts suggesting they completely reject Lydia in the name of good Christian charity. Darcy, however, comes to the rescue by spending both time and money to insure that the reluctant Wickham fulfills his matrimonial obligations to Lydia.

Lizzy is surprised by a visit from Lady Catherine de Bourgh, who has heard that Darcy and Lizzy are to be wed. Lady Catherine pressures Elizabeth to swear she will never marry Darcy, but Lizzy refuses to do so. When his enraged aunt reports this to Darcy, it gives him hope that he might yet have a chance to win Lizzy's affections and he rushes to Longbourn to propose. Lizzy is more than happy to accept his proposal, as she is no longer prejudiced against the still-proud, but very much in love Mr. Darcy.

Sense and Sensibility

Death, Maiden of Teacups, Knight of Teacups, Four of Swords, Ace of Coins, Two of Coins, Four of Coins, Knight of Coins, Lady of Coins, Lord of Coins

When Henry Dashwood dies, he leaves behind a wife and three daughters, Elinor, Marianne, and Margaret. His dying request to his son, John, is to ensure that they are well-provided for, as John is to receive the bulk of his estate, including Norland, his home.

But John's wife Fanny encourages generosity only to herself, and convinces her husband that his stepmother and half-sisters need very little to live on. Fanny makes the widow Dashwood and her daughters so uncomfortable that they soon move from Norland to Devonshire. When they enter that society, an older man, Colonel Brandon, falls in love with the sensitive, passionate, and beautiful Marianne, who considers him too old and unromantic a suitor for her. The more practical, yet very attractive elder sister, Elinor, has already given her heart to her Fanny's brother, Edward Ferrars, but has not received an offer of marriage from him.

While on a walk, Marianne falls and is "rescued" by Willoughby, a dashing young man who seems to share Marianne's every romantic taste and sensibility. It is clear that they are both quite infatuated with one another, and when Willoughby gifts Marianne with a horse, Mrs. Dashwood is sure that they are engaged or will soon be. Elinor, who is less sanguine, wishes her sister wouldn't evince her admiration for Willoughby so openly and publicly.

Soon Willoughby goes away, without having made Marianne an offer of marriage. She believes he will return any day for her. When she sees a rider on horseback, she is sure it is he, but it is, in fact, Edward Ferrars. He seems out of spirits, and leaves for London after a brief visit. Soon thereafter, the Steele sisters are introduced into the sisters' social sphere. It is to Elinor that the younger, prettier sister,

Lucy, confides that she is secretly engaged – to Edward Ferrars! Elinor is heartbroken, but does not openly lose her composure.

When the Jennings invite Elinor and Marianne to London, Elinor is disinclined to go. Her heartache is still fresh. She gives in for Marianne's sake, knowing that she is eager to see Willoughby again. Colonel Brandon meets up with them when they come to town and asks Elinor privately if it is true that Marianne and Willoughby are engaged. Elinor indicates that, although there is no formal engagement, she thinks they will marry. Colonel Brandon seems distraught, but takes his leave with good wishes for them both.

Despite numerous letters, Willoughby does not seem to be in a hurry to be in touch with Marianne. When they see each other at a public gathering, he openly snubs her. A day later, he returns Marianne's letters, writing that he is engaged to another young woman, the wealthy Miss Grey. Colonel Brandon returns, telling Elinor some unknown facts about Willoughby – not only had he been improvident with his income, he had seduced a young woman and left her alone and pregnant.

Marianne, whose romantic sensibilities have been crushed, goes into a decline. Meanwhile, Edward Ferrars' mother discovers that he and Lucy Steele have been secretly engaged. When Edward refuses to break it off with her as his mother commands, she disinherits him for his younger brother, Robert. This means that Edward can not afford to marry Lucy for a long time. Colonel Brandon offers employment to Edward Ferrars, via Elinor, so that he can marry sooner. Marianne, in her great despair, takes a walk in the wet grass and becomes very ill. Elinor expresses her fears for Marianne's life to Colonel Brandon, who offers to drive to Devonshire and fetch their mother, an offer Elinor gratefully accepts. Before she arrives, Willoughby hears of Marianne's illness and comes to the house. While he is not permitted to see her, he confides in Elinor that he made a grave mistake by marrying Miss Grey – he loves Marianne and always will, and now must suffer the consequences of his improvident actions.

Marianne recovers, and both sisters are shocked to learn that Lucy Steele has married Robert Ferrars, who is now the wealthy Ferrars brother. Edward soon comes to ask for Elinor's hand in marriage, explaining that Lucy had ensnared him into a proposal when he was young, and even when he fell in love with Elinor, he felt he had to honor his youthful proposal to Lucy. Her marriage to his brother has freed him to marry the one he truly loves. Elinor accepts him. Marianne eventually falls in love with and marries her faithful suitor, Colonel Brandon, and they are very happy together.

Bibliography

This book is based primarily on the works of Jane Austen, and there are many different editions of each book.
You can read all of these books online (for free) at:
http://www.mollands.net/etexts/

The following books were also helpful:

Austen-Leigh, James-Edward, *A Memoir of Jane Austen* (1870)
Copeland, Edward and Juliet McMaster, *The Cambridge Companion to Jane Austen* (1997)
Henderson, Lauren, *Jane Austen's Guide to Dating* (2005)
Honan, Park, *Jane Austen: Her Life* (1987)
Ray, Joan Klingel, *Jane Austen for Dummies* (2006)
Shields, Carol, *Jane Austen* (2001)
Tanner, Tony, *Jane Austen* (1986)
Tomalin, Claire, *Jane Austen: A Life* (1997)
Tyler, Natalie, *The Friendly Jane Austen* (1999)
Weldon, Fay, *Letters to Alice on First Reading Jane Austen* (1985)

I have read many tarot books over the years. However, in the writing of this book, I have frequently consulted the following:

Greer, Mary, *The Complete Book of Tarot Reversals* (2002)
Riley, Jana, *The Tarot Dictionary and Compendium* (1995)

In addition, all of Mary Greer's works have strongly informed my view of the tarot, as a writer and as a reader. I recommend her book *Tarot for Your Self* to tarot novices who wish to learn more than I could possibly include in this companion book.